T0327924

KAIJU UNLEASHED

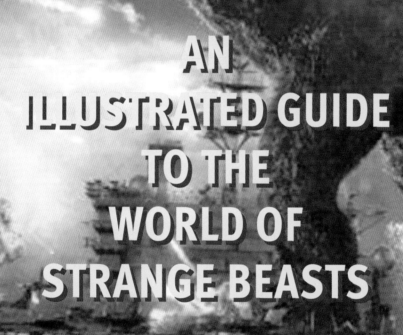

AN
ILLUSTRATED GUIDE
TO THE
WORLD OF
STRANGE BEASTS

Shawn Pryor

EPIC INK

CONTENTS

Page 1:
Terror of Mechagodzilla (1975)

Pages 2–3:
Godzilla vs. Kong (2021)

This page;
Godzilla (1954)

FOREWORD

One of the most perplexing things about the kaiju film genre is that it can be so . . . redemptive. Alongside all the destruction, sacrifice, and punching, there is almost always a hope for brighter days ahead. As society grew, stacking skyscrapers taller and taller like playsets, so, too, did the monsters.

And so, too, did the destruction. From giant apes to radioactive dinosaurs, from stone gods to ancient flying turtles, our eyes are constantly dazzled by the most primal of sights: the annihilation of everything we hold dear. Bridges wrecked. Landmarks smashed. Homes and neighborhoods in flames. By any rights, the kaiju genre should be closely related to horror. After all, very rare is the kaiju, heroic or not, that isn't responsible for the death of hundreds, if not millions.

Yet, we constantly return to the kaiju genre, so much so that Godzilla's total number of films is rapidly approaching 40 in all, and that's alongside dozens of other films, from *Gamera* to *King Kong* to *Daimajin* to *Pacific Rim*.

It is my belief that the kaiju genre offers us, on the surface, not only the basest of thrills, but the genre also reminds us of the potential for humanity to solve, quite literally, the biggest problems. After all, as humans, we measure ourselves by the adversity we face, and the kaiju is a perfect stand-in for the world-shaking moral issues we collectively face alongside our nettlesome individual challenges. We create the beast in order to reassure ourselves that we can slay it, to see if we can measure up to the task. Sometimes, these victories require great sacrifice and redemption, but, in the end, humanity almost always wins, even if it is a bit tenuous at times. And even if it is rarely a lasting victory.

While speaking of human triumphs, let's not forget the directors who worked to bring their visions to life, the actors sweating in their leaden suits, or the computer animators toiling at their stations for hours on end. Thousands upon thousands of people who set out to make giant movie monsters to entertain us, to warn us, to inspire us. Of course, let's also acknowledge the triumph of this book as well! Within the realm of kaiju studies, just as in the fictional worlds of the kaiju, the human spirit remains strong; sometimes tattered, but always indomitable. Always adapting. Always providing new and insightful perspectives.

What you hold in your hands right now is the latest victory over a personal kaiju. Shawn Pryor has faced down the beast of composing, researching, and crafting this book full of unique and interesting insights. This is a victory for Shawn, in particular, but for us as well: we have at our fingertips yet another pathway toward understanding the labor and the triumphs of the kaiju genre. We all benefit from Shawn's victory, and all of those that will follow.

What's next for you?

Look up to the sky. There's something big on the horizon.

—Jason Barr, author of *The Kaiju Film: A Critical Study of Cinema's Biggest Monsters* and *The Kaiju Connection: Giant Monsters and Ourselves*

OPPOSITE:
Godzilla is a global force in the modern day, even welcoming visitors to Tokyo at the Hotel Gracery Shinjuku.

> "
> Monsters are tragic beings. They are born too tall, too strong, too heavy. They are not evil by choice. That is their tragedy.
> —Ishirō Honda, director and co-creator of the kaiju genre
> "

I remember my first kaiju experience quite well. In my early youth, on a summer Saturday evening, I was about to head to bed and my parents were flipping through the many channels on the television, trying to find something to watch. I heard a shrill cry from the television before I could place my right foot on the first step upstairs to my room.

I stopped. The loud and piercing cry rang out once more.

As I turned to see the commotion, I knew what I witnessed would be part of me for the rest of my life. On the TV screen stood a behemoth of a green prehistoric creature, firing atomic breath from its mouth, battling against a menacing, three-headed flying dragon. I quickly returned to the couch and begged my parents to let me stay up and watch the rest of the movie. That night, I witnessed the last forty minutes of *Destroy All Monsters*. When it was over, I was speechless. I wanted to know everything about Godzilla, the King of the Monsters.

From that moment, I spent many late summer evenings of my childhood searching for more Godzilla movies. Many times, movies featuring kaiju would be a part of the local "Creature Feature/Shock Theater" scene, packaged alongside kinetic and action-packed martial arts and horror films. But I only had eyes for the monsters. I couldn't wait to hear that classic Godzilla bellow through the mono television speaker.

As time went on, not only did I witness more of Godzilla's battles, but I was also introduced to many other giant monsters and heroes along the way. The more I saw of these fantastic beasts, the more I wanted everyone to know how awesome they were. I took advantage of any opportunity to introduce a friend or relative to any of the eras of Godzilla or Gamera, I would share my copies of *Starlog* magazine that had articles on the history of Godzilla movies and other kaiju, and there was nothing I wanted more than the twenty-four-inch Godzilla from the Shogun Warriors toy collection.

From the heroic terror of Godzilla and the fire demon Rodan, to the benevolent behemoth Mothra

Best Movies & Shows for Those New to Kaiju

Looking to start your path into kaiju media? Start with this list of classics to make yourself familiar with the genre. These seven are a fantastic gateway to a larger world:

King Kong (1933)
Godzilla (1954)
Ultraseven (1967–1968)
Destroy All Monsters (1968)
Gamera: Guardian of the Universe (1995)
Pacific Rim (2013)
Godzilla Minus One (2023)

and the flying space turtle Gamera, these kaiju of Japanese science fiction are some of the most popular characters of their cinematic genre. The first tokusatsu hero, Ultraman, is also considered part of the genre. Around the world, their exploits and adventures are well known. They present heroism, danger, destruction, lessons of humanity, moments of levity, and plenty of science fiction, fantasy, and action. The popularity of these monsters has only grown, as they've taken over the world, box office, television screens, and streaming apps. The kaiju genre has bled into literature and video games, too, and has inspired countries around the world to create their own monsters and universes that either pay homage to Godzilla (such as the United Kingdom's 1961 film *Gorgo*), create a new universe of deadly kaiju and the threat to civilization (as seen in 2013's *Pacific Rim*), or find a new way discuss

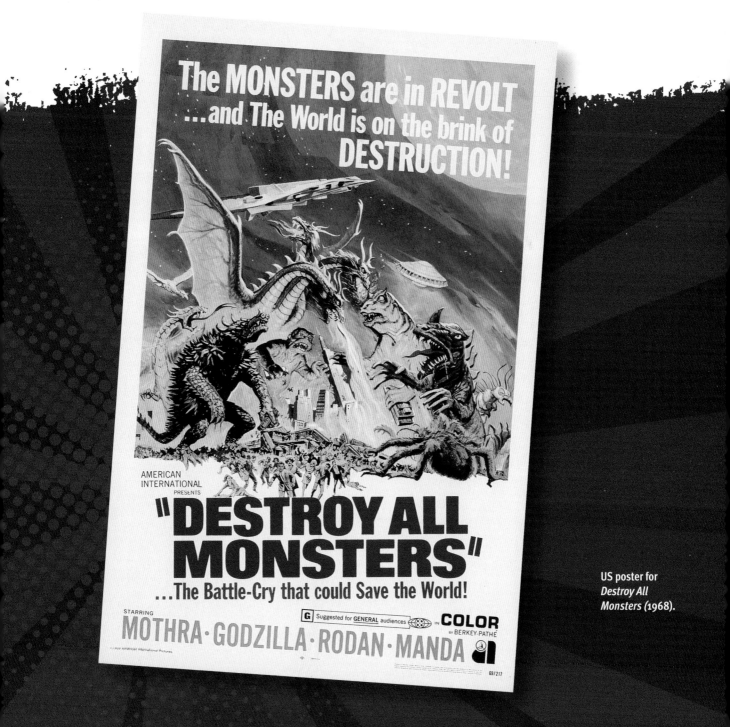

US poster for *Destroy All Monsters* (1968).

as metaphors for the fears of society and the anxiety of the perpetual damage done to the Earth, the lingering effects of war, the fear of advancing technology, and even the fight for humanity. But most of all, they make for fantastic cinema and shows.

These films and shows are successful because they refuse to be bound by rules and have constantly found ways to evolve and change with the decades. For example, in the original *Godzilla* (1954), the massive titular kaiju was awakened by a hydrogen bomb test and sparked fear of a nuclear holocaust in postwar Japan. The latest entries in the film series have shifted from nuclear-related anxieties to the fallout from climate change.

As society and the world change, the kaiju genre will continue to evolve. With each advancement in technology, science, and the environment, fears will circle us because of the aftermath of our actions. The Kaiju genre will represent those fears and hopes throughout its infinite lifespan.

Tomoyuki Tanaka in 1959.

relationships and toxic friendships (as in 2016's *Colossal*). The latest Godzilla film, *Godzilla Minus One*, was released in 2023 and became the most successful Japanese Godzilla movie in the seventy-year history of the franchise, proving that audiences are still showing up for these cinematic events. There are also kaiju conventions where experts and creators talk about the history behind these classics. Even at pop culture and comic book conventions, you'll probably spot fans cosplaying as Godzilla, Ultraman, or characters from *Attack on Titan*.

But what does the word *kaiju* mean?

Kaiju is a Japanese word meaning strange beast or monster, with "kai" meaning unknown or a mystery and "ju" meaning beast. But they are more than just giant creatures. They can be antagonists, protagonists, a force of nature, and even a divine power. The stories they are a part of can serve

The thesis was very simple. What if a dinosaur sleeping in the Southern Hemisphere had been awakened and transformed into a giant by the bomb? What if it attacked Tokyo?
—Tomoyuki Tanaka, creator of Godzilla

This text aims to familiarize you with some of the greatest kaiju ever known, from the strange beasts of Japan to riffs on the genre across the entire world, spanning decades and mediums and including the many creations and characters that Godzilla, the undisputed King of the Monsters, has inspired.

OPPOSITE:
The King of the Monsters in *Godzilla Minus One* (2023).

STRANGE BEASTS

There have been enough kaiju movies over the last seventy years that they can be considered their own genre of film and television. But kaiju media actually belongs to a subgenre of another genre in Japan called tokusatsu, which has been massively popular in Japan for over seventy years and worldwide for over fifty years.

Tokusatsu is a Japanese term for live-action movies or television shows that make extensive use of practical special effects and puppetry. The most popular kinds of tokusatsu are kaiju films like *Godzilla* (1954) and *Gamera the Giant Monster* (1965) and Henshin Hero television shows such as *Kamen Rider* (1971–1973). Series such as *Ultraman* (1966–1967) and *Super Sentai* (1975–present)—with the latter serving as inspiration for the *Power Rangers* franchise in the United States—are a combination of tokusatsu subgenres (which include kaiju, kaijin, Yokai, superheroes, metal heroes, and mecha).

In the early 1950s, producer Tomoyuki Tanaka of Toho Studios in Tokyo was trying to figure out his next feature film. His filmmaking career had started in 1944, and in only ten years he had produced over forty films, including the 1954 films *Shiosai* (aka *The Surf* or *The Sound of the Waves*), based off a novel by Yukio Mishima, and the war dramas *Saraba Rabauru* (aka *Farewell Rabaul*), and *Kimi, Shinitamuo Koto Nakare*.

He was a fan of the Hollywood monster B-movies of the time, which were making their way to Japan. For example, *The Beast from 20,000 Fathoms* (1953) was released and translated for Japanese audiences as *An Atomic Kaiju Appears*, one of the earliest uses of the word kaiju in the title of a movie. So, Tanaka decided to make a monster movie. He combined Japan's fears of atomic weapons and nuclear fallout (inspired by the actual fallout of a United States hydrogen bomb test in the Marshall Islands) and created a massive, radioactive, dinosaur/lizard-like creature that came from the ocean, wreaking havoc on Tokyo. This creature would be known as Godzilla.

KAIJU FACT

Tomoyuki Tanaka worked for Toho Studios for over sixty years, producing over 200 feature-length films, and also handled a majority of Toho's kaiju films from 1954 to 1995. He even produced a quarter of Akira Kurosawa's films. Kurosawa is considered one of the greatest directors in the history of cinema.

OPPOSITE: Japanese poster for *Gamera: The Giant Monster* (1965).

▼▼ SUITMATION ▼▼

Before the first Godzilla movie in 1954, some giant monster movies in the United States used stop-motion and animation techniques to move their creatures across the screen, as in films like *Lost Continent* (1951) and *The Beast from 20,000 Fathoms* (1953). Sometimes they even used actual creatures, such as in *Beginning of the End* (1957) when live grasshoppers were filmed and enlarged for the screen. However, in Japan, director and cinematographer Eiji Tsuburaya felt that kaiju movies needed something different to give their creatures more life and vibrancy. That thing was suitmation.

Suitmation, created by Tsuburaya, is a technique in which an actor puts on a monster suit and performs on a set that uses models, miniatures, and visual effects. It was the opposite of what stop-motion legend Ray Harryhausen was doing in American cinema with films such as *Mighty Joe Young* (1949) and *It Came from Beneath the Sea* (1955). Harryhausen's stop-motion technique, known as Dynamation, would split the background and foreground of a shot into two separate images. He would then animate the model (creature), positioning it frame by frame, then integrate it into the live-action shot.

Tsuburaya was brought on to be the special effects coordinator for the first Godzilla film. The

Suit actor Haruo Nakajima (left) in 1954.

Godzilla suit was designed by Teizō Toshimitsu and Akira Watanabe, with Eiji Tsuburaya supervising the construction of the suit with an emphasis on a dinosaur-like design. Once the design was completed and approved, the suit was built by Kanju Yagi, Yasuei Yagi, and Eizo Kaimai. They used thin bamboo sticks and wire to build the frame of the suit, then reinforced its interior to make sure it was stable and durable. Wooden sandals were put inside the feet of the costume for additional stability.

Using suitmation for the first Godzilla film was dynamic but challenging. In the beginning, the monster suits that the actors wore were over 200 pounds and very rigid because of the rubber, latex, and other materials mixed into the rubber to create the suits at the time, so wearing the monster suits took a toll on the actors. It was also difficult to obtain high quantities of rubber and latex in the wake of World War II. "Since materials were so rare, things like rubber were not available. Instead, they used ready-mixed concrete, so it weighed about 100 kilograms [over 220 pounds]. It was so heavy and hot, and with the lighting, it was even hot just to touch it. I was sweating all over my face, but I did the best I could," said Godzilla suit actor Haruo Nakajima in an interview with *NPR*.

Nakajima was the first actor to don the classic Godzilla suit. He also wore many other kaiju suits when called upon, such as the title character in

KAIJU FACT

The original concept design
for Godzilla was a
whale/gorilla hybrid.

THOSE WHO HAVE WORN THE SUIT

Many actors have donned the Godzilla suit over the decades or performed motion-capture suit acting for the mighty kaiju.

JAPAN

- Haruo Nakajima
- Shinji Takagi
- Isao Zushi
- Toru Kawai
- Kenpachirô Satsuma
- Tsutomu Kitagawa
- Katsumi Tezuka
- Hiroshi Sekita
- Mansai Nomura
- Naoya Matsumoto
- Seiji Onaka
- Mizuho Yoshida

AMERICA

- Kurt Carley
- TJ Storm

東宝
総天然色
FRANKENSTEIN VS. BARAGON
フランケンシュタイン対地底怪獣バラゴン
恐怖の怪人か?・狂悪の新怪獣か?・日米合作の黄金娯楽巨篇!
監督・本多猪四郎
特技監督・円谷英二
製作・田中友幸
脚本・馬淵薫
東宝 ベネディクトプロ作品/東宝配給
ニック・アダムス
水野久美
高島忠夫
土屋嘉男
佐原健二
田崎潤
藤田進
中村伸郎
志村喬
撮影・小泉一
美術・北猛夫
録音・小沼渡
照明・小島正七
音楽・伊福部昭
整音・下永尚
特技スタッフ
撮影・有川貞昌
〃・富岡素敬
美術・渡辺明
照明・岸田九一郎
合成・向山宏
Printed in Japan © TOHO Co., Ltd 1965

CREATIVES WHO WERE INSPIRED BY KAIJU MOVIES

Some recognizable names have been influenced by the Godzilla franchise, including these talented folks:

▶ **Steven Spielberg**—the director of such films as *Jurassic Park*, *Jaws*, *E.T.*, and *Raiders of the Lost Ark*—once called *Godzilla* (1954) the most masterful of all the dinosaur movies, because it made you believe it was really happening.

▶ **Martin Scorsese**, director of *Taxi Driver*, *Raging Bull*, *Goodfellas*, and *Killers of the Flower Moon*, is an admirer of director Ishirō Honda.

▶ **Akira Kurosawa**, director of classic films such as *The Hidden Fortress* and *Seven Samurai* (both influences for George Lucas's *Star Wars*) called *Godzilla* one of his favorite movies of all time and became great friends with director Ishirō Honda. Kurosawa even brought Honda on to consult on his last five films.

▶ **Guillermo del Toro**, director of *Blade II*, *Pan's Labyrinth*, *Hellboy*, and *The Shape of Water*, is a passionate fan of *Godzilla*. His 2013 film, *Pacific Rim*, was heavily influenced by Ishirō Honda, *Godzilla*, and kaiju cinematic lore in general.

Rodan (1956), *Varan* (1958), and *Mothra* (1961); Moguera in *The Mysterians* (1957); Baragon in *Frankenstein vs. Baragon* (1965); and many others. Before filming, Nakajima spent time at Ueno Zoo in Tokyo to study the motion of elephants and bears, as reference for how his own giant beast should move, especially when Godzilla had to walk. Nakajima preferred to shuffle his feet while being filmed in the costume. "No one should ever see the monster's heels. Godzilla won't look strong without that shuffle. The same is true of a sumō wrestler, you know," said Nakajima in an interview with *Nippon.com* in 2014. Due to his versatility as an actor, as he had played many types of roles before Godzilla, he was able to quickly adapt to the role of the mega monster.

The heavy Godzilla suit required two assistants to help Nakajima put it on when it came time to film. As if moving around in a heavy rubber/concrete suit weren't enough, miniatures would explode during filming to give the proper effect of Godzilla destroying Tokyo, and Nakajima would breathe in kerosene fumes from the crushed models smoking under his suited feet.

There were two Godzilla suits created for the production of the film. One was cut in two and used for partial shots of close-ups, one part for the lower half, one part for the upper half and head shots. The second suit was a full-body suit, which Nakajima and Katsumi Tezuka wore during filming early in the production. The actors alternated wearing the suit because they could only be inside it for minutes at a time. But because the shoot was so physical and laborious, Nakajima's time in the full-body suit gave director Ishirō Honda the best footage and scenes for the movie, so Tezuka would only fill in for Nakajima when he became too exhausted to continue. And since they only had two suits to wear, they had to be very careful.

Once Nakajima mastered the suit in the first Godzilla movie, he played the role for twelve films from 1954 to 1972. As the years went along, he taught the next suit actors for Toho Studios.

It was not comfortable at all to perform in the suit, but the overall purpose of suitmation was to create something that made the audience look on in awe instead of wondering if the monster seemed lifelike or not. Filming on *Godzilla* was done at double the frame speed, to make the monster's motions look smooth and slowed down in post-production. Over thirty carpenters were hired to build miniatures and sets for the film. Overall, the film took over fifty days to shoot and the special effects took over seventy days to complete.

OPPOSITE:
Japanese poster for *Franksenstein vs. Baragon* (1965).

> **If Godzilla had been a dinosaur or some other animal, he would have been killed by just one cannonball. But if he were equal to an atomic bomb, we wouldn't know what to do. So, I took the characteristics of an atomic bomb and applied them to Godzilla.**
> **—Ishirō Honda**

O ver the decades, the *Godzilla* films have ranged from deadly serious to science fantasy to completely silly. But throughout all the eras of this great kaiju, the films have served as metaphors for natural disasters, the fear and consequences of atomic weaponry, survivors' guilt, and a primal force that could be a savior or could bring an end to mankind.

In *Godzilla* (1954), director Ishirō Honda uses the King of the Monsters as a metaphor for and a nightmare vision of the aftereffects of a nuclear holocaust. This black-and-white cinematic masterpiece sometimes looks like a classic noir movie, due to the visual tones of black and dark

American promotional art for *Godzilla* (1954).

gray, especially in the night scenes when Godzilla invades Tokyo. And because this Godzilla movie uses suitmation, the lumbering and limiting movement of the suit reads as a primal, powerful force on screen. Godzilla is so large that it takes massive energy for him to move, and each movement can cause destruction. This destruction that Godzilla leaves in his wake again serves as a metaphor for the violence and devastation caused by nuclear weapons (especially summoning up the atomic bombings of Hiroshima and Nagasaki) and the need for peace.

OPPOSITE:
Japanese poster art for *The Return of Godzilla* (1984).

Who are the "Godzilla Fathers"?

The Godzilla Fathers are the people who helped create the mighty cinematic kaiju. They are:

Director: Ishirō Honda
Producer: Tomoyuki Tanaka
Special Effects savant: Eiji Tsuburaya
Composer: Akira Ifukube

▼▼ INITIAL RECEPTION ▼▼

In Japan, *Godzilla* (1954) became an icon of Japanese post-war culture, even though some critics felt the film exploited the atomic bombings that had taken place just nine years before. Still, the film was an immense success overall, becoming the eighth-highest-grossing film in Japan that year. A heavily edited and dubbed American version of *Godzilla* premiered two years later, in 1956. The film was successful and received very good to great reviews in the US, but some American audiences didn't take the film seriously, comparing it to the average monster movie or B-movie fare they had consumed before. The spectacle of Godzilla outweighed the horrors of the atomic bomb, partly due to the way the film was trimmed to make it more American. Though the film is still entertaining, it overlooks the symbolism of Godzilla as a metaphor for the dangers of atomic weapons.

The success of *Godzilla* (1954) led to many sequels, reboots, themes, and audiences of all ages. And with subsequent films came some of Godzilla's most dangerous villains, steadfast allies, and one of the most dangerous human-made weapons used to battle kaiju.

▼▼ DANGEROUS VILLAINS ▼▼

Over the decades, Godzilla has gone toe-to-toe with some of the world's most vile and deadly kaiju. Here are a few of his greatest enemies and their abilities.

▶ **Biollante** — Created from Godzilla's DNA, Biollante is a genetically-made flower-hybrid kaiju that originated as a large, mutated rose. She spews deadly sap from her massive mouth and can move very quickly, despite her size.

◀ **Destoroyah** — This incredibly well-designed kaiju's most effective weapon is the ability to destroy oxygen using the Micro-Oxygen beam he emits from his mouth. He also has a laser horn and chest beam. He is a destructive crustacean that can also transform into multiple forms (Juvenile, Aggregate, Flying, Perfect) and is aware of how wicked and evil he is. Destoroyah truly wants nothing more than to eliminate all life, no matter where he goes.

King Ghidorah — Originally introduced in the Showa Era (the earliest Godzilla Era), this maniacal, three-headed, extraterrestrial flying dragon is one of Godzilla's deadliest foes. This planet destroyer also has magnetic powers, can generate powerful winds, fire gravity beams, and is extremely durable.

Kiryu, aka Millenium Mechagodzilla — The third version of Mechagodzilla, this giant robotic kaiju can use its powerful Absolute Zero Cannon to instantly freeze a combatant. It also has two Maser weapons, a Double Maser Cannon, and a Maser Blade, plus it carries missiles, rockets, and railguns.

Gigan — This space monster has curved blades for hands and a buzzsaw that emerges from his stomach, can fire lasers from head, and can fly at as fast as Mach 3. He is lethal in close combat.

Hedorah — The smog monster kaiju from outer space is an enormous lump of toxic pollution that can wipe out an entire city instantly with its toxic emissions. Hedorah even withstood a full atomic blast from Godzilla!

THE MASER CANNON: THE KILLER WEAPON AGAINST KAIJU

The Maser Cannon is a large, satellite-shaped dish weapon that can fire a laser beam that is usually highly effective against kaiju attacks. It is attached to tanks or large vehicles to be brought into battle. The Maser Cannon has been featured in multiple Toho Studio science-fiction films, eleven Toho Studio Godzilla films, and one Monsterverse film. The premise of the Maser Cannon is akin to the actual Maser devices in the real world. Maser is an acronym for Microwave Amplification by Stimulated Emission of Radiation. In reality, Masers are devices that amplify weak signals. They have been instrumental in intensifying faint signals returned from radar and communication satellites. They have also made it possible to measure faint radio waves emitted by Venus, which helped researchers understand the planet's temperature. The maser is considered the principal precursor to laser technology.

Megaguirus — A flying scorpion kaiju, Megaguirus is one of the fastest-flying kaiju, flying at speeds of Mach 4. She also has a tail stinger and can vibrate so quickly that she disappears, a technique she uses to confuse her prey.

Monster X, aka Kaiser King Ghidorah — Having only made one appearance in the history of Godzilla films, X is one of the strongest kaiju and can steal energy from any kaiju that battles him. He can also acquire energy from the alien race known as the Xiliens with the growths on his tail, and he is able to withstand a full-strength atomic blast. Like the other Ghidorah, he also has gravity beams.

▶ **Orga** — A hunchbacked, giant, mutated version of Godzilla, Orga has similar strength and regeneration abilities to Godzilla. Because of its size and mouth, it was once able to swallow Godzilla whole.

▼ **Mechagodzilla (Showa Era)** — The first version of Mechagodzilla, this kaiju battle-mech was controlled by aliens who wanted to rule the Earth. It can fire missiles from its fingers, toes, and knees and fire energy beams from its eyes. It also has a Cross Attack Beam which fires from its chest. It has the power of flight, a head that can rotate 360 degrees, and has a force field that can protect its entire robotic body.

▶ **SpaceGodzilla** — The Heisei Era's most dangerous foe, SpaceGodzilla is a crystalline Godzilla clone. SpaceGodzilla came to life when some of Godzilla's cells were put into outer space. This kaiju's only mission is to destroy Godzilla so it can be the only Godzilla in the universe. It has crystal shards that protrude from its back and shoulders, can smash foes with its tail, and has a Corona Beam and a Photon Reactive Shield that can deflect energy beams and Godzilla's atomic breath. Due to its build, it's best in close combat.

■ **Super Mechagodzilla** — The second version of Mechagodzilla, this piloted kaiju-mech can hover in the air and has Laser Cannons, a Maser Beam, Shock Anchors that can electrocute kaiju, a Mega Buster beam that it emits from its mouth like Godzilla's atomic breath, paralyzer and tranquilizer missiles, and a Diamond Coating that can absorb energy attacks.

▼▼ GREATEST ALLIES ▼▼

Every hero needs a friend or two when times get rough—or when a deadly kaiju is bent on destroying the world and turning it into their own personal playground. There have been many allies that have fought beside the mighty Godzilla—here are a few highlights.

▲ **Anguirus** — This ankylosaur kaiju was originally an enemy of Godzilla, being the very first kaiju to ever battle Godzilla on film in *Godzilla Raids Again* (1955). He was killed by Godzilla in the film but was brought back years later as an ally in multiple films.

▲ **Jet Jaguar** — A five-foot, nine-inch sentient robot, Jet Jaguar helped Godzilla fight Megalon and Gigan. Even though he is human-sized, Jet can grow to over 160 feet tall to battle kaiju and then return to normal size. Jet is incredibly strong, can fly at super speed, has liquid-nitrogen breath, and can blind his enemies with the built-in spotlights embedded in his eyes.

◄ **King Caesar** — A kaiju that could only be awakened from its slumber with a mythical statue, King Caesar helped Godzilla defeat Mechagodzilla. Caesar can absorb energy blasts with one of his eyes, and fire them back at opponents with the other eye.

▲ **Minilla** — This small kaiju is the son of Godzilla, always ready to help his father in battle—though due to his size and awkwardness, he is rarely much help. He means well. He can't fire atomic breath like his father, but he blows smoke hoops from his mouth. The smoke hoops cause no damage.

Mothra — The peaceful kaiju butterfly that serves as a metaphor for the power and elegance of nature, Mothra's overall goal is to protect humanity and the planet. Like Anguirus, Mothra and Godzilla were once enemies, but later she became an ally in multiple films. She is normally accompanied by two tiny women known as the Twin Fairies. In her larva stage, Mothra uses her mandibles to bite and spit streams of strong silk. In her imago (kaiju butterfly) stage, she can strike enemies with her wings, ram into opponents, use her claws for stabbing or scratching, and is strong enough to lift Godzilla with her claws. She can release poisonous yellow powder from her scales, and her scales can also turn into mirrors to reflect energy beams back toward enemies.

Rodan — This pteranodon kaiju and Godzilla were once enemies, but they agreed to a truce and teamed up to defeat Ghidorah. Rodan has appeared in multiple Godzilla movies and can create destructive shockwaves as he flies, which can destroy anything in his wake. He can also swim and submerge himself underwater, carry large kaiju, fire radioactive wind from his mouth, and create hurricane-strength gusts by moving his wings quickly.

▼▼ INTO THE ERAS ▼▼

For seventy years, Godzilla has been the leader and an icon of kaiju cinema, with films featuring this mighty kaiju broken into eras. The eras correspond to the reign of emperors: the Showa Era (1954–1975, corresponding to the reign of Emperor Shōwa), the Heisei Era (1984–1995) and Millennium Era (1999–2004, both corresponding to the reign of Emperor Emeritus Akihito), and the Reiwa Era (2016–present, corresponding to the reign of Emperor Naruhito Akihito).

3 THE SHOWA ERA (1954-1975)

> The theme of the [first] film, from the beginning,
> was the terror of the bomb.
> Mankind had created the bomb, and now nature
> was going to take revenge on mankind.
> —Tomoyuki Tanaka

The first Godzilla movie marked the beginning of the Showa Era in the kaiju industry. During this period, Godzilla was portrayed as an antagonist, fighting against other kaiju like Anguirus and Mothra.

However, Godzilla underwent a transformation with the release of Ghidorah, the Three-Headed Monster. After that, the King of the Monsters became a heroic figure, famous for battling evil beasts alongside other friendly kaiju. This new image of Godzilla would define the character for years to come.

Godzilla (1954)

Director: Ishirō Honda

Producer: Tomoyuki Tanaka

Writers: Akira Takarada, Momoko Kochi, Akihiko Hirata

Alternate film titles: *Gojira* (Japan), *Godzilla, King of The Monsters* (US), *Godzilla – The most sensational film of the present* (Germany), *Godzilla: Monster of the Sea* (Sweden), *Japan: Under the Terror of the Monster* (Spain), *The Monster of the Pacific Ocean* (Portugal), *Godzilla, the Monster of the Century* (Greece), *Godzilla, The Sea Monster* (Brazil)

Release date: November 3, 1954 (Japan), April 27, 1956 (US)

Lead actors: Akira Takarada, Momoko Kōchi, Akihiko Hirata, Takashi Shimura, Fuyuki Murakami, Sachio Sakai, Ren Yamamoto

Primary Godzilla suit actor: Haruo Nakajima

▼

The debut of Godzilla shows how this prehistoric kaiju was awakened by nuclear tests in the Pacific Ocean. Once awakened, Godzilla goes on a destructive rampage across Tokyo, Japan, summoning up the horrors of nuclear destruction that the Japanese lived through after the United States dropped atomic bombs on Hiroshima and Nagasaki in 1945. That attack destroyed many landmarks, pieces of history, and lives in those regions of the country, and even though the bomb brought an end to World War II, the ramifications for the Japanese were extensive.

KAIJU FACT

"Godzilla" comes from *Gojira* (Japanese). *Gojira* is the combination of two Japanese words: *gorira* (gorilla) and *kujira* (whale).

OPPOSITE:
Godzilla in *Ebirah, Horror of the Deep* (1966).

Years later, on March 1, 1954, a small Japanese fishing boat was exposed to nuclear fallout from the US thermonuclear weapon test at Bikini Atoll. The fishermen were unaware of this until later. Once they found out that they had been exposed to radiation, they contacted the Coast Guard. A few days later, they were tracked down and sent to a hospital, where they were found to be suffering from numerous diseases and severe burns on their skin. These injuries would later inspire the appearance of Godzilla's skin in his film debut.

The overall message of *Godzilla* is to show the negative impact that nuclear weapons can have. Godzilla is an embodiment of immense atomic power; if atomic power were a sentient being, it would be Godzilla. The point of the original *Godzilla* is to discourage the use of nuclear weapons ever again. This black-and-white classic does an excellent job of confirming and validating the fears of nuclear weapons and war, and the damage they cause that affects families for generations.

In an interview with NBC Asian America, William Tsutsui, the author of *Godzilla on My Mind: Fifty Years of the King of Monsters*, said, "Japanese creative artists, filmmakers, novelists, and so forth really couldn't talk about the atomic bombings. It was a topic that could not be discussed. And Japanese people, as well, were very reticent about discussing this tragedy, because it was so horrible, and because they felt a sense of guilt and shame about those events. But when the Japanese had their independence back, and as filmmakers were thinking about giant monsters, people began to think about that connection between monstrosity and the atomic bombing." For those in Japan, the film was the impactful and cathartic validation the viewers needed, with the film expressing the need of humanity to defeat evil—even though the ending of the film is quite somber.

During its first theatrical release in Japan, the movie broke records, hitting Tokyo's highest first-day ticket sales. Eventually, it sold 9.69 million tickets, making it Japan's eighth-most-attended film that year. The movie's total earnings were 183 million yen, well above its budget of 63 million yen. Tim Martin, critic for *The Daily Telegraph*, said in 2014 that the film was "a far cry from its B-movie successors. It was a sober allegory of a film with ambitions as large as its thrice-normal budget, designed to shock and horrify an adult audience."

The American version of *Godzilla* does not have the same impact as the original version. For one, the film was heavily edited, with nearly twenty minutes of footage removed. The cut scenes were the most political of the film and gave it its proper gravitas. Additionally, to give American audiences

Poster for *Godzilla* (1954).

someone they could relate to, new footage was shot with actor Raymond Burr as reporter Steve Martin. Despite Burr's work bringing the seriousness the film deserved, *Godzilla* didn't resonate with American audiences, who mostly saw it as just another creature feature. Though some Japanese Americans were able to view the original version of the film in Japanese neighborhoods during *Godzilla*'s original theatrical run, the edited American version of the film would be the only one available to English-speaking American audiences until 2004.

Anne Allison, a professor of cultural anthropology with a focus on Japanese culture, said in her book, *Millennial Monsters,* that Godzilla has many political and cultural references that can be connected to the experiences of the Japanese people during World War II. Japanese audiences were able to connect emotionally with Godzilla, who they saw as a victim. The movie can also be interpreted as laying blame on the US for Japan's post-war struggles, as it was atomic bomb testing carried out by the US that awakened Godzilla. *Godzilla* is a cultural coping mechanism that helped the people of Japan to move on from the events of the war.

KAIJU FACT

Godzilla's legendary roar was created by rubbing a pine tar-coated leather glove over a double bass string.

☢ *Godzilla Raids Again* (1955)

Director: Motoyoshi Oda
Producer: Tomoyuki Tanaka
Writers: Shigeaki Hidaka, Shigeru Kayama, Takeo Murata
Alternate film titles: *Gojira no hangeki* (Japan), *Gigantis, the Fire Monster* (US), *The King of the Monsters* (Spain/Italy), *The Return of Godzilla* (Belgium), *Godzilla Returns* (Germany), *Godzilla Attacks Again* (Brazil)
Release date: April 24, 1955 (Japan), May 21, 1959 (US)
Lead actors: Hiroshi Koizumi, Minoru Chiaki, Setsuko Wakayama, Takashi Shimura, Masao Shimizu, Sonosuke Sawamura, Seijiro Onda, Yoshio Tsuchiya
Primary Godzilla suit actor: Haruo Nakajima

——— ▼ ———

This sequel was quickly pushed into production due to the success of *Godzilla* (1954). *Godzilla Raids Again* also marks the first time that Godzilla battles another kaiju on film. The monster-versus-monster motif would become the focus of all future Godzilla films.

When two pilots, Shoichi Tsukioka and Koji Kobayashi, must land on Iwato Island due to a malfunction, they discover that Godzilla has returned, and he is battling a kaiju named Anguirus. When the pilots return to Osaka, they team with scientists and find out that both kaiju are around

Godzilla faces Anguirus in *Godzilla Raids Again* (1955).

A climactic battle from *Mothra vs. Godzilla* (1964).

the same age and have had a rivalry for millions of years. Daisuke Serizawa, the inventor of the Oxygen Destroyer weapon used against Godzilla in his last appearance, has since died and destroyed the formula for the weapon. As Godzilla and Anguirus battle through Osaka, Tsukioka and Kobayashi try to find a way to end Godzilla's devastation.

Godzilla Raids Again was not received well in Japan by critics even though it did well at the box office, earning 170 million yen against a budget of 32 million yen. Tomoyuki Tanaka, the producer, later admitted that the crew did not have enough preparation time to make the film better and that, in his eyes, *Godzilla Raids Again* was unsuccessful. The negative reception led Toho Studios to put any future Godzilla movies on hold until 1962 (*King Kong vs. Godzilla*, which will be discussed in Chapter 8).

In America, movie producer Paul Schreibman acquired the rights to the film, had it re-edited, added stock footage from other sci-fi movies of the time, and, perhaps most egregiously, changed Godzilla's name to Gigantis, the Fire Monster. Godzilla's classic roar was also changed for the release. Schreibman thought audiences would accept "Gigantis" as a monster that they had never seen before—but the gambit was not successful. It was the only time that Godzilla's name would ever be changed.

KAIJU FACT

In the 1980s, *Godzilla vs. Mothra* was released on VHS under that title, but because it still had the original English voiceover dubbing from *Godzilla vs. The Thing* (1964), Mothra is called "the Thing" instead.

☢ *Mothra vs. Godzilla* (1964)

Director: Ishirō Honda
Producer: Tomoyuki Tanaka
Writer: Shin'ichi Sekizawa
Alternate film titles: *Mosura tai Gojira* (Japan), *Godzilla vs. The Thing* (US/England), *Godzilla vs. Mothra* (US), *Godzilla Against Mothra* (Mexico), *Mothra Against Godzilla* (France), *Godzilla Against "The Thing"* (Belgium), *Godzilla and the Prehistoric Caterpillars* (Germany), *Godzilla Against the Monsters* (Spain), *Watang in the Fabulous Empire of Monsters* (Italy), *Mothra Meets Godzilla* (Sweden), *Panic in Tokyo: Godzilla and Monster Mothra* (Netherlands), *Godzilla Against the Holy Island* (Brazil)
Release date: April 29, 1964 (Japan), November 25, 1964 (US)
Lead actors: Akira Takarada, Yuriko Hoshi, Hiroshi Koizumi, Yū Fujiki, Emi and Yumi Itō, Yoshifumi Tajima
Primary Godzilla suit actor: Haruo Nakajima

——— ▼ ———

Mothra vs. Godzilla was the fourth Godzilla film in the Showa Era, following 1962's *King Kong vs. Godzilla*, which was the second-highest-grossing film in the history of Japan at the time. *Mothra vs. Godzilla* marked the first time Toho Studios brought in a kaiju from another of their franchises. When a giant egg washes up on shore, reporter Ichiro Sakai and photographer Junko Nakanishi, with the help of Professor Miura, investigate. Business tycoon Kumayama claims to have bought the egg from the local villagers and intends to turn it into a tourist attraction, preventing further investigation of the egg.

When the Shobijin, two tiny twin fairies, find Kumayama, they tell him that they are from Mothra Island and that the egg belongs to Mothra. But Kumayama is focused on the money that can be made from the spectacle of the egg and the Shobijin. He tries to capture the fairies, but they escape. Before heading back to Mothra Island, they ask Ichiro, Junko, and Miura to help them get the egg back before it hatches. Unfortunately, shortly after, Godzilla is awoken and attacks the city, getting closer to the egg. Mothra swoops in to save the egg and attacks Godzilla, but the King of the Monsters ends up killing Mothra. The egg hatches and twin larvae emerge and attack Godzilla with sprays of silk, until Godzilla falls and sinks down to the depths of the sea.

William Fischer of *Collider* listed this film as the third best of the Showa Era. "Even more impressive is the marionette work done with Mothra and the puppeteering of her larval twins," Fischer wrote. "Such unorthodox foes to fight give Godzilla some of his most unique battles in the series."

☢ Ghidorah, The Three-Headed Monster (1964)

Director: Ishirō Honda
Producer: Tomoyuki Tanaka
Writers: Shinichi Sekizawa
Alternate film titles: *Three Giant Monsters: The Greatest Battle on Earth* (Japan),

Ghidrah, the Three-Headed Monster (US), *Ghidrah, Monster of 3 Heads* (Spain/Mexico), *Ghidrah, the Monster of Three Heads* (Argentina), *Ghidorah, Monster of Monsters* (Turkey), *Ghidrah The Tricephalic Monster* (Brazil)
Release date: December 20, 1964 (Japan), September 13, 1965 (US)
Lead actors: Yosuke Natsuki, Yuriko Hoshi, Hiroshi Koizumi, Akiko Wakabayashi, Takashi Shimura, Hisaya Itō, Akihiko Hirata
Primary Godzilla suit actor: Haruo Nakajima

——— ▼ ———

After destroying alien lives on Venus, Ghidorah, a three-headed dragon kaiju from outer space, takes his powerful, destructive evil to Earth, ready to burn the planet to a crisp. It will take a team-up between Godzilla, Rodan (in his first appearance since his film debut in 1956), and Mothra to deal with the cosmic threat. This film marks the very first time that Godzilla is a protector and guardian of Earth, as opposed to just being an unchecked destructive menace, and the first time these three kaiju are allies.

Perhaps the most compelling part of the film is the fact that the kaiju heroes don't want to save

Ghidorah, The Three-Headed Monster (1964)

King Ghidorah and Godzilla in *Invasion of Astro-Monster* (1965).

the Earth. When Mothra confronts a quarreling Godzilla and Rodan, she pleads with them to help defend Earth against Ghidorah, and Godzilla essentially roars no. He and Rodan have always had problems with man, and man does not like them, so why should they help? Mothra calls them stubborn and goes to battle Ghidorah on her own. Only when Mothra is being beaten by Ghidorah do Godzilla and Rodan recognize Mothra's bravery and decide to join the fight.

Ghidorah, the Three-Headed Monster would become the fourth-highest-earning film in Japan from 1964 to 1965. During pre-production of the film, the set that was built of Mt. Fuji was constructed at 1/25th scale and took over 12,000 hours to complete. Movie critic Leonard Maltin called the film "one of the better Toho monster rallies."

☢ *Invasion of Astro-Monster* (1965)

Director: Ishirō Honda
Producer: Tomoyuki Tanaka
Writer: Shin'ichi Sekizawa
Alternate film titles: *Great Monster War* (Japan), *Monster Zero* (US), *Invasion Planet "X"* (France), *The Monsters Invade the Earth* (Spain), *Monsters of the Galaxies* (Mexico), *Command from the Dark* (Germany), *The Space Monsters Are Attacking* (Finland), *Monster Invasion* (Poland), *Year 2000: The Invasion of the Astro Monsters* (Italy), *Attack from the Unknown* (Czechoslovakia), *Invasion from Space* (Yugoslavia)
Release date: December 19, 1965 (Japan), July 29, 1970 (US)
Lead actors: Akira Takarada, Nick Adams, Yoshio Tsuchiya, Kumi Mizuno, Jun Tazaki, Akira Kubo, Keiko Sawai
Primary Godzilla suit actor: Haruo Nakajima

▼

When a two-man spacecraft piloted by an American and a Japanese astronaut finds a strange planet

behind Jupiter called Planet X, they land on the it and encounter the Controller of Planet X, who asks the astronauts if Earth would be willing to help them. The Controller wants Godzilla and Rodan, and in return, the people of Earth will be gifted a miracle drug that can cure any disease. Seeing how this would rid the Earth of two deadly kaiju, they

KAIJU FACT

During the production of *Invasion of Astro-Monster*, American actor Nick Adams spoke his lines in English and the Japanese actors said their lines in Japanese so that Adams could keep his voice in the American version of the film.

agree to the deal. The Controller eventually acquires Godzilla and Rodan, then sends back a message that if the Earth refuses to surrender to him and Planet X, they will send Godzilla, Rodan, and King Ghidorah, under the control of the aliens, to destroy the planet. The aliens arrive on Earth and unleash the kaiju onto the world as mankind attempts to find a way to free Godzilla and Rodan from alien control.

This film in the Showa series begins the push toward a kid-friendly Godzilla. The story is simple but fun. My favorite part of the film is a scene where Godzilla does a little jump dance; it is the most ridiculous thing, but it's so fun that you just accept it and continue watching the film. The American version of the film, which didn't premiere until five years after its release in Japan, stayed close to the original version of the film, only cutting three minutes and making minimal scene shifts.

Ebirah, Horror of the Deep (1966)

Director: Jun Fukuda
Producer: Tomoyuki Tanaka
Writer: Shin'ichi Sekizawa
Alternate film titles: *Gojira Ebira Mosura: Nankai no Daikettō* (Japan), *Godzilla vs. the Sea Monster* (US), *The Monsters from the Sea* (Spain), *Godzilla versus the Terror of the Seas* (Mexico), *The Return of Godzilla* (Italy), *Ebrirah: Monster Island* (Turkey)
Release date: December 17, 1966 (Japan), 1969 (US)
Lead actors: Akira Takarada, Kumi Mizuno, Akihiko Hirata, Jun Tazaki, Hideo Sunazuka, Chotaro Togin, Toru Ibuki, and Toru Watanabe
Primary Godzilla suit actor: Haruo Nakajima

——— ▼ ———

The first film in the Showa Era not directed by Ishirō Honda

starts with teenage Ryota and his friends being shipwrecked on Letchi Island. As they look for Ryota's brother, Yata, they find out that the island is being used by the Red Bamboo, a terrorist group that has enslaved the native people of Infant Island (formerly known as Mothra Island). The Red Bamboo has plans to launch a nuclear stockade of weapons, but Ryota and the others discover that Godzilla is on the island and hope that maybe he can stop the terrorists. But that's not all Godzilla has to worry about; he's going to have to battle the crustacean kaiju Ebirah and the deadly Giant Condor. But Godzilla won't face this menace alone, as Mothra joins the battle.

Ishirō Honda did not direct *Ebirah, Horror of the Deep*, due to scheduling conflicts and because he felt that he had made too many kaiju movies and it was time to step away from the genre for a bit. This

Godzilla and Mothra take on their underwater foe in *Ebirah, Horror of the Deep* (1966).

film is lighter in tone than previous kaiju movies, and the quick pace emphasizes the expediency of the threat of nuclear warfare, a terrorist group, and two evil kaiju all on the brink of destroying Japan and the world. Even with all that drama, this film continues the trend of the time of Godzilla becoming more camp, due to a push to make the series more kid-friendly to increase ticket sales and compete with the rise in popularity of television in Japan. Released as *Godzilla vs. the Sea Monster* in the United States, it was the first Godzilla film to not be shown in American movie theaters. Instead, it debuted on television sometime in 1969.

☢ *Son of Godzilla* (1967)

Director: Jun Fukuda
Producer: Tomoyuki Tanaka
Writers: Shin'ichi Sekizawa, Kazue Shiba
Alternate film titles: *The Battle of Monster Island: Son of Godzilla* (Japan), *Son of Godzilla* (US), *Frankenstein's Monsters Hunt Godzilla's Son* (West Germany), *Frankenstein's Island* (Germany)
Release date: December 16, 1967 (Japan), 1969 (US)
Lead Actors: Tadao Takashima, Bibari Maeda, Akira Kubo, Akihiko Hirata, Kenji Sahara, Yoshio Tsuchiya
Primary Godzilla suit actors: Haruo Nakajima, Hiroshi Sekita

Big Shoes to Fill

Director Jun Fukuda had a big act to follow after Ishirō Honda, but he had a successful run as director during the Showa Era, including on the following Godzilla films:

Ebirah, Horror of the Deep (1966)
Son of Godzilla (1967)
Godzilla vs. Gigan (1972)
Godzilla vs. Megalon (1973)
Godzilla vs. Mechagodzilla (1974)

Godzilla protects Minilla from Kamacuras in *Son of Godzilla* (1967).

KAIJU FACT

Kazue Shiba was the first woman to write a Godzilla movie.

When United Nations scientists on an island in the South Pacific try to solve an oncoming world food shortage, they create a climate experiment that ends up whipping up a radiation storm. The storm affects the already large mantises on the island, mutating them into kaiju called the Kamacuras. The Kamacuras find a kaiju egg, which hatches to reveal an infant Godzilla, Minilla. Godzilla rescues Minilla and adopts him as his own. But Godzilla is going to have his hands full, trying to both raise a son and defeat the Kamacuras and the Kumonga, a gigantic spider.

Some view Minilla as the Scrappy-Doo of the kaiju world because he brings little to the table and gets himself into trouble more than he helps. But he has an undying love for his new dad, and Godzilla will destroy anyone who puts a claw on him.

ROAR!
HAVE YOU EVER SEEN A MONSTER
HATCHED FROM A MONSTER EGG?
NO?
YOU WILL!
IN TOHO'S PRODUCTION
SON OF GODZILLA
EEK!
with
TADAO TAKASHIMA
BEVERLY MAEDA
AKIRA KUBO

There are some minor similarities between *Son of Godzilla* and *Ebirah, Horror of the Deep*. Both films take place on an island in the South Pacific that contains plenty of kaiju, and both films have similar endings, with people waving goodbye to the kaiju as the island is frozen (*Son of Godzilla*) or destroyed (*Ebirah, Horror of the Deep*). Both films also have a "native" female character. These similarities could be due to director Jun Fukuda and composer Masaru Sato, who both worked on the films. Like *Ebirah*, *Son of Godzilla* also made its US debut on television.

One unique aspect of *Son of Godzilla* is the debut of the MusukoGoji suit, which has a longer neck, higher-placed eyes, and a thick nose. This suit was designed to make Godzilla look more fatherly and taller compared to Minilla.

☢ *Destroy All Monsters* (1968)
Director: Ishirō Honda
Producer: Tomoyuki Tanaka
Writers: Ishirō Honda, Kaoru Mabuchi

Alternate film titles: *Monster Total Advancement* (Japan), *Godzilla: Blitz Battle* (Japan re-release), *The Invaders Attack* (France), *The Awakening of the Monsters* (Brazil), *Starfield Monsters* (Turkey), *The Heirs of King Kong* (Italy), *Extraterrestrial Invasion* (Spain), *Frankenstein and the Monsters from Space* (Germany), *Operation Monsterland* (England), *The Monsters are Threatening the World* (Finland), *All Monsters Must Be Destroyed* (Sweden)
Release date: August 1, 1968 (Japan), May 28, 1969 (US)
Lead actors: Akira Kubo, Jun Tazaki, Yukiko Kobayashi, Kyōko Ai, Yoshio Tsuchiya, Kenji Sahara
Primary Godzilla suit actor: Haruo Nakajima

———— ▼ ————

In what was originally to be the final film in the Godzilla franchise, *Destroy All Monsters*, the twentieth Toho kaiju film, sees the return of director Ishirō Honda, special-effects master Eiji Tsuburaya, and composer Akira Ifukube. In this kaiju mega-battle spectacular set in the year 1999, humanity has finally corralled all the kaiju on Earth and placed them in the Ogasawara Islands in an installation called "Monsterland," where the kaiju

Destroy All Monsters (1968) lobby card.

KAIJU FEATURED IN DESTROY ALL MONSTERS

NEW SUITS

GODZILLA
This film marks the debut of the SoshingekiGoji Godzilla suit, featuring a bell-shaped body with a highly prominent breastbone, a long neck, and defined eyebrows.

ANGUIRUS
A brand-new suit was built for Anguirus's appearance in *Destroy All Monsters*, as the creature becomes an ally to Godzilla. The new suit was made of leather on the back and had thorns made of polished balsa wood painted with polyester resin.

REPURPOSED SUITS/PROPS

MINILLA
The Minilla suit had modifications to its face and was refurbished from *Son of Godzilla* (1967).

MOTHRA
The larval form of Mothra was borrowed from earlier Toho films, but with some significant changes. Compared to previous versions, she sits closer to the ground and appears shorter. Her body is a deeper brown than the Second Generation Mothra. Her head is tiny, with the forehead not even reaching the top of the body. The sockets around Mothra's eyes are slightly more rounded but less deep, making the eyes more visible.

KUMONGA
Kumonga's head has six eyes that are usually blue. However, they shift to red when the monster is agitated in the *Son of Godzilla* and are permanently red in *Destroy All Monsters*.

RODAN
The Rodan suit used in *Destroy All Monsters* is technically the second-generation Rodan from *Invasion of the Astro-Monster*.

VARAN
This marks the second and final appearance of Varan in the Showa Era, following his debut in 1958.

GOROSAURUS
This is the second appearance of the massive atomic descendant of the Allosaurus since his debut in *King Kong Escapes* (1967).

KING GHIDORAH
Jiro Shirasaki, an art assistant, repaired the suit in various ways. He created new wings around the existing framework using Indian cloth. New die-cut scales were affixed to the monster's upper body, and new scales for the lower body and legs were handmade by cutting up rubber bicycle tires. The suit was also freshly painted with a blend of gold-colored rubber adhesive.

BARAGON
A new head was created for the suit, which looked almost the same as the original, except for the shape of the ears and its horn being pointed in a different direction. Despite being restored in time for filming, the suit was hardly used in the movie.

MANDA
The prop's head was replaced with a new design that lacked the previous ornate features such as spikes, horns, whiskers, and mane. As a result, the second-generation Manda now resembled its original concept as a gigantic snake, although it still had four legs. Along with the refurbished prop, a miniature model of Manda was also created for wide shots.

PREVIOUS FOOTAGE

KAMACURAS
Previous footage from his appearance in *Son of Godzilla* was used for this film.

can live in peace and scientists can study them. Humanity no longer has to worry about the kaiju being a threat.

But when a group of female aliens called the Kilaaks find Monsterland, they use their mind-control powers to send the kaiju on a destructive rampage all over the world. It's up to Captain Katsuo Yamabe and his team to find a way to end the Kilaaks's mind control over Godzilla and the others. Little do they know that even if they can find the solution, the Kilaaks have a dangerous and deadly last resort that they'll use against the Earth.

This film is not perfect by any means, but seeing so many kaiju on screen is amazing, and it's worth watching for the excellent final battle alone. With the success of *Destroy All Monsters*, Toho decided to continue the Godzilla film franchise. Steve Biodrowski of *Cinefantastique* had a mixed, but overall positive, review of the film, saying it "is too slim in its storyline, too thin in its characterizations, to be considered a truly great film

. . . But for the ten-year-old living inside us all, it is entertainment of the most awesome sort." *Destroy All Monsters* is also a cult favorite among Godzilla fans. In Steve Ryfle and Ed Godziszewski's 2017 book, *Ishiro Honda: A Life in Film, from Godzilla to Kurosawa*, which covers Honda's filmography, they call this film the "last truly spirited entry" in Toho's initial series of kaiju films. "It's an audacious and simple story, a bounty of monsters and destruction, and a memorably booming soundtrack from Akira Ifukube."

All Monsters Attack (1969)

Director: Ishirō Honda
Producer: Tomoyuki Tanaka
Writer: Shin'ichi Sekizawa
Alternate film titles: *Godzilla, Minilla, Gabara: All Monsters Attack* (Japan), *Godzilla's Revenge* (US), *Minya, Son of Godzilla* (US alternate title), *The Return of Gorgo* (Italy), *The Island of Monsters* (Spain)
Release date: December 20, 1969 (Japan), December 8, 1971 (US)
Lead actors: Tomonori Yazaki, Hideyo Amamoto, Kenji Sahara, Machiko Naka, Tomonori Yazaki, Hideyo Amamoto, Sachio Sakai, and Kazuo Suzuki
Primary Godzilla suit actor: Haruo Nakajima

—— ▼ ——

The first Godzilla film to sell under two million tickets in Japan, this coming-of-age story meant for children is one of the most critically panned films in the Showa Era. *All Monsters Attack* is centered on a young, lonely boy named Ichiro

Kaiju square off in *Destroy All Monsters* (1968).

Miki, who is bullied. To escape his problems—and reality—he dreams of going to Monster Island, where he meets Godzilla's son, Minilla. Minilla and Ichiro share a common bond—their parents are always busy and they are both trying to learn how to stand up to those that are tormenting them. Together, Ichiro and Minilla must find a way to confront their fears.

The majority of *All Monsters Attack* contains previous footage from *Ebirah, Horror of the Deep*, *King Kong Escapes*, *Son of Godzilla*, and *Destroy All Monsters*. Because of the amount of previously recorded footage used, filming took only a little over a month. It would be nine years before Ishirō Honda would direct another Godzilla film.

☢ *Godzilla vs. Hedorah* (1971)
Director: Yoshimitsu Banno
Producer: Tomoyuki Tanaka

Writers: Yoshimitsu Banno, Kaoru Mabuchi
Alternate film titles: *Gojira Tai Hedora* (Japan), *Godzilla vs. the Smog Monster* (US), *Monster Hedorah* (Turkey), *Hedorah, the Toxic Bubble* (Spain), *Satan's Creature* (Netherlands), *Godzilla Against Monsters of Smog* (Mexico), *Godzilla Against Hedorah* (Poland), *Frankenstein's Battle Against the Devil's Monster* (Germany), *Godzilla: Fury of the Monster* (Italy)
Release date: July 24, 1971 (Japan), February 1972 (US)
Lead actors: Tomonori Yazaki, Eisei Amamoto, Kenji Sahara, Machiko Naka
Primary Godzilla suit actor: Haruo Nakajima

——— ▼ ———

For a film that seriously intends to discuss the dangers of pollution in a postwar Japan, *Godzilla vs. Hedorah* is a delicate balance of serious, humorous, and flat-out absurd. Hedorah comes to Earth as a microscopic alien and begins to feed on the planet's pollution, causing it to grow to kaiju size and evolve.

A scene from *All Monsters Attack* (1969).

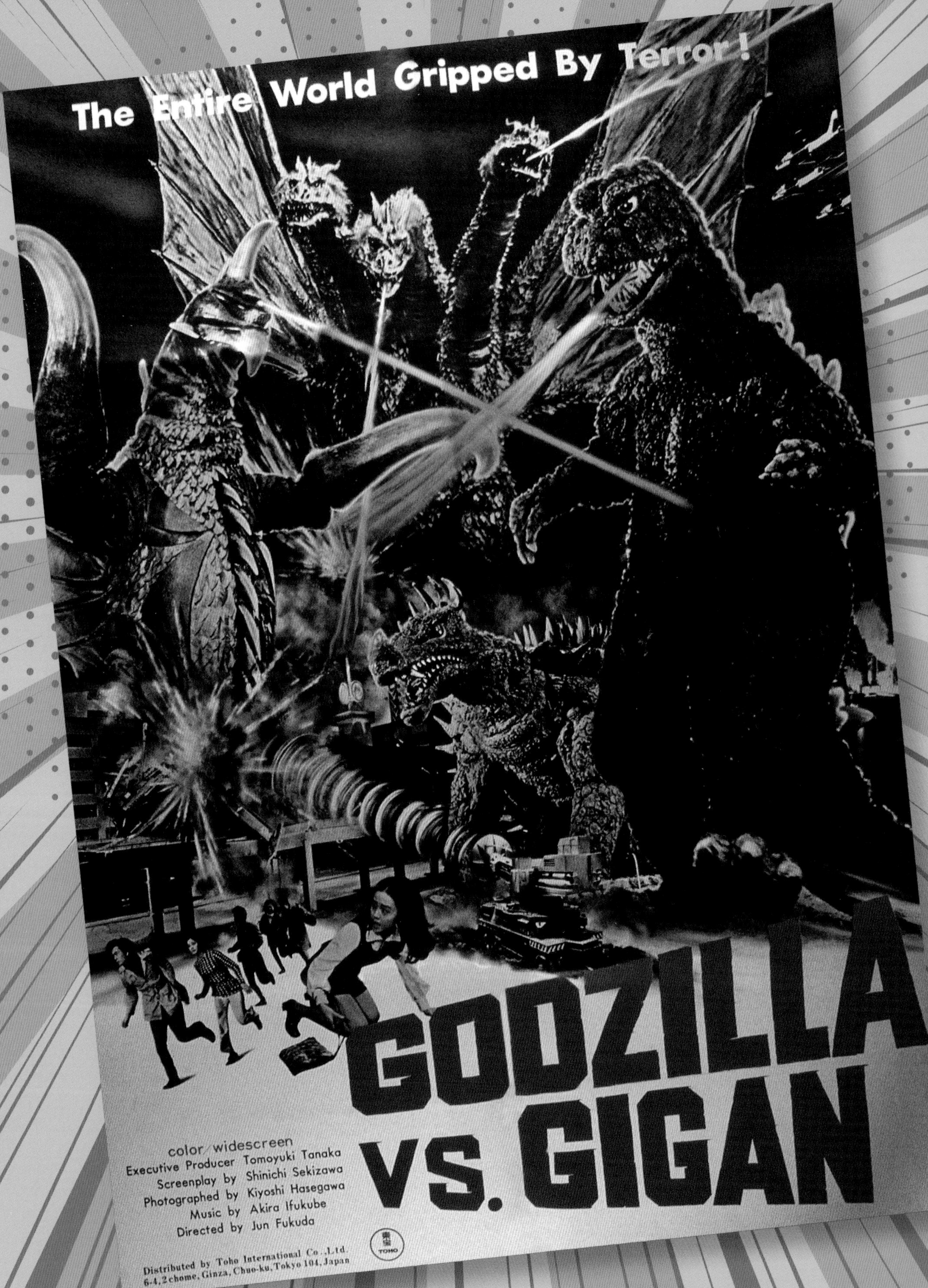

The Entire World Gripped By Terror!
GODZILLA
VS. GIGAN
color/widescreen
Executive Producer Tomoyuki Tanaka
Screenplay by Shinichi Sekizawa
Photographed by Kiyoshi Hasegawa
Music by Akira Ifukube
Directed by Jun Fukuda
TOHO
Distributed by Toho International Co., Ltd.
6-4, 2 chome, Ginza, Chuo-ku, Tokyo 104, Japan

Hedorah gains the ability to spew acid mists and sludge, fire crimson laser beams, and become aquatic, fly, or walk on land. It will take Godzilla and a group of scientists to defeat this mysterious monster. In one of the most ridiculous scenes in Godzilla history, while attempting to chase Hedorah, Godzilla uses his atomic breath to propel himself into the air and fly with ease, defying the laws of physics.

One positive thing about *Hedorah* is that Yasuyuki Inoue's design of this pollution kaiju is pure ecological terror for its time—especially when the monster's brain eerily creeps out from the

KAIJU FACT

The suit actor for Hedorah, Kenpachiro Satsuma, had appendicitis during filming. Due to the amount of time needed to take the Hedorah suit off, doctors had no choice but to perform the appendectomy while he was still wearing the suit.

many cracks on his head. The design gets across the need to provide a clean and safe Earth for the next generation. Even though the film attempts to be an anti-pollution story, it was panned by Japanese film critics. Author Steve Ryfle said in his book, *Japan's Favorite Mon-Star: The Unauthorized Biography of "The Big G,"* "The problem is that its treatment of pollution is visually didactic and dramatically childish . . . the issue of pollution is reduced to terms a child can understand (a monster) and its root causes are never discussed, making it hard to take the picture seriously." Vincent Canby, a *New York Times* critic, said that Godzilla in the film looks like "a sort of Japanese Smokey the Bear [sic] . . . looking as embarrassed and pious as an elderly clergyman at a charity masquerade ball."

☢ *Godzilla vs. Gigan* (1972)

Director: Jun Fukuda
Producer: Tomoyuki Tanaka
Writers: Shinichi Sekizawa
Alternate film titles: *Earth Attack Command: Godzilla vs. Gigan* (Japan), *Godzilla on Monster Island* (US), *Godzilla Against the Giants* (Turkey), *War of the Monsters* (England) *The Planet of Godzilla* (Belgium), *Galien, the Monster of the Galaxies Attacks the Earth* (Spain), *Godzilla Versus the Giants* (Italy), *Godzilla Against Gigan* (Poland), *Frankenstein's Hell Brood* (Germany), *Earth Objective: Mission Apocalypse* (France)
Release date: March 12, 1972 (Japan), August 1977 (US)
Lead actors: Hiroshi Ishikawa, Yuriko Hishimi, Minoru Takashima, Tomoko Umeda, Zan Fujita, Toshiaki Nishizawa, Kunio Murai
Primary Godzilla suit actor: Haruo Nakajima

——— ▼ ———

Godzilla and Anguirus team up to protect Japan and the Earth from an all-new kaiju, the cyborg-bladed space dinosaur Gigan. King Ghidorah also returns as an antagonist, having been brought to Earth by the M Space Hunter Nebula Aliens, who are space cockroaches disguised as human beings. (They also have a secret base that fronts as an amusement

The King of the Monsters takes on the pollution kaiju in *Godzilla vs. Hedorah* (1971).

OPPOSITE: Poster for *Godzilla vs. Gigan* (1972).

park.) It is also one of the first Godzilla films where the titular character draws blood.

Like *Godzilla vs. Hedorah*, the tone of this movie is all over the place and maintains a kid-friendly appeal. A number of changes were made in the American version of *Godzilla vs. Gigan*, including the new title *Godzilla on Monster Island*, even though Monster Island is not in the film. Additional cuts were made to get the film a G rating from the Motion Picture Association of America, including removing some harsh language and some of the

more violent or bloody fight scenes. Critic Scott Meek of *Time Out* said of the film, "Although Godzilla doesn't really cut it in the special effects department, he does have a certain lumbering charm. So does the script." Bob Chapman of *Escapist Magazine* wrote, "This one takes a while to get going, but as payoff you get Godzilla and Anguirus fighting new enemy Gigan and Ghidorah on one of the series' most unique battlefields: a Godzilla-themed amusement park."

Jet Jaguar takes on Megalon in *Godzilla vs. Megalon* (1973).

☢ *Godzilla vs. Megalon* (1973)

Director: Jun Fukuda
Producer: Tomoyuki Tanaka
Writers: Jun Fukuda, Takeshi Kimura, Shin'ichi Sekizawa
Alternate film titles: *Gojira tai Megaro* (Japan), *Godzilla vs. Megalon* (US), *At the Borders of Reality* (Italy), *King Kong: Demons from Outer Space* (Germany), *Gorgo and Superman Meet in Tokyo* (Spain), *Godzilla 1980* (France), *Planetary Titans* (Mexico)
Release date: March 17, 1973 (Japan), April 28, 1976 (US)
Lead actors: Katsuhiko Sasaki, Yutaka Hayashi, Hiroyuki Kawase, Kanta Mori, Kotaro Tomita, Ulf Otsuki
Primary Godzilla suit actor: Shinji Takagi

——— ▼ ———

Originally meant as a solo debut movie for the character Jet Jaguar, Godzilla was brought into the mix because Toho Studios felt the new character wouldn't be able to carry the film on their own. When nuclear testing is performed near the Aleutian Islands, the test creates dangerous seismic aftershocks which effect Japan and Monster Island. Even worse, the nuclear tests have also caused a series of environmental disasters and damaged the undersea world of Seatopia. Enraged, the Emperor of Seatopia calls

reviewed *Godzilla vs. Megalon* and said that this movie completed the canonization of Godzilla. He also noted that it was a wildly preposterous, imaginative, and funny film that often intentionally aimed for comedy. Canby also observed that the movie demonstrated the rewards of friendship between humans and monsters and had a gentle tone.

Over time, the film has become one of the most well-known kaiju films in the United States. However, its success may have contributed to the Western perception of kaiju films as cheap, comedic, and campy entertainment for children that should not be taken seriously. The film received renewed attention after being featured on *Mystery Science Theater 3000* in 1991.

One of the most memorable (and meme-able) scenes in the film happens when Jet Jaguar is holding Megalon still so Godzilla can dropkick the kaiju. Godzilla's dropkick consists of him taking a brief run, then sliding on the tip of his tail with his body held horizontal for what seems to be a mile before he kicks Megalon in the chest with both of his feet. The dropkick is so ridiculous—yet cool—that they perform it a second time.

Poster for *Godzilla vs. Megalon* (1973).

upon their kaiju, Megalon, to destroy Japan for the damage done to their world. It will take inventor Goro Ibuki, his creation Jet Jaguar, and his friends to help Godzilla defeat Megalon and Gigan, who the Hunter Nebula aliens have loaned to Seatopia.

This film has a new Godzilla suit, the MegaroGoji, which was made in one week. Three minutes of footage were removed from the initial American release of the film so it could receive a G rating. Even though *Godzilla vs. Megalon* contains new kaiju footage, it still uses a lot of footage from previous Godzilla films to save money, which lowers the quality of the story, making the film negatively received in Japan. It was one of the least viewed Godzilla films in the Showa Era with box-office receipts in Japan being much lower than the previous films. However, in America, *Godzilla vs. Megalon* was well received by critics. On July 12, 1976, *New York Times* film critic Vincent Canby

KAIJU FACT

This is the only Godzilla film without a major female character. Previous major Showa Era heroines include journalist Naoko Shindo in *Ghidorah, The Three-Headed Monster* (1964), played by Yuriko Hoshi; Emiko Yamane in *Godzilla* (1954) and *Godzilla, King of the Monsters* (1956), played by Momoko Kochi; and archeologist Saeko Kanagusuku in *Godzilla vs. Mechagodzilla* (1974), played by Reiko Tajima.

☢ *Godzilla vs. Mechagodzilla* (1974)

Director: Jun Fukuda
Producer: Tomoyuki Tanaka
Writers: Jun Fukuda, Shin'ichi Sekizawa, Masami Fukushima, Hiroyasu Yamamura
Alternate film titles: *Gojira tai Mekagojira* (Japan), *Godzilla vs. The Bionic Monster* (US) *Godzilla vs. The Cosmic Monster* (US-reissue), *Terror of Mechagodzilla* (Poland), *Godzilla Against the Mechagodzilla* (Hungary), *Godzilla vs. Cyber-Godzilla, the Destruction Machine* (Spain), *King Kong vs. Godzilla* (Germany), *MechaKing Against Godzilla* (Mexico), *Godzilla vs. the Robot* (Italy)

The titular kaiju go head-to-head in *Godzilla vs. Mechagodzilla* (1974).

Release date: March 21, 1974 (Japan), November 19, 1976 (US)
Lead actors: Masaaki Daimon, Kazuya Aoyama, Reiko Tajima, Bellbella Lin, Hiromi Matsushita, Akihiko Hirata, Hiroshi Koizumi, Goro Mutsumi, and Shin Kishida
Primary Godzilla suit actor: Isao Zushi

———— ▼ ————

This film, released in the twentieth anniversary year of the original Godzilla movie, marks Jun Fukuda and Masaru Sato's final time with the franchise and the debut of Mechagodzilla, one of Godzilla's most popular and dangerous adversaries.

When an ancient prophecy about a monster that will destroy the Earth is translated by archeologist Saeko Kanagusuku, Godzilla emerges from Mount Fuji and goes on a rampage. Godzilla's kaiju ally, Angurius, tries to stop Godzilla's fury and upon battling him realizes that the kaiju he's battling is a phony Godzilla. Godzilla finally arrives and is able to show that the fraudulent kaiju is Mechagodzilla, a robotic duplicate under the control of the Black Hole Planet 3 aliens, whose goal is to take over the world. This film also features the debut of the kaiju King Caesar, the ancient protector of Okinawa.

The jazz-influenced score is enthralling and adds so much to the film, while the special effects are vivid and fresh. *Godzilla vs. Mechagodzilla* is a refreshing entry in the franchise after the previous campier films and was a critical and commercial success in both Japan and America.

Terror of Mechagodzilla (1975)

Director: Ishirō Honda
Producer: Tomoyuki Tanaka
Writer: Yukiko Takayama
Alternate film titles: *Mechagodzilla's Counterattack* (Japan), *The Terror of Godzilla* (US), *Battle in Outer Space* (Turkey), *Monsters from an Unknown Planet* (England), *Monsters of the Lost Continent* (France), *Monsters from an Unknown Planet* (England), *Destroy Kong! The Earth is in Danger!* (Italy), *The Devil's Spawn* (Germany), *The Fury of the Monsters* (Brazil), *Mechakong* (Mexico)
Release date: March 15, 1975 (Japan), March 1977 (US)
Lead actors: Katsuhiko Sasaki, Tomoko Ai, Akihiko Hirata, Tadao Nakamaru, Goro Mutsumi, Masaaki Daimon, Katsumasa Uchida
Primary Godzilla suit actor: Toru Kawai

————— ▼ —————

The final film in the Showa Era and the last Godzilla film directed by Ishirō Honda, *Terror of Mechagodzilla* is not as lighthearted as the previous Godzilla fare. Picking up directly after *Godzilla vs. Mechagodzilla*, scientist Shinzo Mafune teams up with the Black Hole Planet 3 aliens to help them rebuild Mechagodzilla and also gives them access to the dinosaur kaiju known as Titanosaurus so that they can rule the planet. Once Titanosaurus and Mechagodzilla unleash their fury on Tokyo, Godzilla must face these two on his own. It takes both the Japan Self Defense Force and INTERPOL to help Godzilla save Tokyo.

KAIJU FACT

Godzilla vs. Mechagodzilla is the first film in which the monster suit actors are given credit on screen.

During the 1970s, the three major Japanese studios—Shochiku, Toho, and Nikkatsu—faced severe financial difficulties. As a result, they had limited funding to produce innovative films or support new talent. This led to a decline in Japanese-produced movies that could generate revenue in international markets. In 1975, the Japanese film industry's market share of box office receipts fell below fifty percent. *Terror of Mechagodzilla* was not meant to be the final Godzilla film in the Showa Era, but due to this continued decline of the film industry in Japan and lower box office returns, Godzilla would not return to the big screen for almost a decade.

OPPOSITE:
A battle sequence featuring Godzilla, Mechagodzilla, and Angurius in *Godzilla vs. Mechagodzilla* (1974).

The French poster for *Terror of Mechagodzilla* (1975).

4 **THE** **THE HEISEI ERA** **(1984-1995)**

> " The reckless ambitions of Man are often dwarfed by their dangerous consequences. For now, Godzilla, that strangely innocent and tragic monster, has gone to earth. Whether he returns or not or is never again seen by human eyes, the things he has taught us remain.
> —Raymond Burr as Steve Martin in *Godzilla 1985* "

After a nine-year absence in Japan, the Heisei Era of Godzilla launched in 1984. The era marks the reboot of the franchise, which kept the 1954 film in the canon and completely ignored the other films of the Showa Era. The decision to do this was made to bring Godzilla back to his serious and bleak beginnings. Originally, producer Tomoyuki Tanaka offered legendary director Ishirō Honda the chance to relaunch the franchise, but Honda refused. He had been turned off by the number of campy and kid-friendly Godzilla movies of the 1970s. He also felt that Godzilla should never return, due to the death of Eiji Tsuburaya in January 1970, who was a major influence in the creation of the kaiju.

For this era, the executives and directors made sure to introduce new kaiju, which would allow them to create merchandise and products for ancillary sales. There was not a years-long, pre-built schedule for the Heisei Era films, unlike the current American movie studio system, but a shared continuity within the era was established. Koji Hashimoto directed the first film in the Heisei Era and Kenpachiro Satsuma handled the suitmation for the entire era, wearing the more menacing "84Goji" Godzilla suit.

The Return of Godzilla rebooted the franchise and shared continuity with the Heisei films that came after it. Most of the films' titles in Japan include the word *versus*, leading to the nickname "VS. Series."

☢ *The Return of Godzilla* (1984)
Director: Koji Hashimoto
Producers: Tomoyuki Tanaka, Fumio Tanaka
Writers: Hideichi Nagahara
Alternate film titles: *Godzilla 1985* (US), *Godzilla: The Return of the Monster* (West Germany), *Godzilla Returns* (Norway), *Godzilla-85* (Sweden), *The Return of Godzilla 1986* (Mexico)
Release date: December 15, 1984 (Japan), August 23, 1985 (US)

KAIJU FACT

A 20-foot-tall animatronic Godzilla was built for *The Return of Godzilla* (1984) and was heavily promoted. But due to technical issues, it was primarily used for close-up shots and facial movements and reactions. A massive Godzilla foot was also made for certain crushing scenes in the film.

OPPOSITE:
Poster art for
Godzilla vs. King Ghidorah (1991).

Godzilla makes his way into the city to wreak havoc in *The Return of Godzilla* (1984).

Lead actors: Keiju Kobayashi, Ken Tanaka, Yasuko Sawaguchi, Shin Takuma, Yosuke Natsuki
Primary Godzilla suit actor: Kenpachiro Satsuma

— ▼ —

The Return of Godzilla takes place thirty years after the original *Godzilla* film (1954). The Japanese government attempts to keep Godzilla's return to Japan under wraps after a fishing boat is attacked and the only survivor claims that Godzilla was the aggressor. The secret doesn't remain a secret for long, after Godzilla creates tensions in the Cold War by destroying a Soviet nuclear submarine and activating a Soviet nuclear missile in the process, which is now heading toward Tokyo. Japan is faced with two nuclear dangers and hope for survival is slim.

The American version of the film, *Godzilla 1985*, was distributed by New World Pictures. New World added new footage for the film, and actor Raymond Burr reprised his role of Steve Martin from the original American *Godzilla: King of the Monsters* (1956). He only agreed to return if the American producers took the film seriously.

Even though Burr does a fantastic job in the film, there were still many edits made that shortened scenes or removed them altogether, and some of the American-produced scenes during serious moments of the film are interrupted by light nonsense or egregiously blatant shots of Dr. Pepper (thanks to a nice product placement deal with New World). One of the most bizarre changes in the New World Pictures version appears on the Russian submarine. In the original version, when the submarine is attacked by Godzilla, a Russian officer tries to prevent the nuclear weapons from firing and dies in the process. In the New World Pictures version, the film is edited to make the officer press the launch button purposely. Though the scene can easily be read as American producers pushing their own agenda during the Cold War, producer Anthony Randel said that the scene was done as a "joke" and no one thought about the ramifications. Since 1999, the New World Pictures version of this film has not been available for sale.

The Godzilla suit that Kenpachiro Satsuma wore for *The Return of Godzilla* was extremely heavy, and it wasn't built to properly fit him. Like the trials original suit actor Hauro Nakajima faced during the filming of *Godzilla* (1954), Satsuma lost a lot of weight during filming. Thankfully, more secure and safer suits were built for Satsuma for the sequels. *The Return of Godzilla* was a success in Japan, but the critically and commercially panned *Godzilla 1985* from New World Pictures would be the last Toho Godzilla that had a full American cinematic release for fifteen years.

☢ *Godzilla vs. Biollante* (1989)
Director: Kazuki Omori
Producers: Tomoyuki Tanaka, Shogo Tomiyama
Writers: Kazuki Omori, Shinichiro Kobayashi
Alternate film titles: *Godzilla Counterattacks* (Portugal), *Godzilla 2* (Mexico), *Godzilla 1990* (Thailand), *Big Dinosaurs* (Taiwan, China), *Godzilla: The Ancient Giant* (Germany), *Godzilla Against Biollante* (Poland/France/Italy/Spain)

Release date: December 16, 1989 (Japan), 1992 (US—home video)

Lead actors: Kunihiko Mitamura, Yoshiko Tanaka, Masanobu Takashima, Megumi Odaka, Toru Minegishi, Ryunosuke Kaneda, Koji Takahashi, Manjot Bedi

Primary Godzilla suit actor: Kenpachiro Satsuma

——— ▼ ———

The second film in the Heisei Era picks up where *The Return of Godzilla* left off. With Tokyo still reeling from the devastating effects of the mighty Godzilla, scientists are on the hunt for tissue samples that Godzilla left in his wake. They find them, only to have the samples stolen by a group called Bio-Major, and *then* they are stolen from Bio-Major by a man known as SSS9. SSS9 heads to the Middle East and gives them to Dr. Genichiro Shiragami, who is attempting to breed a new species of plant in the desert. His experiment fails when Bio-Major bombs the doctor's lab, killing his daughter.

Years later, Japan has finally recovered from Godzilla's attack, but Dr. Genichiro Shiragami, still grieving the death of his daughter, has acquired more Godzilla tissue samples. The government hopes that a bioweapon can be created to stop Godzilla once he returns from the volcanic tomb he fell into at the end of *The Return of Godzilla* (1984).

KAIJU FACT

Special effects director Koichi Kawakita first thought to use stop-motion and cell animation during the final battle between Godzilla and Biollante, but opted instead for practical effects for budgetary reasons and due to operating on a tight production schedule.

Godzilla takes on Biollante in the 1989 movie *Godzilla vs. Biollante.*

An epic battle from *Godzilla vs. King Ghidorah* (1991).

Instead, Shiragmai uses the samples to create a dangerous plant-based kaiju, the deadly Biollante.

Godzilla vs. Biollante is the first "kaiju vs. kaiju" Godzilla movie in the Heisei Era and features an all-new kaiju, Biollante. Biollante was created for a contest that Toho ran, in which contestants submitted solicited script ideas. Shinichiro Kobayashi was the winner, and his idea was adapted into a screenplay for filming. The film has fantastic monster battles, and for a massive plant kaiju, the Biollante suit has a lot of movement and flexibility. A favorite among fans, *Godzilla vs. Biollante* was one of the most expensive Godzilla movies ever made at the time.

☢ *Godzilla vs. King Ghidorah* (1991)

Director: Kazuki Omori
Producers: Tomoyuki Tanaka, Shogo Tomiyama
Writer: Kazuki Omori
Alternate film titles: *Godzilla: Duel of the Megasaurians* (Germany), *Godzilla Against the Evil Monster* (Brazil), *Godzilla Against King Ghidrah* (Portugal), *The War of the Dinosaurs* (Argentina), *War Dragon Godzilla* (Hong Kong, China) **Release date:** December 14, 1991 (Japan), April 28, 1998 (US—home video)
Lead actors: Anna Nakagawa, Kosuke Toyohara, Megumi Odaka, Kiwako Harada, Akiji Kobayashi, Katsuhiko Sasaki, Chuck Wilson, So Yamamura
Primary Godzilla suit actor: Kenpachiro Satsuma

——— ▼ ———

This film brings back one of Godzilla's biggest foes, opening the door for the return of other classic Showa Era foes in future films. In *Godzilla vs. King Ghidorah*, Godzilla has lain dormant in the Sea of Japan for over two years after his battle with Biollante. When the Futurians arrive in Japan from the year 2204, they warn that Godzilla will soon return and destroy everything. The Futurians plan to go back to 1944 and remove young Godzilla from Lagos Island (the birthplace of the King of the Monsters, located between the larger islands of Luol and Kwajalein in the Marshall Islands) before it can be bombarded by nuclear testing. The Futurians' plan is successful, but they leave creatures known as Dorats on the island instead. The nuclear fallout causes them to evolve and become King Ghidorah, who the Futurians then release on modern-day Japan, fulfilling their true plan. The government tries to find a way to bring back Godzilla to save humanity.

There's a scene in this movie that is a bit difficult to parse. An old man looks at Godzilla, at eye level, from a skyscraper window. During World War II, we find out, Godzilla defended this man's platoon during a battle. For a moment, there seems to be admiration and respect between man and beast. Then, Godzilla blasts his atomic breath into the building, blowing it to pieces and killing the old man.

The film also faced some controversy for a scene in which a younger Godzilla kills American soldiers on Lagos Island. CNN and the Associated Press reported on that particular scene, as well as the scene in which the Futurians' plan to subjugate Japan before it can become a superpower. In an interview with CNN, director Kazuki Omori clarified that the movie was not specifically anti-US, but rather an attempt to explore the identity of the Japanese people. Still, it would be several years until the film was released in the United States.

☢ *Godzilla vs. Mothra* (1992)

Director: Takao Okawara
Producers: Tomoyuki Tanaka, Shogo Tomiyama
Writer: Kazuki Omori
Alternate film titles: *Return of the Dinosaur* (Russia), *Godzilla and Mothra: The Battle for Earth* (US), *Butterfly Dragon Mothra* (Taiwan, China), *Godzilla vs. Super Mothra* (India), *Godzilla and Mothra* (Portugal), *Godzilla's Dragon War of the Four Seas* (Hong Kong, China), *Godzilla: Battle of the Saurian Mutants* (Germany), *Godzilla: The Mutant Dinosaur* (Argentina)
Release date: December 12, 1992 (Japan), April 1998 (US —home video)

Lead actors: Tetsuya Bessho, Satomi Kobayashi, Takehiro Murata, Megumi Odaka, Shiori Yonezawa, Akiji Kobayashi, Keiko Imamura, Sayaka Osawa
Primary Godzilla suit actor: Kenpachiro Satsuma

—— ▼ ——

An archeological research team visits Infant Island as the Earth is dealing with the ramifications and environmental disturbances of a meteor that impacted the Ogasawara Trench. During their exploration, they meet two tiny twin fairies known as the Cosmos who reveal that the Earth is fighting back against the harm caused by humans. The fairies inform the research team that an evil creature

The Japanese poster for *Godzilla vs. Mothra* (1992).

Godzilla vs. Mothra remains the highest-grossing film in Godzilla's history. It was also the second-highest-grossing film at the Japanese box office that year, behind *Jurassic Park*.

named Battra has been sent to destroy humanity. In response to their call for help, the Cosmos summon Mothra to battle Battra. However, the situation becomes more complicated when Godzilla also appears, and the three-way battle puts Japan in danger of being destroyed.

This film represents Battra's debut and only cinematic appearance. Two Godzilla suits were used during the filming of *Godzilla vs. Mothra*. The BatoGoji suit was a sleek and sturdy Godzilla suit with expressive eyes, more flexibility in the biceps, and an electronic head that could tilt independently. The BioGoji suit had larger teeth and was heavier than the BatoGoji suit. Akira Ifukube won a Japanese Academy Award for his musical score for *Godzilla vs. Mothra*.

☢ *Godzilla vs. Mechagodzilla II* (1993)

Director: Takao Okawara
Producers: Tomoyuki Tanaka, Shogo Tomiyama
Writer: Wataru Mimura
Alternate film titles: *Jurasic City – Godzilla v/s Mechagodzilla* (India), *Birth of the Dinosaur* (Taiwan, China), *Godzilla Against Mechagodzilla II* (Poland), *Legend of the Dinosaur 2* (Russia)
Release date: December 11, 1993 (Japan), August 1999 (US—home video)
Lead actors: Masahiro Takashima, Ryoko Sano, Megumi Odaka, Daijiro Harada, Kenji Sahara, Akira Nakao
Primary Godzilla suit actor: Kenpachiro Satsuma

In *Godzilla vs. Mechagodzilla II*, Mechagodzilla and Rodan are brought back, following the successful revivals of King Ghidorah and Mothra in the franchise's previous two films. The United Nations Godzilla Countermeasure Center has created Mechagodzilla as the ultimate anti-Godzilla weapon. Meanwhile, on the radiation-polluted Adonoa Island, scientists discover a perfectly intact Pteranodon egg, only to be attacked by its nestmate, the kaiju Pteranodon Rodan. Godzilla, knowing the egg is that of his kin, also arrives on the island to claim it, but the scientists manage to escape with the egg as Godzilla and Rodan battle. When the egg

Godzilla, Rodan, and Mechagodzilla in *Godzilla vs. Mechagodzilla II* (1993).

hatches into a baby Godzillasaurus, G-Force (an international military unit formed by the United Nations and the Japanese Self-Defense Force) plans to use the infant to lure Godzilla over to the Ogasawara Islands, where Mechagodzilla awaits. Rodan interferes with the plan by intercepting the convoy carrying BabyGodzilla (named by a scientist), and this sets up a final battle between Godzilla, Rodan, and Mechagodzilla near Makuhari Bay.

This film is not a remake, reimagining, or sequel to the original *Godzilla vs. Mechagodzilla*. Its title was chosen to avoid confusion with the 1974 film as the two films' Japanese titles both translate to *Godzilla vs. Mechagodzilla*. *Godzilla vs. Mechagodzilla II* marks the first time that Rodan was not portrayed using suitmation; puppets and props were used instead. Godzilla is on screen for twenty-seven minutes, one of his longest stints on film.

☢ *Godzilla vs. SpaceGodzilla* (1994)

Director: Kensho Yamashita
Producers: Tomoyuki Tanaka, Shogo Tomiyama
Writer: Hiroshi Kashiwabara

Alternate film title: *Godzilla Against Cosmicgodzilla* (Poland)
Release date: December 10, 1994 (Japan), 1999 (US—home video)
Lead actors: Jun Hashizume, Megumi Odaka, Zenkichi Yoneyama, Akira Nakao, Yosuke Saito, Koichi Ueda, Kenji Sahara, Towako Yoshikawa, Akira Emoto
Primary Godzilla suit actor: Kenpachiro Satsuma

——— ▼ ———

Godzilla cells that were sent into space, either via Biollante's remains after the battle in *Godzilla vs. Biollante* (1989) or Godzilla flesh from Mothra's claws after she went into space in *Godzilla vs. Mothra* (1992), fall into a black hole, and then exit from a white hole in space, giving rise to a mutant monster named SpaceGodzilla, who plans to destroy Godzilla and take control of Earth. In the meantime, G-Force has built a new anti-Godzilla machine called Moguera, a kaiju-sized robot designed to destroy Godzilla. Moguera's first combat mission is to face SpaceGodzilla, and it fails to stop the monster from approaching the Earth. SpaceGodzilla defeats Godzilla and then turns the city of Fukuoka into his own crystal fortress. To save his adopted

A scene from *Godzilla vs. SpaceGodzilla* (1994), featuring the titular characters and BabyGodzilla.

GODZILLA SPECIAL EFFECTS DIRECTORS OVER THE ERAS

The films of Godzilla would not be what they are today without the heavy lifting that's done by the special effects implemented in every movie. These are a few contributors who have helped give Godzilla and his fellow kaiju life.

SHOWA ERA

EIJI TSUBURAYA AND ISHIRŌ HONDA

Honda and Tsuburaya were frequent collaborators. Tsuburaya directed or received credit for the special effects in all of Honda's kaiju films until he died in 1970. During the filming of *All Monsters Attack* (1969), Tsuburaya's failing health prevented him from handling the special effects, so Honda took over, with assistance from Teruyoshi Nakano. Despite this, Tsuburaya was still given honorary credit as the film's special effects supervisor.

SADAMASA ARIKAWA

Arikawa was a cinematographer and special effects director mentored by Eiji Tsuburaya. He began his career as a cameraman and was responsible for filming effects for every Toho science-fiction movie from 1954 to 1966. After Tsuburaya's death, Arikawa succeeded him as the special effects director for the Godzilla series. He started unofficially with *Ebirah, Horror of the Deep* (1966) and officially with *Son of Godzilla* (1967) and held the role until *Destroy All Monsters* (1968).

YOSHIO TABUCHI

Tabuchi served as assistant director of special effects (uncredited) for *All Monsters Attack* (1969) and first assistant director of special effects (also uncredited) on *Godzilla vs. Hedorah* (1971), *Godzilla vs. Gigan* (1972), *Godzilla vs. Megalon* (1973), and *Terror of Mechagodzilla* (1975).

TERUYOSHI NAKANO

After handling most of the special effects on Ishirō Honda's behalf (uncredited) for *All Monsters Attack* (1969), following the death of Tsuburaya and Arikawa's departure, Teruyoshi contributed to the special effects work in an official capacity starting with *Godzilla vs. Hedorah* (1971) and running through *The Return of Godzilla* (1984).

HEISEI ERA

KŌICHI KAWAKITA

The director of special effects for every film in the Heisei Era except *The Return of Godzilla* (1984), Kōichi also has a number of uncredited acting roles in Godzilla films from the Showa Era, Heisei Era, and the Millennium Series.

MAKOTO KAMIYA

The assistant director of special effects for *Godzilla vs. Biollante* (1989), *Godzilla vs. King Ghidorah* (1991), and *Godzilla vs. Mechagodzilla II* (1993, uncredited), Makoto later became the director of special effects for the Millennium Series' *Godzilla, Mothra, and King Ghidorah: Giant Monsters All-Out Attack* (2001).

MILLENIUM SERIES

KENJI SUZUKI

Suzuki was the first assistant special effects director for almost every Heisei Era Godzilla

Crew members prepare Godzilla for his close-up in 1994's *Godzilla vs. SpaceGodzilla*.

EIICHI ASADA

Asada was the director of special effects for *Godzilla: Tokyo SOS* (2003) and *Godzilla Final Wars* (2004). He also worked (uncredited) on Showa Era projects *Godzilla vs. Megalon* (1973), *Godzilla vs. Mechagodzilla* (1974), and *Terror of Mechagodzilla* (1975), and was the first assistant director of special effects for the Heisei Era film *The Return of Godzilla* (1984).

YOSHIKAZU ISHII

Ishii served as first assistant director of special effects on *Godzilla Final Wars* (2004).

film except *The Return of Godzilla* (1984) and would later be promoted to director of special effects for the Millennium Series films *Godzilla 2000: Millennium* (1999) and *Godzilla vs. Megaguirus* (2000).

YUICHI KIKUCHI

After handling the role of first assistant director of special effects for *Godzilla vs. Megaguirus* (2000) and *Godzilla, Mothra, and King Ghidorah: Giant Monsters All-Out Attack* (2001), Yuichi became the director of special effects on *Godzilla Against Mechagodzilla* (2002).

SHOREI NOMA

Noma was the first assistant director of special effects for *Godzilla Against Mechagodzilla* (2002).

REIWA ERA

KATSURO ONOUE

Onoue served as the associate director, VFX creative director, and director of special effects on *Shin Godzilla* (2016).

SHINJI HIGUCHI

Higuchi held multiple roles on *Shin Godzilla* (2016), including co-director and storyboard artist, as well as working in the visual effects department.

KIYOKO SHIBUYA

The visual effects director for *Godzilla Minus One* (2023), Shibuya was inspired to work in visual effects after watching *Star Wars* (1977) and *Back to the Future* (1985).

son, BabyGodzilla, from being trapped in SpaceGodzilla's deadly crystals, Godzilla teams up with Moguera in the hopes of defeating his extraterrestrial doppelganger.

Though it was much larger than the Godzilla suit, the SpaceGodzilla suit was made with fiber-reinforced plastic, which made it lighter than the Godzilla suit. The lighter weight made it easier for suit actor Ryo Hariya to move around in it. It was designed by Minoru Yoshida, who had worked as a designer on a lot of the Heisei Era Godzilla movies. SpaceGodzilla was designed to pay homage to Biollante, incorporating tusks and a hissing roar reminiscent of the monster. Special effects artist Koichi Kawakita incorporated crystals into SpaceGodzilla's design and added a horn on its head to imply radar abilities and hint at its power.

🌀 Godzilla vs. Destoroyah (1995)

Director: Takao Okawara
Producers: Tomoyuki Tanaka, Shogo Tomiyama
Writer: Kazuki Omori
Alternate film titles: *The Last Godzilla* (India), *Dinosaur Empire* (Taiwan, China), *Godzilla Meets Destoroyah* (Sweden), *Godzilla the Final Chapter: Deadly Battle of the Century* (Hong Kong, China), *Godzilla Against Destroyer* (Argentina/Poland), *Godzilla Against Absolute Destroyer* (Greece)
Release date: December 9, 1995 (Japan), January 19, 1999 (US—home video)

Godzilla unleashes his atomic breath in *Godzilla vs. Destoroyah* (1995).

Lead actors: Takuro Tatsumi, Yoko Ishino, Yasufumi Hayashi, Megumi Odaka, Sayaka Osawa, Masahiro Takashima, Momoko Kochi, Akira Nakao
Primary Godzilla suit actor: Kenpachiro Satsuma

———— ▼ ————

Godzilla vs. Destoroyah is the final Godzilla film of the Heisei Era. After uranium deposits under Baas Island explode, Godzilla transforms into the super-powerful Burning Godzilla. However, his nuclear heart becomes uncontrollable and could possibly explode, posing a threat to the planet. When the construction of the Tokyo Bay bridge and underwater tunnel wakes up a colony of Precambrian crustaceans that were mutated by the Oxygen Destroyer used to kill the first Godzilla in 1954, the creatures merge together and form an evil abomination called Destoroyah. Even though the people of Japan need Destoroyah to fight Godzilla (and hope that it kills him before his overloaded heart destroys the world), Destoroyah's only goals are terror and destruction, leaving little room for hope in Japan.

After its release, Toho decided to place any future Godzilla plans on hold to make room for Sony/TriStar Pictures' *Godzilla* (1998), which was supposed to be the start of a Hollywood trilogy that would've kept Toho from making another Godzilla movie for many years. But the new millennium brought a different turn of events.

OPPOSITE: BabyGodzilla, Godzilla's adopted son, in *Godzilla vs. SpaceGodzilla* (1994).

KAIJU FACT

Ryu Hariken was the suitmation actor for BabyGodzilla, aka Godzilla Junior. His nickname is "Hurricane."

5 A NEW MILLENNIUM

> ## Witness! A new era of Godzilla!
> —Japanese tagline for
> *Godzilla 2000: Millennium* (1999)

f the American Godzilla movie from 1998 had been both critically and commercially successful, there's a chance that the Millennium Series of Godzilla films would've happened at a much later date, if at all. But since *Godzilla* (1998) was controversial and universally panned, plans for two more sequels at the American studio were terminated. Toho decided that it would be best to revitalize the franchise, rebooting the series and again ignoring every film after the original *Godzilla* (1954). In fact, this series of films would see multiple reboots, in order to tell a variety of stories and experiment with storytelling without having to worry about continuity.

▾▾ THE MILLENNIUM SERIES ▾▾

Godzilla 2000: Millennium (1999)

Director: Takao Okawara
Producers: Shogo Tomiyama, Kazunari Yamanaka
Writers: Hiroshi Kashiwabara, Wataru Mimura
Alternate film titles: *Godzilla 2000* (US), *The Return of Godzilla* (Poland), *Godzilla 2000 vs. the Extraterrestrial Squid* (Mexico)
Release date: December 11, 1999 (Japan), August 18, 2000 (US)

Lead actors: Takehiro Murata, Hiroshi Abe, Naomi Nishida, Takeo Nakahara, Mayu Suzuki, Shiro Sano
Primary Godzilla suit actor: Tsutomu Kitagawa

▾

After Y2K, the Godzilla Prediction Network (GPN) is formed to study and track Godzilla's movements when he appears on the coast of Nemuro and

OPPOSITE:
Poster art for
Godzilla (2014).

A new era dawns for the King of the Monsters in *Godzilla 2000: Millennium* (1999).

A crew member (and Godzilla) on the set of *Godzilla vs. Megaguirus* (2000).

ultimately destroys the city. Before this tragedy, a 60-million-year-old rock is discovered, and without warning, it begins to float and heads towards a meeting with Godzilla in Tokai Mura. During their encounter, Godzilla uses his powerful atomic breath to break the rock, revealing a UFO. The UFO and Godzilla engage in battle, with the UFO ultimately blasting Godzilla back into the sea. Later, the UFO heads towards Shinjuku, where the final battle between the UFO and Godzilla commences. The UFO transforms into a monster called Orga and attempts to take Godzilla's DNA so it can convert itself into a Godzilla clone, making Orga one of Godzilla's most challenging foes to date.

TriStar Pictures acquired the license to give *Godzilla 2000* a full cinematic release in the US, instead of a limited theatrical run in big market cities. It was the first Godzilla film to be shown in a theater since *Godzilla 1985*. Sony (owners of TriStar Pictures) spent over a million dollars to re-edit the film and dub it, and another ten million dollars in marketing.

The American Sequel that Wasn't

Mike Schlesinger oversaw the American version of *Godzilla 2000* and planned to produce an American-made sequel to the film titled *Godzilla Reborn*, which would feature Godzilla fighting a giant lava bat monster called Miba in Hawaii. The project was approved by Toho and even greenlit by Sony, but it was ultimately cancelled by Sony's new head of production because they did not want to produce films with low budgets of just $5 to $10 million. The American release of *Godzilla 2000* also only earned $10 million at the box office, leaving executives wary of a sequel.

I feel that this was TriStar's way of apologizing to Toho to keep their video distribution deal with Toho intact due to their production of *Godzilla* (1998) being the controversial mess that it was.

☢ *Godzilla vs. Megaguirus* (2000)

Director: Masaaki Tezuka
Producers: Shogo Tomiyama, Kazunari Yamanaka
Writers: Hiroshi Kashiwabara, Wataru Mimura
Alternate film title: *Exterminate Godzilla* (Mexico)
Release date: December 16, 2000 (Japan), July 13, 2002 (US—G-FEST), 2004 (US—home video)
Lead actors: Misato Tanaka, Shosuke Tanihara, Masanobu Katsumura, Mansaku Ikeuchi, Hiroyuki Suzuki, Masato Ibu, Yuriko Hoshi
Primary Godzilla suit actor: Tsutomu Kitagawa

—— ▼ ——

In another reboot of the Godzilla franchise that ignores every Godzilla film except the original, Japan has been dealing with attacks from Godzilla since he first appeared in 1954. When Godzilla returns to wreak havoc on Japan, scientists have developed two new weapons for self-defense: a state-of-the-art ship called the Gryphon and the Dimension Tide, a device that can create artificial black holes. During a test of the Dimension Tide, strange eggs start appearing in Shibuya, which hatch into terrifying monsters called Meganurons.

The Meganurons require water to grow, so they break the water mains to flood the city. As they multiply and grow, they begin to feed on the energy of humans, which gives them the power to transform into giant dragonfly monsters called Meganuras. The Meganuras target Godzilla to take his energy to feed their queen, the horrifying Megaguirus, which leads to a battle between Godzilla, Megaguirus, and the people of Japan.

Godzilla vs. Megaguirus is the second-lowest-earning film in the Millennium Series and the last Godzilla film to be produced and released in the twentieth century. The GiraGoji suit was used during filming and was digitally placed into footage of Godzilla's original attack from the 1954 film. The scales on this particular Godzilla suit are more detailed and deep, his dorsal plates are large and jagged with a purple tint, and his head shape is thinner, making him look more reptilian. Godzilla also has a prominent frown on his face, and the eyes are a darker green. Critical reception of the film was mixed, with Mike Bogue of American Kaiju writing, "Though not the best of the post-Showa Godzilla movies, Godzilla vs. Megaguirus is one of the most entertaining." In his review for The Spinning Image, Andrew Pragasam called the film a "flawed, but entertaining comic book extravaganza."

☢ Godzilla, Mothra, and King Ghidorah: Giant Monsters All-Out Attack (2001)

Director: Shusuke Kaneko
Producers: Hideyuki Honma, Shogo Tomiyama
Writers: Keiichi Hasegawa, Masahiro Yokotani, Shusuke Kaneko
Alternate film titles: The Invasion of Godzilla (Mexico), The Great Battle of Monsters (Poland)
Release date: December 15, 2001 (Japan), July 19, 2003 (US—G-Fest)
Lead actors: Chiharu Niiyama, Ryudo Uzaki, Masahiro Kobayashi, Shiro Sano, Kaho Minami, Shin'ya Owada, Kunio Murai, Hiroyuki Watanabe, Hideyo Amamoto
Primary Godzilla suit actor: Mizuho Yoshida

In yet another continuity reboot following the poor performance of Godzilla vs. Megaguirus, the people of Japan have put the horrors of World War II and Godzilla behind them. However, the destruction of a US submarine raises concerns for Admiral Tachibana. Meanwhile, his daughter Yuri is working on a docudrama and learns about the legend of three guardian monsters that are believed to be awakened by an old man named Hirotoshi Isayama. Isayama explains to Yuri that Godzilla embodies the restless souls of the victims of the Pacific War and he has returned to take revenge on the nation for forgetting the suffering that the war brought. Yuri and her team set out to investigate, while Admiral Tachibana and the Guardian Monsters—Baragon, Mothra, and Ghidorah—try to defeat a Godzilla hellbent on vengeance.

Godzilla, Mothra, and King Ghidorah was an immense success for Toho, which allowed the studio to continue the Millennium Series for three more films. The kaiju battles are quite violent

Poster art for Godzilla, Mothra, and King Ghidorah: Giant Monsters All Out Attack (2001).

and the film's tone is darker, in an attempt to make Godzilla feel like a threat to everything and everyone. The story delves into the politics of war and those who are left behind to deal with the after-effects. Critic Kevin L. Lee of *Film Inquiry* said of the film, "Though short on humor or deep substance, both political and emotional, it has consistently stirring action sequences, tight pacing, and a likable female lead. This is efficient monster entertainment, and if you're already a Godzilla fan, this is surely one of the best installments in the franchise." This also marks one of the few times that Ghidorah is portrayed as a hero (and also as shorter than Godzilla—in previous appearances, Ghidorah is much larger). Mothra is also smaller here, and her poison powder and hurricane wind attacks are replaced with stingers. In his first appearance since *Destroy All Monsters* (1968), Baragon's heat ray is also removed for this movie.

☢ *Godzilla Against Mechagodzilla* (2002)
Director: Masaaki Tezuka
Producers: Shogo Tomiyama, Takahide Morichi
Writer: Wataru Mimura

Poster art for *Godzilla Against Mechagodzilla* (2002).

KAIJU FACT

Mechagodzilla is called Kiyru (Machine Dragon) in this film to distance the character from previous versions of Mechagodzilla.

Alternate film title: *The Return of Mechagodzilla* (*Powrót Mechagodzilli*; Poland)
Release date: November 2, 2002 (Japan), June 24, 2004 (US—Godzilla's 50th anniversary year)
Lead actors: Yumiko Shaku, Shin Takuma, Kana Onodera, Ko Takasugi, Yusuke Tomoi, Koichi Ueda, Kumi Mizuno, Akira Nakao
Primary Godzilla suit actor: Tsutomu Kitagawa

Yet again, Toho reboots the franchise continuity. When an all-new Godzilla (following the death of the original in 1954) attacks Japan in 1999, the attack prompts the government to dig up the bones of the original Godzilla from 1954 to create a Mechagodzilla called Kiryu. Kiyru is deployed to battle the new kaiju, but when the sound of Godzilla's roar activates the soul of the original Godzilla within Kiyru, Kiryu goes awry. Scientist Tokumitsu Yuhara repairs the error caused by Godzilla's scream, but the government and Kiryu pilot Akane Yashiro must decide if it's worth using the mechanical kaiju again as Godzilla returns for another battle.

Godzilla Against Mechagodzilla is the second-highest-grossing Godzilla film of the Millennium Series. It has a compelling story and manages to be both entertaining and fun. Plus, it's just downright cool to see the skeleton of the original Godzilla. Witney Seibold of *Nerdist* also called *Godzilla Against Mechagodzilla* "the strongest Millennium film."

☢ *Godzilla: Tokyo S.O.S.* (2003)

Director: Masaaki Tezuka
Producers: Shogo Tomiyama, Kazunari Yamanaka
Writers: Masaaki Tezuka, Masahiro Yokotani
Alternate film titles: *Godzilla X Mothra X Mechagodzilla: Tokyo SOS* (Japan), *Godzilla: Tokyo in Danger* (Mexico)
Release date: December 13, 2003 (Japan), 2004 (US—home video)
Lead actors: Noboru Kaneko, Miho Yoshioka, Mitsuki Koga, Chihiro Otsuka, Masami Nagasawa, Tatsuki Omori, Koichi Ueda, Yumiko Shaku, Akira Nakao, Hiroshi Koizumi
Primary Godzilla suit actor: Tsutomu Kitagawa

——— ▼ ———

Godzilla: Tokyo S.O.S. is the first direct sequel in the Millennium Series. A year after Kiryu's battle with Godzilla, the Shinjobin—the twin fairy priestesses of Mothra—appear in Japan to tell the government that the reason why Godzilla keeps coming back is because of the use of the original Godzilla bones inside of Kiryu. That use violates the natural order of kaiju and nature itself. Both Kiryu and Godzilla's bones must be sent to the ocean to restore peace. With the government refusing to terminate the

Kiryu program, Godzilla makes his way back to Tokyo yet again, and now Mothra and her two twin larvae, along with Kiryu, must battle Godzilla to the death.

Ken Eisner of *Variety* enjoyed *Godzilla: Tokyo S.O.S.*, saying, "Monster effects for Godzy and Mothra (aka Mosura) are as cheesy as ever, while Mecha gets more hi-tech lensing. Still, helmer Masaaki Tezuka, who has made a few of these before, does an above-average job of pulling the disparate elements together and finishing off Godzilla."

☢ *Godzilla: Final Wars* (2004)

Director: Ryuhei Kitamura
Producers: Shogo Tomiyama, Kazunari Yamanaka
Writers: Wataru Mimura, Isao Kiriyama
Alternate film titles: *Godzilla: The Final Battle* (Latin America), *Godzilla: The Last War* (Poland), *Godzilla: Final Battle* (Brazil), *Godzilla: The Final War* (Greece)
Release date: December 4, 2004 (Japan), November 29, 2004 (US—Toho premiere)
Lead actors: Masahiro Matsuoka, Rei Kikukawa, Don Frye, Maki Mizuno, Kazuki Kitamura, Kane Kosugi, Akira Takarada, Jun Kunimura, Kumi Mizuno, Kenji Sahara
Primary Godzilla suit actor: Tsutomu Kitagawa

Godzilla returns to Tokyo again in *Godzilla: Tokyo S.O.S.* (2003).

The final Godzilla film for over a decade and the final film of the Millennium Series, *Godzilla: Final Wars* commemorates Godzilla's fiftieth anniversary. Set in the future, an alien invasion by the Xiliens brings about multiple kaiju attacks all over the world that destroy most of humanity. The Xiliens are controlling some of the kaiju, making them attack against their will. A group of Earth Defense Force (the military organization created by the United Nations to protect mankind from kaiju) survivors head to the South Pole, where Godzilla has been placed in a frozen prison, while another group plans to sneak onto the Xiliens' mothership and defeat them. Godzilla is freed and is willing to

The Japanese poster for *Godzilla: Final Wars* (2004).

take on every kaiju, but he hasn't forgotten what civilization did to him. And even if he can free the kaiju from the controls of the Xiliens, in the final act of the movie he will still have to deal with the Xiliens' dangerous kaiju, Monster X, who morphs into the mighty Keizer Ghidorah. If this was a video game, this would be what one would call a boss battle.

This film included every single kaiju Toho had ever created, even beasts like Hedorah who had been archived for over thirty years. Multiple CGI kaiju were also created specifically for the film, including Toho's take on the American Godzilla from 1998, named Zilla. (And yes, Zilla catches a beatdown.) It can be a fun ride, and seeing so many kaiju in one film makes this worth the price of admission for some, but one's mileage as a viewer may vary. Unfortunately, *Godzilla: Final Wars* was critically panned and wasn't the success that Toho had thought it would be, which put future live-action Godzilla plans on hold. It went on to become the lowest-grossing film of the Millennium Series.

▼▼ REIWA ERA ▼▼

☢ *Shin Godzilla* (2016)
Directors: Hideaki Anno, Shinji Higuchi
Associate Director: Katsuro Onoue
Producers: Minami Ichikawa, Akihiro Yamauchi
Writer: Hideaki Anno
Alternate film titles: *Godzilla–The Return* (Sweden), *Godzilla's Return* (Finland), *Authentic Godzilla* (Taiwan, China), *Godzilla Resurges* (Mexico), *True Godzilla* (Hong Kong, China)
Release date: July 29, 2016 (Japan), October 11, 2016 (US limited release)
Lead actors: Hiroki Hasegawa, Yutaka Takenouchi, Satomi Ishihara, Ren Osugi, Akira Emoto, Kengo Kora, Mikako Ichikawa, Jun Kunimura, Pierre Taki
Primary Godzilla suit actor: Mansai Nomura

The first Godzilla film of the Reiwa Era was also

was a complete reboot of the franchise, featuring a Godzilla attack in modern Japan. In Tokyo Bay, a creature with gills mutates due to nuclear waste and the carelessness of humans. Footage of the creature appears on social media, which prompts the government's emergency cabinet to meet to assess the situation. Despite an evaluation to the contrary, the creature is able to walk on land, causing widespread panic. The cabinet sends a defense team to kill the monster, but it evolves and starts overheating with radiation. The monster retreats to the bay, leaving the city to fear its return. Later, it

reappears in a new form. Now immensely tall and indestructible, Godzilla is truly born and wreaks havoc on Tokyo again.

The "Shin" series of films directed by Hideaki Anno and Shinji Higuchi (including this film, *Shin Ultraman, Shin Kamen Rider,* and *Evangelion: 3.0+1.0 Thrice Upon A Time*) are a franchise of unconnected Japanese film reboots of popular science fiction series. *Shin Godzilla* was one of the most successful Godzilla films since the 1960s and received plenty of critical praise. It also received seven Japanese Academy Awards. This was the first Godzilla film in which the titular character is not said to be a reptile and his origin is not connected to nuclear bomb testing.

☢ *Godzilla Minus One* (2023)

Director: Takashi Yamazaki
Producers: Minami Ichikawa, Hisashi Usui, Shuji Abe
Writer: Takashi Yamazaki
Release date: November 1, 2023 (Japan), November 10, 2023 (US)
Lead actors: Ryunosuke Kamiki, Minami Hamabe, Yuki Yamada, Munetaka Aoki, Hidetaka Yoshioka, Sakura Ando, Kuranosuke Sasaki

——— ▼ ———

In *Godzilla Minus One*, fighter pilot Koichi Shikishima is caught up in the horror of a devastated postwar Japan. After refusing to take his own life during a kamikaze mission, Shikisima returns to Tokyo, grappling with survivor's guilt. As he attempts to rebuild his life and help rebuild his city, in hopes of finding some form of normalcy again, a horrifying Godzilla steps into an already battle-worn Tokyo and begins destroying everything in his path. An all-volunteer force attempts to find a solution to rid themselves of this monster.

Godzilla Minus One is the most successful Godzilla movie of all time in Japan and the world. It's considered a cinematic masterpiece by many, and possibly the best Godzilla film ever made,

ニッポン対ゴジラ。

シン・ゴジラ

JULY 29, 2016

The Japanese poster for *Shin Godzilla* (2016).

GODZILLA SUITS THROUGH THE ERAS

SHOWA ERA

SHODAIGOJI SUIT (1954)

The first Godzilla suit features a heavy lower-body base, a round head with pronounced brows, and tiny arms.

GYAKUSHUGOJI SUIT (1955)

This suit was slimmer with a smaller head, to make the suit more agile and flexible.

KINGOJI SUIT (1962)

One of the more popular designs in Godzilla's history, this suit has a reptilian feel and a stocky build, with human-style eyes on the side of the head instead of the front and much larger hands. There are no ears on this suit, and the tail has a smooth underside.

MOSUGOJI SUIT (1964)

This suit features a sleek body with sharp claws, pronounced hands, and front-facing eyes centered on the face. The face is slender with furrowed brows, moveable eyes, and an elongated tongue. In the fandom, the MosuGoji suit is regarded as the best.

DAISENSOGOJI SUIT (1965–1966)

With a larger head than previous suits, this suit also has a thinner body and fingers placed closer together on the hands. The eyes can also move.

MUSUKOGOJI SUIT (1967)

A wide-loaded suit with a large neck, weirdly shaped dorsal plates, and a very chunky face, the MusukoGoji is one of the ugliest Godzilla suits in the Showa Era.

SOSHINGEKIGOJI SUIT (1968–1972)

A beautifully designed suit, the SoshingekiGoji has even proportions, a sturdy breastbone, a head that is properly shaped and that fits the body, and eyelids that can flutter.

MEGAROGOJI SUIT (1973–1975)

The MegaroGoji has a simple muzzle, large brows, and big eyes that make the King of the Monsters resemble a canine. The plain, streamlined body had a short neck and fat dorsal plates.

HEISEI ERA

84GOJI SUIT (1984)

This suit is an amalgam of the ShodaiGoji and MosuGoji suits, making Godzilla look menacing and dangerous.

BIOGOJI/GHIDOGOJI SUIT (1989–1991)

Stocky with a triangle-shaped body, very long neck, and pronounced teeth, this suit turned Godzilla into a vicious kaiju.

BATOGOJI SUIT (1992)

Sleek and powerful with very sharp teeth and piercing, expressive eyes, the BatoGoji suit has additional flexibility at the biceps and rearranged dorsal plates.

MILLENNIUM SERIES

MIREGOJI/GIRAGOJI SUIT (1999)

Inspired by the KinGoji suit, this suit had highly detailed scales that are prominently displayed. The dorsal plates on the back are large and jagged, with a subtle rose tint. The shape of the head is thinner, giving Godzilla a more reptilian appearance. As with other suits, Godzilla's mouth and eyes feature the trademark "frown."

SOKOGEKIGOJI SUIT (2001)

With its extended pointer and thumb claws, the suit puts a significant emphasis on musculature. The eyes have no pupils or irises, enhancing Godzilla's evil nature. Standing over seven feet, it is also the tallest suit.

RADOGOJI SUIT (1993)

With a wider head, higher-placed tail, smaller shoulders, and slimmer legs with a big body, this suit looks more top heavy when compared to previous models.

MOGEGOJI/DESUGOJI SUIT (1994–1995)

Perfectly proportioned, this suit was modified in *Godzilla vs. Destoroyah*. Pieces of the costume were removed and 200 orange lights were added, then covered with transparency plates. A steam mechanism was also added, which when combined with the glowing orange lights puts Godzilla in "critical mass" mode.

KIRYUGOJI SUIT (2002–2003)

This suit reduced the size of the head and made the overall creature smaller, similar to Godzilla's appearance in the Heisei Era. The dorsal plates have lost their purplish hue and returned to the classic bone-white color, but they remain jagged like the dorsal plates on the MireGoji/GiraGoji suit. Godzilla's skin color has also reverted to the traditional charcoal black from the MireGoji/GiraGoji green.

FINALGOJI SUIT (2004)

The arms and legs of this Godzilla suit are slimmer than usual, allowing the actor to fit perfectly into it. The suit's thighs are smaller, and the tail from the KiryuGoji suit is reused. This suit also has more noticeable ears than previous designs.

capturing the despair of people struggling in a devastated postwar Japan. *Godzilla Minus One* dares to discuss the travesties of war, the value of life, and the choice to live even in the most hopeless of situations. Though Godzilla is the attraction, this period piece dives deep into the human element, allowing the viewer to really care about the characters who are trying to survive the catastrophic series of events they face.

Dana Stevens of *Slate* wrote of *Minus One*, "It's the rare kaiju movie that cares this deeply about the inner lives and motivations of the people scurrying out of the way of the monster's ginormous thudding feet." Tara Brady of *The Irish Times* stated, "This prequel . . . yokes American imperialism, postwar malaise, survivor guilt, and weaponized atomic power to produce the best action film of the year."

The Japanese IMAX poster for *Godzilla Minus One* (2023).

▾▾ AN AMERICAN ABOMINATION ▾▾

☢ *Godzilla* (1998)
Director: Roland Emmerich
Producers: Roland Emmerich, Ute Emmerich, William Fay, Robert N. Fried, Cary Woods, Dean Devlin
Writers: Dean Devlin, Roland Emmerich
Alternate film title: *Godzilla Attacks New York* (Portugal)
Release date: May 19, 1998 (US), July 11, 1998 (Japan)
Lead actors: Matthew Broderick, Jean Reno, Maria Pitillo, Hank Azaria, Kevin Dunn, Harry Shearer, Frank Welker
Primary Godzilla suit actor: Kurt Carley

——— ▾ ———

If you make a Godzilla movie where the kaiju's strength is limited and he doesn't have his classic Atomic Breath, then it's not a Godzilla movie. It's just shoddy film of a giant lizard running amok in New York City.

During a nuclear test performed by the French government, a lizard nest becomes mutated. Years later, a colossal lizard makes its way toward New York City. To study the creature, the US government sends Dr. Niko Tatopoulos, an expert on the effects of radiation on animals. The news outlets call the monster "Godzilla." When the creature appears, a massive battle with the military ensues. To make matters worse, Niko discovers that Godzilla has laid 200 eggs in a nest ready to hatch.

The cast of *Godzilla*, while talented, are saddled with characters so two-dimensional and stale that you hope and pray that Godzilla will step on them. Since this version of Godzilla was put together by Roland Emmerich and Dean Devlin, the creators behind the allusion-laden *Independence Day*, viewers get blatant homages throughout the movie to films like *Alien* and *Jurassic Park*. An early script written by Ted Elliot and Terry Rossio convinced Emmerich and Devlin that it was possible to make a Godzilla film set in the US, though they agreed to do the movie only if they could throw out

Poster for *Godzilla* (1998).

The Monsterverse's primary focus is on Godzilla and King Kong, but other Toho kaiju, such as Rodan, Mothra, and King Ghidorah, have also appeared, as well as original, non-Toho kaiju such as the Mantleclaw, Endoswarmer, Frost Vark, and the Brambleboar.

▼▼ FILMS ▼▼

☢ Godzilla (2014)

Director: Gareth Edwards
Producers: Mary Parent, Brian Rogers, Thomas Tull, Jon Jashni
Writers: David Callaham, Max Borenstein
Release date: May 16, 2014 (US), July 25, 2014 (Japan)
Lead actors: Ken Watanabe, Bryan Cranston, Aaron Taylor-Johnson, Elizabeth Olsen, Sally Hawkins, Juliette Binoche, David Strathairn

——— ▼ ———

The second American-produced Godzilla movie was the debut of the Monsterverse, and it gives us so much more than Sony's *Godzilla* (1998). *Godzilla* (2014) sincerely tries to be a more faithful adaption of Toho Studios' previous works.

This film introduces viewers to Monarch, an American-Japanese task force investigating a mining collapse in the Philippines in 1999. Dr. Ishiro Serizawa, Dr. Vivienne Graham, and their team discover a large underground cave that contains a massive, fossilized skeleton and two spores. A few days later, in Janjira, Japan, a nuclear power plant is

Elliot and Rossio's script and do whatever they wanted instead.

There is nothing redeeming about this film, even though it grossed over $379 million at the box office on a $150-million budget. If you feel the need to watch anything that deals with this version of Godzilla, then watch the animated *Godzilla: The Series*. It respects the lore, adds depth to all the characters, and gives Godzilla back his strength and his atomic breath.

▼▼ GODZILLA IN THE MONSTERVERSE ▼▼

The Monsterverse is a shared universe that features a number of kaiju and other large monsters who appear in films, television series, and animated series produced by American mass media company Legendary Pictures. Legendary Pictures decided to produce their own Godzilla film after acquiring the licensing rights from Toho Studios in 2009.

KAIJU FACT

The temperature of Godzilla's Atomic Breath is 500,000 degrees Celsius.
Do not ask Godzilla to make you a grilled cheese sandwich; he'll disintegrate the bread—and you.

Poster for *Godzilla: King of the Monsters* (2019).

rocked by what appears to be a massive earthquake. Nuclear physicist Joe Brody survives the tragedy, but his wife, Sandra, and the investigative team are killed. The Japanese government quarantines Janjira and evacuates everyone permanently. Fifteen years later, Joe's son, Ford, travels to Japan to collect his father, who has trespassed in the Janjira quarantine area. Together, they discover the truth about the accident: the spores were Massive Unidentified Terrestrial Organisms (MUTOs) that eat trapped radiation. The MUTOs escape and causes destruction in Honolulu, as Godzilla emerges from the depths to fight them.

Godzilla (2014) gained critical acclaim and was a box office success, earning over half a billion dollars worldwide. Bryan Cranston and Ken Watanabe are fantastic, and the film teases you for a long time before it *finally* becomes Godzilla's movie in the third act, but it is truly worth the wait.

☢ *Godzilla: King of the Monsters* (2019)

Director: Michael Dougherty
Producers: Mary Parent, Brian Rogers, Thomas Tull, Jon Jashni, Alex Garcia
Writers: Michael Dougherty, Zach Shields
Alternate titles: *Godzilla II: King of the Monsters* (International)
Release date: May 31, 2019 (US/Japan)
Lead actors: Ken Watanabe, Sally Hawkins, David Strathairn, Kyle Chandler, Vera Farmiga, Mille Bobby Brown, Bradley Whitford, O'Shea Jackson Jr., Zhang Ziyi, Charles Dance, Aisha Hinda, Thomas Middleditch

—— ▼ ——

In this riveting sequel to 2014's *Godzilla*, more kaiju (classified as "Titans") wake up from their slumber on Earth to cause chaos across the planet. Monarch believes that most of these Titans are friendly and should be protected, but eco-terrorist Alan Jonah has other plans. Jonah and his crew steal a sonar device called the Orca, which can communicate with the Titans, and unleash Monster Zero (King Ghidorah) to wreak the destruction of humankind.

Godzilla must team up with Mothra and Rodan to battle the sinister King Ghidorah.

The monster fights in this movie are fantastic, but there are times when the acting feels flat and sometimes slows the film to a crawl. But the viewing audience isn't here for the humans. The story is good and the Titans look amazing—you won't be able to take your eyes off them. The Titans were produced with motion-capture suits, with motion-capture acting by TJ Storm, Jason Liles, Alan Maxson, and Richard Dorton.

▼▼ *SERIES* ▼▼

☢ *Monarch: Legacy of Monsters* (2023–)

Alternate titles: *Project Monarch: The Puzzle of the Mysterious Organization and Monsters* (Mandarin), *The Monarch Organization and the Mysterious Beasts* (Cantonese)
Release Date: November 17, 2023

GODZILLA'S EVOLVING POWERS

Over the decades, Godzilla's powers and abilities have grown. Some appear in multiple films, but some are used only once and then abandoned. Here are some of his ever-changing power sets.

- **Atomic Breath – First featured in *Godzilla* (1954)**
  Originally, Godzilla's atomic breath was more of a vapor, but over the decades it has become a more concentrated and powerful beam, more like a laser blast.

- **Flying Ability with His Atomic Breath – First featured in *Godzilla vs. Hedorah* (1971)**
  Used only in this film, Godzilla blew his atomic breath toward the ground, and the power of the blast pushed him into the air. It is one of the most ridiculous abilities given to Godzilla during the Showa Era.

- **Metal Manipulation – First featured in *Godzilla vs. Mechagodzilla* (1974)**
  Absorbing the power of a major lightning storm, Godzilla was able to turn himself into a magnet to pull his mechanical doppelganger close enough to destroy him. Does it make sense? No. Is it cool? Yes.

- **Nuclear Pulse Attack – First featured in *Godzilla vs. Biollante* (1989)**
  Godzilla can charge up and release a nuclear pulse, a powerful attack that unleashes a wave of atomic energy and obliterates anything nearby.

- **Spiral Heat Ray – First featured in *Godzilla vs. King Ghidorah* (1991)**
  The spiral heat ray is one of the most unique versions of Godzilla's atomic breath, an ultra-focused beam emitted from his mouth. This beam is accompanied by electricity along his dorsal spikes and a spiral of excess energy surrounding the main beam.

- **Burning G Spark Heat Ray – First featured in *Godzilla: Final Wars* (2004)**
  Possibly Godzilla's most powerful ray, this form of blast hits his enemies so hard that it can send them into outer space. Ask Keizer Ghidorah. Oh, that's right, you can't—Godzilla destroyed him with his heat ray!

- **Full Body Atomic Rays – First featured in *Shin Godzilla* (2016)**
  In *Shin Godzilla* (2016), the titular character was able to project atomic rays from various parts of his body, causing immense destruction.

Poster for *Monarch: Legacy of Monsters* (2023–).

Taking place after the events of *Godzilla* (2014), this series follows half-siblings Cate and Kentaro Randa as they attempt to discover their family's deep connection to the Monarch organization. As they follow the clues that bring them closer to what they're looking for, they discover more Titans and a man named Lee Shaw, who knows enough that Monarch considers him a threat to their future.

A series that operates in parallel storylines set in 2015 and the 1950s–1980s, this is the first Godzilla television or streaming series to not feature the character's name in the title. *Legacy of Monsters* made its debut on Apple TV+ to positive reviews.

6 KING KONG

It was beauty killed the beast!
—Robert Armstrong as Carl Denham
in *King Kong* (1933)

Poster for *King Kong* (1933).

I n the pre-Code era of American cinema, before proper laws and regulations in cinema were standard, *King Kong* was one of the greatest films produced. It predates *Godzilla* by twenty-plus years, but since the term kaiju didn't come around until the 1950s, it's better known as a "monster movie." Since RKO Pictures lent *King Kong* to Toho Studios in the 1960s to star in a couple of films, that technically makes him a kaiju! Though *Godzilla* is still seen as the "first" kaiju movie, *King Kong* deserves a nod.

What makes the movie so important is its special effects, led by stop-motion animator Willis H. O'Brien and his assistant, Buzz Gibson. The stop-motion effects were state-of-the-art at the time. O'Brien and Gibson were able to blend together live-action footage and the separately filmed stop-motion footage. Rear-screen projection techniques were also used to blend scenes and miniatures with real footage of the actors. *King Kong* director Merian C. Cooper started his film career as a documentarian for explorers and later took his talents to Hollywood. He said the idea for *King Kong* came to him in a dream, in which a giant gorilla attacked New York City. The mighty roar of King Kong was created by Murray Spivack, who combined the recordings of captive tigers and lions

and then played them backward and slowed down. Additionally, it is one of the first films in cinematic history to have a sequel (*Son of Kong*).

▼▼ INITIAL RECEPTION AND CHANGE ▼▼

The film was a massive success at the box office, having multiple releases in the 1930s and 1950s. Since the film was created and released before the Motion Picture Production Code took effect, the film had to undergo additional censoring for later

OPPOSITE:
King Kong shows off his might in his 2005 film.

A scene from *King Kong* (1933).

releases, with multiple scenes removed or trimmed down to fit the Code. For decades it was thought that the original film print of *King Kong* had been lost to time, but in 1969 a print of the original, uncensored version was found, which contains controversial scenes such as King Kong biting a man in New York and dropping a woman to her death after realizing that she isn't Ann Darrow, as well as a brutal scene in which the creatures of Skull Island eat some of the crew members of Captain Englehorn's ship.

Since that uncensored cut was found, multiple studios have had a hand in properly restoring the film to its best quality. In 2005, Warner Bros. was able to do a fully digital 4K restoration of the film (including a four-minute overture) using the best film prints and materials they could find.

Even with all the innovation that went into the making of *King Kong* and the film's subsequent success, there are many scenes that don't sit well with modern viewers. The film's depiction of the villagers on Skull Island is quite racist, reflecting the ignorance of the times. Directors Merian C. Cooper and Ernest Schoedsack said that the film had no hidden meanings and that Cooper's point of the film was to give a story of how a primitive animal was destroyed by current civilization.

In Japan, the film was such a success in 1933 that a short, comedic film produced by Shochiku Kinema (*Japanese King Kong*) was made later that year.

▼▼ FILMS ▼▼

☢ *King Kong* (1933)

Directors: Merian C. Cooper, Ernest Schoedsack
Producers: David O. Selznick, Merian C. Cooper, Ernest Schoedsack
Writers: James Creelman, Ruth Rose
Alternate film titles: *King Kong, the Eighth Wonder of the World* (France) *The Fable of King Kong – An American Film Sensation* (Germany)
Release date: March 2, 1933 (US), September 14, 1933 (Japan)
Lead actors: Fay Wray, Robert Armstrong, Bruce Cabot, Frank Reicher

A kaiju-sized ape called King Kong is taken from his home on the mysterious and dangerous Skull Island to be exhibited in New York. Kong becomes obsessed with Ann Darrow, who tagged along with filmmaker Carl Denham and ship captain Jack Driscoll to capture Kong, and he pursues her during his rampage in New York. In perhaps the most iconic scene, King Kong swats at biplanes while

"THE MOST AWESOME THRILLER OF ALL TIME"
the one and only
KING KONG
with
FAY WRAY
ROBT. ARMSTRONG
BRUCE CABOT

MERIAN C. COOPER
ERNEST B. SCHOEDSACK
PRODUCTION

FROM A STORY BY
EDGAR WALLACE
AND
MERIAN C. COOPER

DAVID O. SELZNICK
Executive Producer

hanging off the top of the Empire State Building. The image has been aped (no pun intended) across entertainment media in the decades since.

One of the ground-breaking special-effects monster movies of its time, *King Kong* is perhaps best known for its stop-motion animation, rear projection, miniatures, and matte paintings. A large mechanical model of Kong's head and shoulders was built for close-up shots of the giant ape, and special-effects operators could control the mouth and eyes to make it seem as if it were a living creature.

KAIJU FACT

King Kong was preserved for the United States National Film Registry in 1991.

☢ *Son of Kong* (1933)

Director: Ernest Schoedsack
Producer: Ernest Schoedsack
Writer: Ruth Rose
Alternate film titles: *The Revenge of Kong* (Japan), *The Son of King Kong* (Portugal/Brazil), *Kong's Son* (Finland), *King Kong's Son* (Germany)
Release date: December 22, 1933 (US), December 1934 (Japan)
Lead actors: Robert Armstrong, Helen Mack, Frank Reicher, John Marston, Victor Wong, Lee Kohlmar, Ed Brady

——— ▼ ———

Released just nine months after *King Kong* to capitalize on its success, this lackluster sequel has filmmaker Carl Denham fleeing Kong's rampage in New York. He and Captain Englehorn, the ship captain from the original *King Kong*, leave the city and build a failing cargo business, struggling to make any money hauling cargo throughout Asia. They later return to Skull Island in the hopes of finding lost treasure and end up meeting Kong's son, a friendly, twelve-foot-tall albino gorilla who protects Denham and the others during their deadly adventure.

The poster for *King Kong* (1933).

A scene on Skull Island in *Son of Kong* (1933).

Son of Kong used a decent amount of footage from the original *King Kong* to save money. Perhaps unsurprisingly, the film was critically panned. The story aims for adventurous but often ends up comical, unlike the serious tone of *King Kong*. The film was still a success for RKO Radio Pictures in 1933, due to its very low budget, but King Kong wouldn't be seen again on the big screen for thirty years.

☢ *King Kong Escapes* (1967)

Director: Ishirō Honda
Producer: Tomoyuki Tanaka
Writer: Kaoru Mabuchi
Alternate film titles: *King Kong's Counterattack* (Japan), *King Kong – Frankenstein's Son* (West Germany), *King Kong Gets Out* (Netherlands), *King Kong on the Island of Terror* (Finland), *The Revenge of King Kong* (France/ Belgium), *Wrath of the Monsters* (Turkey), *King Kong Has Not Died* (Mexico)
Release date: July 22, 1967 (Japan), June 19, 1968 (US)
Lead actors: Akira Takarada, Mie Hama, Rhodes Reason, Linda Miller, Hideyo Amamoto
Primary Kong suit actor: Haruo Nakajima

———— ▼ ————

Kong in *King Kong Escapes* (1967).

Godzilla director Ishirō Honda helmed the second King Kong film by Toho (the first being *King

KAIJU FACT

In the original television airing of *King Kong Escapes*, Dr. Who's death scene was removed because at the time it was thought to be too horrific.

Kong vs. Godzilla in 1962), in which King Kong is captured by the villainous Dr. Who (no relation to the popular British science-fiction character) and forced to find Element X. Who's creation, a robotic duplicate of King Kong called Mechani-Kong, had previously failed to find the element. King Kong eventually escapes and takes on Mechani-Kong in a fight to the death.

King Kong Escapes was co-produced by American studio Rankin/Bass, known for the classic Christmas specials *Rudolph the Red-Nosed Reindeer*, *Santa Claus is Coming to Town*, and animated series such as *Thundercats* and *Silverhawks*. The film is loosely based on episodes of the popular animated *The King Kong Show*, produced by Rankin/Bass and Toei Animation, which aired from 1966 to 1969 in the United States and Japan. The film is entertaining and doesn't take itself too seriously—though it *is* a little jarring to hear Paul Frees, the voice of such iconic Rankin/Bass characters as Jack Frost, Burgermeister Meisterburger, and Santa Claus himself, provide voice-dubbing for Hideo Amamoto's Dr. Who.

☢ *King Kong* (1976)

Director: John Guillermin
Producer: Dino De Laurentiis
Writer: Lorenzo Semple, Jr.
Release date: December 17, 1976 (US), December 18, 1976 (Japan)
Lead actors: Jeff Bridges, Charles Grodin, Jessica Lange
Primary Kong suit actor: Rick Baker

King Kong

Dino De Laurentiis
présente
un film de
John Guillermin
avec **JEFF BRIDGES · CHARLES GRODIN** et **JESSICA LANGE**
musique   John Barry   Panavision° Color

THE THREE JAPANESE KING KONG RIP-OFFS YOU'LL NEVER SEE

Japan loved *King Kong* (1933) so much that in the 1930s studios created rip-offs based on the giant ape. These films pre-date *Godzilla* (1954) by twenty years. They were only ever released in Japan to avoid copyright infringement lawsuits and have been lost to time, so they will unfortunately likely never be recovered.

▶ *Wasei Kingu Kongu* (1933) (*Japanese-made King Kong*)
This short 30-minute silent comedy tells the story of a poor man in need of money because his girlfriend's father refuses to allow her to marry someone of such low means. Inspired by RKO Studios' King Kong, he decides to dress up as an ape and pretend to be the great ape at a local theater, with much success.

▶ *Edo ni Arawareta Kingu Kongu* (1938) (*King Kong Appears in Edu*)
In this silent film, King Kong kidnaps the daughter of a wealthy man to appease his master.

▶ *Kingu Kongu Zenkouhen* (1938)
No information about this film survives, but some believe that it is part two of *King Kong Appears in Edu*.

Jessica Lange is scooped up by the great ape in *King Kong* (1976).

In this blockbuster reimagining of the 1933 film, a research trip spearheaded by oil tycoon Fred Wilson hopes to find oil reserves on a hidden island in the Indian Ocean. Paleontologist Jack Prescott sneaks onto the ship and tries to warn the crew about the dangers of the island and joins the journey. Along the way, they rescue a woman in a life raft named Dwan, an aspiring actress who was the lone survivor of a shipwreck. Upon arriving at the island, they

Who Is Konga?

Konga is a British film that attempted to capitalize on the popularity of *King Kong*. Released in 1961, the movie stars Michael Gough (Alfred Pennyworth in the Batman quadrilogy, 1989–1997) as scientist Dr. Charles Decker, who has returned from Africa with the knowledge of how to grow animals and plants to giant sizes. He brings a baby chimpanzee, Konga, back to test his growth serum, which turns Konga into a menacing, kaiju-sized gorilla. Decker goes mad and commands Konga to go to London and kill all his scientific rivals. Chaos ensues.

find the natives who live in fear of King Kong and kidnap Dwan as a sacrifice. Kong and Dwan share a special bond, though Dwan is later rescued by Prescott. Though the island's oil is unusable, Wilson decides to take Kong to New York City to use as an exhibit, which goes completely awry after Kong thinks that Dwan is being assaulted by reporters. Kong takes Dwan, and Prescott must find a way to

rescue her and hopefully keep Kong from being killed so he can take him somewhere safe.

This version of *King Kong* uses the energy crisis of the 1970s as inspiration for updating the original film. The film opts to not have stop-motion creatures on the hidden island to focus more on the relationship between Kong and Dwan, but Kong does end up battling a giant Boa constrictor on the island after it tries to eat Dwan. Legendary special effects creative Rick Baker donned the King Kong suit for the film. A forty-foot-tall animatronic version of Kong was also built and was supposed to be heavily used in the film, but due to constant technical issues, it was seldom used. The film also marks the debut of actress Jessica Lange. The film was a mild success, earning $90 million at the box office on a $24-million budget, but it was not enough to quickly greenlight a sequel.

☢ *King Kong Lives* (1986)

Director: John Guillermin
Producers: Dino De Laurentiis, Ronald Shusett, Martha Schumacher
Writers: Ronald Shusett, Steven Pressfield
Alternate film titles: *King Kong 2* (International)
Release date: December 19, 1986 (US), December 27, 1986 (Japan)
Lead actors: Linda Hamilton, Brian Kerwin, John Ashton, Peter Michael Goetz, Frank Maraden, and Jimmie Ray Weeks
Primary Kong suit actors: Peter Elliott, George Yiasomi (Antoni)

The sequel to 1976's *King Kong* takes place ten years after that first film. King Kong survived his long fall from the World Trade Center and is in a coma at the Atlantic Institute, led by Dr. Amy Franklin. King Kong's heart is failing, so Dr. Franklin prepares an artificial heart to keep Kong alive, but she needs a blood transfusion from another giant ape for the surgery to be successful. Hank Mitchell, an explorer and adventure seeker, finds a giant female ape—Lady Kong, naturally—and the blood transfusion works. King and Lady Kong escape the institute, and Lady Kong becomes pregnant with King Kong's child. But the military is, of course, on the hunt for the apes.

The film was a massive flop, earning only $4 million on an $18-million budget, and was critically panned due to a lackluster story and poor special effects. It would be the last King Kong film for almost two decades.

One of the most adorable kaiju in *King Kong Lives* (1986).

☢ *King Kong* (2005)

Director: Peter Jackson
Producers: Jan Blenkin, Carolynne Cunningham, Fran Walsh, Peter Jackson
Writers: Fran Walsh, Philippa Boyens, Peter Jackson
Release date: December 14, 2005 (US)
Lead actors: Naomi Watts, Jack Black, Adrien Brody, Thomas Kretschmann, Colin Hanks, Jamie Bell, Evan Parke, Lobo Chan, Kyle Chandler
Primary Kong suit actor: Andy Serkis (motion capture)

—— ▼ ——

A pensive Kong in the 2005 remake, *King Kong*.

This blockbuster remake from director and King Kong fan Peter Jackson is a tribute to and extension of the 1933 original, following a majority of the 1933 story with bigger and bolder special effects and stronger characterization. Andy Serkis does a fantastic job handling the motion-capture acting for Kong, displaying the emotion, range, and action, giving the movie the life it needs. The CG monsters and action that takes place on Skull Island and the growing relationship and trust between Kong and Ann are what make the film special (even if it's a bit over-long). The film was a financial success, grossing over $550 million on a $200-million budget.

☢ *Kong: Skull Island* (2017)

Director: Jordan Vogt-Roberts

Producers: Eric McLeod, Edward Cheng

Writers: Dan Gilroy, Max Borenstein, Derek Connolly (from a story by John Gatins)

Alternate film titles: *King Kong: Giant God of Skull Island* (Japan)

Release date: March 10, 2017 (US), March 25, 2017 (Japan)

Lead actors: Tom Hiddleston, Samuel L. Jackson, John Goodman, Brie Larson, Tian Jing, John Ortiz, Terry Notary, John C. Reilly

Primary Kong suit actor: Terry Notary (motion capture suit)

——— ▼ ———

After the Vietnam War, a group of scientists with a military escort, including former British SAS tracker James Conrad and photographer Mason Weaver, led by Colonel Preston Packard, attempt to explore an unknown island in the Pacific. Little do they know that they've ventured into the deadly world of Kong, and the many other sinister monsters that occupy the land.

The second film in the Monsterverse, *Skull Island* is adventurous, thrilling, and at moments quite scary. The special effects and CG blend in very well with the film, and the characters, though some of them are one-note, are carried by fantastic performances from Samuel L. Jackson and John C. Reilly. *Kong: Skull Island* also received an Academy Award nomination for Best Visual Effects.

The poster for *Kong: Skull Island* (2017).

KAIJU FACT

In *Kong: Skull Island* (2017), Senator Al Willis and his assistant, Secretary O'Brien, are an ode to Willis O'Brien, the creator of the stop-motion effects for the 1933 *King Kong* and an inspiration for future special effects creatives.

> Godzilla has disappeared without a trace. As for King Kong,
> our International Communications Satellite is
> following him. And strangely enough, we wish him
> luck on his long, long journey home.
> —Michael Keith as Eric Carter in *King Kong vs. Godzilla* (1962)

OPPOSITE:
The Japanese
poster for *Godzilla
vs. Kong* (2021).

The poster for
*King Kong vs.
Godzilla* (1962).

The road to King Kong and Godzilla facing each other on the big screen started in 1958. Willis O'Brien, a pioneer of stop-motion animation in cinema and the force behind the original *King Kong* (1933), wrote a treatment in which King Kong battled a monster made by Dr. Frankenstein's grandson, with the climax taking place in San Francisco. It was titled *King Kong vs. Frankenstein* and was meant to be a sequel to *King Kong*, taking place after the original film and removing *Son of Kong* (1933) from continuity.

Movie producer John Beck agreed on the sequel idea from O'Brien and called on George Yates to write the screenplay, which could then be shown to investors to build hype and acquire funding for production. Yates had a lot of experience writing monster and science-fiction films. His credits included classics like *Them!* (1954) and *It Came from Beneath the Sea* (1955). But when no American studio was interested in making the film, Beck went to Toho to see if they were interested. Toho purchased the rights to use King Kong from RKO Pictures to make *King Kong vs. Godzilla*, and in exchange, Toho gave Beck film distribution rights for the United States, Canada, and the United Kingdom.

In Japan, King Kong was very popular, so it made sense for Toho to take a chance on making

KONG

金刚的身体细部，如一根手指，长度与直径数字都比均高30米的中国本土树木更大。

IMAX® 大银幕的水晶画质，**丛林奇景令人沉醉。** 所呈现的世界非常宽广，同时也能完美的观察金刚的肢体细节。

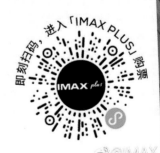

@IMAX

their own Kong movie. It would be the third film for both King Kong and Godzilla, and would help relaunch Godzilla back to stardom.

Though they don't exactly get along in the 1962 feature, currently, King Kong and Godzilla are allies, meeting for the first time in the Monsterverse in *Godzilla vs. Kong* (2021) and reteaming in *Godzilla X Kong: The New Empire* (2024).

☢ *King Kong vs. Godzilla* (1962)

Director: Ishirō Honda
Producer: Tomoyuki Tanaka
Writer: Shinichi Sekizawa
Alternate film titles: *The Triumph of King Kong* (Italy), *King Kong Fighting Dinosaur* (Taiwan, China), *Wrath of Monsters* (Turkey), *Godzilla Against King Kong* (Chile), *The Return of King Kong* (West Germany)
Release date: August 11, 1962 (Japan), June 26, 1963 (US)
Lead actors: Tadao Takashima, Kenji Sahara, Yu Fujiki, Ichiro Arishima, Jun Tazaki, Akihiko Hirata, Mie Hama, Akiko Wakabayashi
Primary Kong suit actor: Shoichi Hirose
Primary Godzilla suit actor: Haruo Nakajima, Katsumi Tezuka

In this "East meets West" battle of kaiju, Godzilla awakens from his prison of ice from the final act of *Godzilla Raids Again* (1955) and begins his journey back to Japan for revenge. When members of the Pacific Pharmaceutical Company find King Kong on Faro Island, they decide to bring Kong back to Japan as an exhibit. Of course, Kong escapes, and the great ape and Godzilla cross paths and enter a fight to determine who is truly king of the monsters.

The success of *King Kong vs. Godzilla* revitalized the Godzilla franchise for Toho, who hadn't released a film featuring Godzilla in nine years. The popularity of this film brought along more

KAIJU FACT

Before *King Kong vs. Godzilla* (1962) was released in Japan, part of Toho's promotional efforts included "interviews" with King Kong and Godzilla, like a press conference before a big boxing match.

The world's best-known kaiju square off in *King Kong vs. Godzilla* (1962).

OPPOSITE: Chinese poster art featuring Kong to announce the release of *Godzilla vs. Kong* (2021) in IMAX in that country.

THE UNMADE SEQUELS

. . . .

Because of the success of *King Kong vs. Godzilla* (1962), Toho pushed forward on pre-production for a sequel, tentatively titled *Continuation: King Kong vs. Godzilla*. Screenwriter Shin'ichi Sekizawa completed a script for the film, but the project was canceled and Toho opted to make *Mothra vs. Godzilla* (1964) and *Frankenstein vs. Baragon* (1965) instead.

During the Heisei Era, Toho again attempted to produce a new Godzilla vs. King Kong film, but Turner Entertainment, who owned the exclusive rights to King Kong at the time, refused to let Toho use the character, leading to the project being scrapped. Toho would then attempt to have Godzilla face Mechani-Kong in a film, but that project was also cancelled.

OPPOSITE:
A Chinese IMAX poster for *Godzilla vs. Kong* (2021) featuring Godzilla.

The King of the Monsters shows off his talents in *King Kong vs. Godzilla* (1962).

Godzilla films in the Showa Era, as well as an animated series called *The King Kong Show* (1966) and another Toho Kong film, *King Kong Escapes* (1967), based on the animated series.

The original US release of *King Kong vs. Godzilla* added new footage directed by Thomas Montgomery, including news broadcasts to move the story along and make it relatable to American audiences. Even with these additional scenes, so many edits and cuts were made that the US runtime was only 91 minutes instead of the original 97. If you can find the original Japanese version (available in the Godzilla: Showa Era Criterion Collection), watch that instead.

☢ Godzilla vs. Kong (2021)
Director: Adam Wingard
Producers: Kenji Okuhira, Yoshimitsu Banno, Jon Jashni, Thomas Tull
Writers: Eric Pearson, Max Borenstein
Alternate film titles: *Kong vs. Godzilla* (Indonesia), *Godzilla vs. King Kong* (China)
Release date: March 31, 2021 (US), July 2, 2021 (Japan)
Lead actors: Alexander Skarsgård, Millie Bobby Brown, Rebecca Hall, Brian Tyree Henry, Shun Oguri, Eiza González, Julian Dennison, Lance Reddick, Kyle Chandler, Demián Bichir, Kaylee Hottle
Primary Kong suit actor: Eric Petey (motion capture)

——— ▼ ———

In the fourth film in the Monsterverse Era, humanity is trying to co-exist with the Titans after the battle between Ghidorah and Godzilla. However, Godzilla begins another reign of terror, forcing humanity to call on another legend to stop him: Kong. Representatives from Monarch travel to Skull Island, where they discover a mysterious young girl who can communicate with Kong and who warns him of the impending danger. As Godzilla continues to destroy everything in

IMAX
#IMAX3D哥斯拉大战金刚#

GODZILLA

哥斯拉的皮肤坚不可摧,不会被常规武器损坏,能够承受猛烈的炮火,如坦克炮弹、火箭甚至导弹。

在 IMAX® 影厅观赏《哥斯拉大战金刚》,可以感受到沉浸式的观影体验,细致感受哥斯拉皮肤的纹理和坚硬质感。

即刻扫码,进入「IMAX PLUS」购票

微博 @IMAX

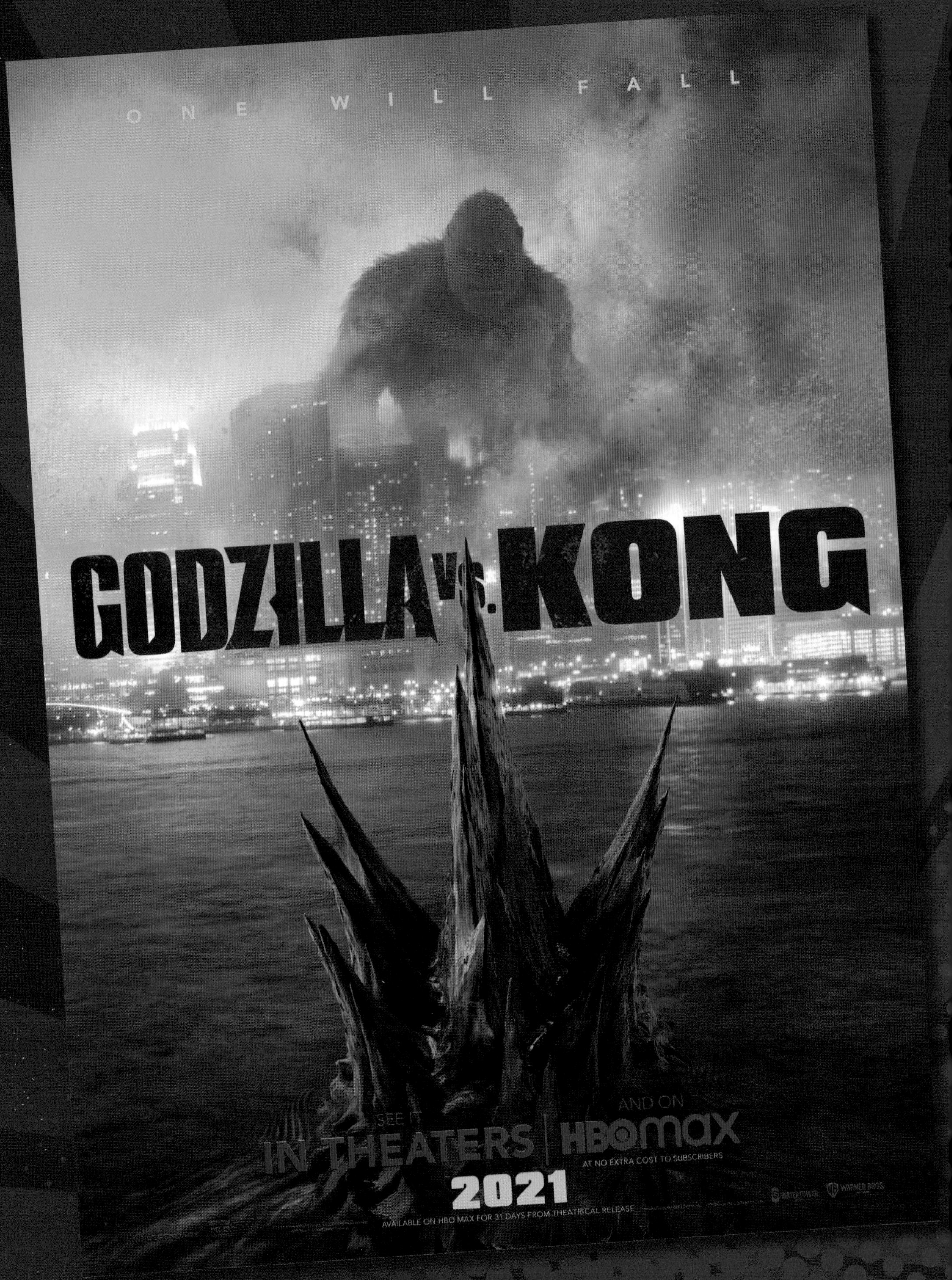
ONE WILL FALL
GODZILLA vs. KONG
SEE IT
IN THEATERS
AND ON
HBO max
AT NO EXTRA COST TO SUBSCRIBERS
2021
AVAILABLE ON HBO MAX FOR 31 DAYS FROM THEATRICAL RELEASE

A team-up for the ages in *Godzilla x Kong: The New Empire* (2024).

his path, it becomes clear that Apex Cybernetics, a rival tech company to Monarch that wants to control all the Titans so they can take over the world, is somehow involved in the Titan's destructive behavior. It is revealed that the Godzilla wreaking havoc is actually Mechagodzilla, so Godzilla and Kong must battle for the right to be king of the monsters and to stop the real threat that faces them.

Godzilla vs. Kong was a box-office success in 2021, even as the world continued to deal with the Covid pandemic, guaranteeing that the Monsterverse would continue. The motion capture and CGI for the Titans is texture-rich and heavily detailed, although the Mechagodzilla design was a bit lacking. Still, it doesn't take away from the fact that this version of Mechagodzilla is a pure threat.

☢ *Godzilla x Kong: The New Empire* (2024)

Director: Adam Wingard
Producers: Adam Wingard, Jen Conroy, Jay Ashenfelter, Dan Lin, Roy Lee, Yoshimitsu Banno, Kenji Okuhira
Writers: Terry Rossio, Simon Barrett, Jeremy Slater, Adam Wingard
Release date: March 29, 2024 (US), April 26, 2024 (Japan)

Lead actors: Rebecca Hall, Dan Stevens, Brian Tyree Henry, Rachel House, Alex Ferns, Kaylee Hottle

▼

Set three years after *Godzilla vs. Kong* (2021), Godzilla maintains peace between humans and Titans by defending the Earth and Kong now lives in Hollow Earth, on a mission to find more of his species. Along the way, Kong befriends a young Titan ape named Suko who takes Kong to meet the leader of the tribe, the villainous Skar King, who also controls an ice-powered Titan named Shimo. A battle between Kong, Skar King, and Shimo ensues. Meanwhile, Godzilla begins to build up his strength by absorbing radiation because he knows a major threat is coming. The King of the Monsters, Kong, and Monarch will need to work together to eliminate their adversaries.

Though *Godzilla x Kong: The New Empire* was a financial success, it received mixed reviews, mostly due to comparisons to *Godzilla Minus One* (2023). Owen Gleiberman of *Variety* felt that the film suffered from being released so soon after *Minus One*, calling *Minus One* a film of "lyrical majesty" and *The New Empire* a "product." Alissa Wilkinson of the *New York Times* said, "The meaning of these films isn't in metaphor at all. It's in punching."

OPPOSITE: An American poster for *Godzilla vs. Kong* (2021).

8 GAMERA

Created by Masaichi Nagata, Yonejiro Saito, Noriaki Yuasa, and Hidemasa Nagata, *Gamera* was created for Daiei Film, a rival to Toho Studios, to compete with *Godzilla* (1954) and capitalize on that film's success. Before making *Gamera*, Daiei distributed foreign films such as *King Kong* (1933), and produced the popular *Zatoichi* (aka *The Blind Swordsman*) film series. They were also known for producing some of monumental director Akira Kurosawa's early films. In 1965, they were ready to fully enter the world of kaiju.

A flying prehistoric turtle, Gamera is a protector of humankind and loves children. The turtle design is possibly inspired by the Black Tortoise, one of the four Chinese constellations from mythology based in East Asia. Co-creator Masaichi Nagata said that he thought of a tortoise flying alongside his airplane during a flight, then later shared his idea with producer Yonejiro Saito. They began to put together ideas for Gamera's debut.

Gamera's name comes from the Japanese words *kame* (meaning "turtle") and *-ra* (a suffix used in most kaiju names). Gamera has had four reboots in the last sixty years, ranging from kid-friendly to grim and dark. The first Gamera suit that was used for filming was built by Kanju and Yasuei Yagi. It stood six-and-a-half feet tall and weighed over 100 pounds. A much heavier second suit was built for scenes in which Gamera breathed fire, with additional protection to keep whoever was wearing the suit safe.

OPPOSITE: Despite his appearance, Gamera is a great friend to children.

A poster for *Gamera: The Giant Monster* (1965).

▾▾ THE SHOWA ERA (1965-1980) ▾▾

☢ *Gamera: The Giant Monster* (1965)

Director: Noriaki Yuasa
Producer: Hidemasa Nagata
Writer: Nisan Takahashi
Alternate film titles: *Gammera the Invincible* (US), *Gamera – Frankenstein's Monster from the Ice* (Germany), *The World Under Terror* (Spain)
Release date: November 27, 1965 (Japan), December 15, 1966 (US)
Lead actors: Eiji Funakoshi, Junichiro Yamashita, Michiko Sugata, Harumi Kiritachi, Jun Hamamura, Yoshiro Uchida
Primary Gamera suit actor: Kazuo Yagi

—— ▼ ——

The debut of Gamera comes off as a *Godzilla* lite. American military jets attack enemy bombers, leading to the detonation of an atomic bomb by one of the enemies. The blast from the nuclear explosion frees Gamera from his ice prison, where he was in suspended animation. Gamera then rampages through Japan with the Japan Self-

Gamera in his 1965 debut film.

Defense Force scrambling to find a way to stop this deadly kaiju.

Gamera's debut is the only time when he is an antagonist and is the only film in which Gamera does not fight a kaiju. *Gamera: The Giant Monster* (1965) is also the only black-and-white film in the franchise.

☢ *Gamera vs. Barugon* (1966)

Director: Shigeo Tanaka
Producer: Masaichi Nagata
Writer: Nisan Takahashi
Alternate film titles: *Giant Monster Duel: Gamera vs. Barugon* (Japan), *War of the Monsters* (US), *Godzilla – The Dragon from the Jungle* (West Germany), *Warning! The Monsters Arrive* (Italy), *Gamera Against the Monster Barugon* (Brazil), *The Monsters of the End of the World* (Spain)
Release date: April 17, 1966 (Japan), 1967 (US television)
Lead actors: Kojiro Hongo, Kyoko Enami, Yuzo Hayakawa, Takuya Fujioka, Koji Fujiyama, Sho Natsuki, Yoshiro Kitahara, Ichiro Sugai
Primary Gamera suit actor: Teruo Aragaki

—— ▼ ——

The first Gamera film in color picks up where *Gamera: The Giant Monster* (1965) left off, with the Z-Plan Rocket—a spacecraft created by Japan, the United States, and the Soviet Union to capture Gamera and send him away from Earth—taking the heroic space turtle to Mars. The rocket is struck by a meteor, freeing Gamera. Meanwhile, on Earth, a

GAMERA VS BARUGON

MONSTERS OF 80 & 70 TONS

IN A FIGHT-TO-THE-DEATH THAT DESTROYS JAPAN'S PORT CITIES OF OSAKA AND KOBE!

COLOR   SCOPE

Release date: March 15, 1967 (Japan), 1968 (US—television release)

Lead actors: Kojiro Hongo, Reiko Kasahara, Taro Marui, Yoshio Kitahara, Sho Natsuki, Kichijiro Ueda, Naoyuki Abe

Primary Gamera suit actor: Teruo Aragaki

——— ▼ ———

Volcanic eruptions around and near Mount Fuji give the heroic Gamera the chance to eat molten magma for energy. But the volcanic activity also affects Mount Futago, where a dormant kaiju, the winged Gyaos, awakens from its slumber. Gamera must now pursue Gyaos and bring its deadly rage to an end.

Daiei Film president Masaichi Nagata brought back Noriaki Yuasa to both direct the film and

A poster for *Gamera vs. Barugon* (1966).

The Japanese poster for *Gamera vs. Gyaos* (1967).

rare gem is discovered and taken to Japan, only for it to actually be an egg that hatches into Barugon, a kaiju reptile. As the Japan Self-Defense Force tries to find a way to defeat the threat, Gamera returns to Earth to battle Barugon and save the citizens of Japan.

This film marks the first time Teruo Aragaki took on the role of Gamera. He would play the role for two more films, making him the only actor in Gamera's history to play the role more than twice. In the Showa Era of Gamera, this film is the only one not directed by Noriaki Yuasa, though Yuasa did play a pivotal role in the production, as the director of special effects. Unfortunately, the film underperformed, making less than the first Gamera movie.

☢ *Gamera vs. Gyaos* (1967)

Director: Noriaki Yuasa
Producer: Hidemasa Nagata
Writer: Nisan Takahashi
Alternate film titles: *Giant Monster Dogfight: Gamera vs. Gyaos* (Japan), *Return of the Giant Monsters* (US), *Boyichi and the Supermonster* (Philippines), *Gamera Against the Monster Gaos* (Italy)

KAIJU FACT

Gamera vs. Gyaos (1967) marks
the debut of Gyaos, Gamera's
greatest foe, who would be
featured in eight Gamera films.

handle the special effects. He also decided that
Gamera vs. Gyaos would be aimed toward a younger
audience, in hopes of a better box office turnout. It
was successful, pulling in close to 40 million yen in
profits. The Gamera suit used in the movie was from
the previous film, though the eyes were changed to
make the kaiju look friendlier.

Japanese poster
art for *Gamera vs.
Viras* (1968).

☢ *Gamera vs. Viras* (1968)

Director: Noriaki Yuasa
Producer: Hidemasa Nagata
Writer: Nisan Takahashi
Alternate film titles: *Gamera vs. Space Monster Viras*
(Japan), *Destroy All Planets* (US), *Destroy The Whole Earth*
(Brazil), *The Invincible Monster* (Italy)
Release date: March 20, 1968 (Japan), 1970 (US—
television release)
Lead actors: Kojiro Hongo, Michiko Yaegaki, Mari Atsumi,
Junko Yashiro, Yoshiro Kitahara, Carl Craig, Toru Takatsuka
Primary Gamera suit actor: Teruo Aragaki

▼

An alien race known as the Virans come to Earth
to conquer it, seeking a way to control Gamera
and send him to destroy Japan. Meanwhile,
two Boy Scouts, Masao and Jim, sneak into a
miniature submarine at the aquarium, which
leads to them meeting Gamera. The Virans
capture Gamera and the boys, then threaten to
kill the children if Gamera does not obey them.
The two Boy Scouts have to find a way to break
Gamera free of the Virans' control. But if they're
able to do that, Gamera will still have to battle the
deadly Viras, a kaiju created by the merged bodies
of the Virans.

    Gamera vs. Viras is the second of the Gamera
films to offer kid-friendly fare. But don't let that title
fool you: it doesn't mean that the violence becomes
subdued. In this film, for example, there's a scene
in which Viras stabs Gamera multiple times in his
underbelly.

☢ *Gamera vs. Guiron* (1969)

Director: Noriaki Yuasa
Producer: Hidemasa Nagata
Writer: Nisan Takahashi
Alternate film titles: *Gamera vs. Giant Evil Beast Guiron*
(Japan), *Attack of the Monsters* (US), *The Attack of the
Monsters* (Brazil)
Release date: March 21, 1969 (Japan), 1970 (US—
television release)

Lead actors: Nobuhiro Kajima, Christopher Murphy, Miyuki Akiyama, Eiji Funakoshi, Kon Omura, Yuko Hamada, Edith Hansen, Reiko Kasahara, Hiroko Kai

Primary Gamera suit actor: Umenosuke Izumi

▼

When two young boys find a spaceship on Earth, their curiosity gets the best of them and they decide to board it, accidentally launching themselves into space toward an asteroid field and, later, the planet Terra. Gamera, aware of the danger the children are in, leaps into action to save them from crashing into the asteroids, and he later battles Terra's deadly monster, Guiron.

Guiron is a relatively simple but effective kaiju design: a quadrupedal beast with a knife head. It's ridiculous, but it works. *Gamera vs. Guiron* did not have a theatrical release in the US, instead making its debut on television, where it was edited to trim down the violence. Originally, the film was also meant to feature a new kaiju called Monga, but due to budget constraints, the team instead added Space Gyaos into the mix. As you might be able to guess, Space Gyaos was just the Gyaos suit painted silver.

GAMERA'S POWERS AND WEAKNESSES

· · · · · · · · · · · · · · · · · · · ·

POWERS

DURABILITY
Gamera has a strong upper shell that can bombard and deflect weaponry, and he can also withdraw into his shell to avoid most attacks. It is 100 times stronger than diamond.

ENERGY IMMERSION AND PROJECTION
The Showa Era Gamera feeds on fire and other heat sources and can even eat coal. Once he builds up his energy, he can also fire immense heat rays from his mouth.

FLIGHT
Gamera can fly at speeds of Mach 3 to Mach 3.5 by pulling his appendages into his shell. He can fly into space and across multiple planets and galaxies. He can also do a flying spin attack which makes him look like a Frisbee.

CLAWS
Gamera's claws are very sharp and he uses them frequently in close combat. They also release a liquid that stuns his enemies.

WEAKNESSES

FREEZING TEMPERATURES
Gamera's major weakness is extreme cold, due to his need for warmth. This weakness only appeared in Gamera's earlier films, and is no longer used in modern films.

PARASITES
Gamera's internal organs are easily affected by deadly parasites.

UNDERBELLY
Although his shell is strong, Gamera's underbelly is very soft, meaning opponents often try to stab or blast him there to cause damage.

Japenese poster art for *Gamera vs. Zigra* (1971).

☢ *Gamera vs. Jiger* (1970)

Director: Noriaki Yuasa

Producer: Hidemasa Nagata

Writer: Nisan Takahashi

Alternate film titles: *Gamera vs. Giant Demon Beast Jiger* (Japan), *Gamera vs. Monster X* (US), *Gamera Against Jiggar – Frankenstein Demon Threatens the World* (West Germany)

Release date: March 21, 1970 (Japan), 1970 (US—television release)

Lead actors: Tsutomu Takakuwa, Kelly Varis, Katherine Murphy, Sanshiro Hono, Franz Gruber

Primary Gamera suit actor: Umenosuke Izumi

— ▼ —

When a strange statue is taken from Wester Island, a kaiju named Jiger emerges and wreaks havoc on Osaka, Japan. As Jiger and Gamera battle in Osaka, Jiger places a parasitic egg into Gamera's lung, making the giant turtle deathly ill. Scientists try

The Japanese poster for *Gamera vs. Jiger* (1970).

to cure Gamera, but two young boys, Hiroshi and Tommy, who are friends to Gamera, decide to steal a miniature submarine at the site and enter Gamera's body to destroy the parasite and save him themselves.

In a movie that combines *Fantastic Voyage* (1966) with kaiju, director Noriaki Yuasa does a lot on a limited budget. The low budget stemmed from Daiei's financial troubles at the time, due to Masaichi Nagata's extravagant spending habits and a decline in movie theater attendance across the board.

☢ *Gamera vs. Zigra* (1971)

Director: Noriaki Yuasa

Producer: Hidemasa Nagata

Writer: Nisan Takahashi

Alternate film title: *Gamera vs. Deep Sea Monster Zigra* (Japan)

FILM PRODUKCJI JAPOŃSKIEJ

SUPERPOTWÓR

REŻYSERIA NORIAKI YUASA

宇宙怪獣ガメラ
produkcja:
Daiei, Tokio

WYSTĘPUJĄ : MACH FUMIAKE, KEIKO KUDO, KOICHI MAEDA

An international poster for *Gamera: Super Monster* (1980).

Release date: July 17, 1971 (Japan), 1987 (US)
Lead actors: Eiko Yanami, Reiko Kasahara, Mikiko Tsubouchi, Koji Fujiyama, Isamu Saeki
Primary Gamera suit actor: Umenosuke Izumi

▼

An extraterrestrial woman from the planet Zigra and her spaceship are causing several earthquakes worldwide, and two children at a marine park are caught in the middle of the chaos. Gamera must fight the monstrous Zigra starship—which also morphs into a deadly alien shark—to protect the children and save the Earth.

A sequel called *Gamera vs. the Two Headed Monster* was to go into development, but it was canceled due to Daiei Films going bankrupt.

☢ *Gamera: Super Monster* (1980)
Director: Noriaki Yuasa
Producer: Hirozaki Oba
Writer: Nisan Takahashi
Alternate film title: *Space Monster Gamera* (Japan)
Release date: March 20, 1980 (Japan), 1983 (US)
Lead actors: Mach Fumiake, Yaeko Kojima, Yoko Komatsu, Keiko Kudo, Koichi Maeda

The first Gamera film in nine years, *Gamera: Super Monster* was supposed to revitalize the franchise and hopefully help the new Daiei Film Releasing stay afloat. But in the end, due to budgetary constraints, the film is essentially just a Gamera clip show, presenting footage from previous films, and is one of the least-liked films in Gamera's history. Even iconic Gamera director Noriaki Yuasa loathed the film so much that he purposely killed Gamera at the end, in the hopes of protecting the character from being bastardized further. A commercial and critical flop, *Gamera: Super Monster* was the final Gamera film directed by Yuasa—and the last Gamera film for fifteen years.

KAIJU FACT

So much previous footage was used in *Gamera: Super Monster* that it includes just two minutes of new footage of Gamera.

THE UNMADE GAMERA FILMS

Gamera vs. the Space Icemen
A race of ice-based aliens invades Earth and plan on returning the planet to the Ice Age. Gamera must battle the Ice Giant and assorted icemen in order to save the planet.

Gamera vs. the Two-Headed Monster W
Not much is known about this unmade film, but the monster that Gamera would've faced (W) resembles a two-headed flying dragon.

Gamera vs. Phoenix
An all-new Gamera arrives from beneath the desert to battle the menacing firebird known as Phoenix. An illustrated version of the unproduced screenplay was published in 1995.

Godzilla vs. Gamera
In what could've been one of the biggest team-ups in Japan in 2002, Kadokawa (owners of Gamera) approached Toho to see if they would be interested in co-producing a crossover film. Toho passed.

Gamera 3D
This was supposed to be a 40-minute film of Gamera battling a kaiju named Midora. It was to be filmed in IMAX and shown in IMAX theaters.

▼▼ THE HEISEI ERA (1995–2015) ▼▼

☢ Gamera: Guardian of the Universe (1995)
Director: Shusuke Kaneko
Writer: Kazunori Ito
Producers: Yasuyoshi Tokuma, Hiroyuki Kato, Seiji Urushido, Shigero Ono
Release date: March 11, 1995 (Japan), April 16, 1997 (US limited release)
Lead actors: Tsuyoshi Ihara, Shinobu Nakayama, Ayako Fujitani, Yukijiro Hotaru, Hirotaro Honda, Hatsunori Hasegawa
Primary Gamera suit actors: Takateru Manabe, Jun Suzuki

—— ▼ ——

A reboot of the franchise, *Gamera: Guardian of the Universe* is the first Gamera film in the Heisei Era. The titular kaiju returns to battle his lifelong rival, Gyaos. This version of Gyaos is made up of three winged creatures, instead of just one, as previously depicted, and can also upgrade to the 280-foot-tall

KAIJU FACT

Gyaos was portrayed by suit actor Yuhmi Kaneyama, one of the first female suit actors.

Super Gyaos by feeding on humans, wildlife, livestock, and anything else that it can find. But the military thinks that Gamera is the problem, not Gyaos.

Daiei Films worked together with Toho to help bring this film to life, and director Shusuke Kaneko ended up directing the entire trilogy (including this film, *Gamera 2: Attack of the Legion*, and *Gamera 3: Revenge of Iris*). *Gamera: Guardian of the Universe* removed itself from the kid-friendly Showa Era in the kaiju's fortieth anniversary year and reaped the benefits: it was a commercial and critical success.

Gamera 2: Attack of the Legion (1996)

Director: Shusuke Kaneko
Producers: Miyuki Nanri, Naoki Sato, Tsutomu Tsuchikawa
Writer: Kazunori Ito
Release aate: July 13, 1996 (Japan), 2003 (US—DVD release)
Lead actors: Toshiyuki Nagashima, Miki Mizuno, Tamotsu Ishibashi, Mitsuru Fukikoshi, Ayako Fujitani
Primary Gamera suit actor: Akira Ohashi

▼

The second film of the Heisei Gamera trilogy introduces an

all-new kaiju known as Legion. Legion are silicon-based symbiote insectoid aliens, consisting of Soldier Legions that attack in swarms, and the massive Mother Legion, who has a microwave shell that fires an intense blast, red-rod crimson tendrils, and sharp-tipped arms and legs. She can also fly and produce electromagnetic waves. Originally, either Barugon or Guiron was going to face off against Gamera in this film, but the creative team opted to create a new kaiju instead, which paid off. The film was a critical and commercial success, raking in 6.5 million yen in Japan, and it's considered one of the best Gamera films.

Gamera 3: Revenge of Iris (1999)

Director: Shusuke Kaneko
Producers: Yasuyoshi Tokuma, Hiroyuki Kato, Kazuhiko Ishikawa, Kiyosh Ono, Naomasa Tsuruta
Writers: Kazunori Ito, Shusuke Kaneko

OPPOSITE: The Japanese poster for *Gamera: Guardian of the Universe* (1995).

Gamera takes on his rival, Gyaos, in *Gamera: Guardian of the Universe* (1995).

Alternate film titles: *Gamera 3: Awakening of the Evil God* (Japan), *Gamera 3: Evil God Irys' Awakening* (Germany), *Gamera, Absolute Guardian of the Universe* (UK)

Release date: March 6, 1999 (Japan), 2003 (US—DVD release)

Lead actors: Shinobu Nakayama, Ai Maeda, Ayako Fujitani, Yu Koyama, Nozomi Ando, Takahiro Ito, Senri Yamazaki, Toru Tezuka, Yukijiro Hotaru

Primary Gamera suit actors: Hirofumi Fukuzawa, Akira Ohashi

———— ▼ ————

OPPOSITE:
A scene from *Gamera: The Giant Monster* (1965).

Gamera in his 1995 film.

The fantastic final film in the Gamera Heisei trilogy, *Revenge of Iris*, has a great premise: What if a child could power a kaiju with its rage? A young girl named Ayana, who lost her family during the battle of Gamera and Legion, blames Gamera for the death of her family and befriends the sinister

Iris, which grows into a giant-sized kaiju and begins a path of destruction, feeding off the child's anger. Gamera then faces off against his most monstrous foe. This film acts an allegory for working one's way through grief.

☢ *Gamera the Brave* (2006)

Director: Ryuta Tasaki
Producer: Kazuo Kuroi
Writer: Yukari Tatsui
Release date: April 29, 2006 (Japan), 2008 (US—DVD release)
Lead actors: Ryo Tomioka, Kaho, Kanji Tsuda, Susumu Terajima, Kaoru Okunuki, Megumi Kobayashi, Shingo Ishikawa, Shogo Narita
Primary Gamera suit actor: Toshinori Sasaki

———— ▼ ————

In the year 1973, Gamera makes the biggest sacrifice to save humankind, taking his own life to defeat a flock of Gyaos. Thirty years later, a young boy finds what he thinks is a regular turtle egg, but when it hatches, it is actually the reincarnated Gamera (named Toto by the boy). When Zedus, a deadly sea lizard kaiju that can emit acid from its claws and tongue, emerges off the coast of Isehima, Gamera (Toto) arrives to eliminate the deadly threat.

Returning to Gamera's more kid-friendly roots, *Gamera the Brave* was a box office failure. The fandom had come to expect the more adult and meaningful tone of director Shusuke Kaneko's

KAIJU FACT

The roars used for Gamera in *Gamera the Brave* (2006) come from Universal creature features *The Deadly Mantis* and *The Land Unknown*, as well as the 1976 *King Kong* remake.

SANDY FRANK, THE MAN WHO LED THE GAMERA RENAISSANCE IN AMERICA

American television producer Sandy Frank, who came to prominence producing game shows during the 1970s and '80s, made his biggest splash in television when he adapted Tatsunoko Productions' action-packed anime series *Science Ninja Team Gatchaman* for American audiences. *Battle of the Planets*, as it was called in the US, featured a group of teenage superheroes known as the G-Force that defended the Earth from the forces of Spectra and their evil leader Zoltar. In first-run syndication, *Battle of the Planets* was very popular from 1978–1980, and reruns stayed in syndication for years.

Frank worked with Daiei Films to acquire the airing rights to four Showa Era Gamera films: *Gamera: The Giant Monster*, *Gamera vs. Barugon*, *Gamera vs. Guiron*, and *Gamera vs. Zigra*. The films were completely redubbed, and new title credits were added. They were frequently on television during the '80s, and all four were later featured on *Mystery Science Theater 3000*.

trilogy and was disappointed by this entry. However, the film did receive a warm reception from critics. Even Katsuhito Ishii, the director of the 2015 short film *Gamera*, views *Gamera the Brave* as one of his favorite movies and cites it as a major inspiration for his film. In a review at *Dread Central*, critic Andrew Kasch gave the film 3.5 out of 5 stars, stating, "Even with its kid-centric approach, *Gamera the Brave* is guaranteed to please most kaiju enthusiasts, and the new franchise should be enough to fill the empty hole left in Godzilla's absence."

Gamera (2015 Short Film)

For the fiftieth anniversary of the Gamera franchise, the Kadokawa Corporation produced a Gamera short film, directed by Katsuhito Ishii. In this final film in the Heisei Era, Gamera battles Gyaos and a never-before-seen kaiju (an unnamed tentacled monster). It premiered at the 2015 New York Comic Con.

9 RODAN

RODAN

**Monster of monsters! Big as a skyscraper!
When he moves, the whole Earth quivers and quakes
and an abyss of horror opens up!
—trailer voiceover for the US release of *Rodan* (1957)**

odan, a prehistoric kaiju Pteranodon with massive wings, was created by writer Ken Kuronuma, who was inspired by a news story about an American fighter pilot, Captain Thomas F. Mantell of the Kentucky Air National Guard. Mantell blacked out and died in a plane crash while purportedly chasing an unidentified flying object in 1948. Director Ishirō Honda, who had directed the successful *Godzilla* (1954) and *Half*

Human (1955), was selected by producer Tomoyuki Tanaka to helm the film. Kaiju and tokusatsu are heavily celebrated and admired in Japan, so to have someone as celebrated as Ishirō Honda direct the film meant a lot. It also meant that Tanaka and Honda, two experienced filmmakers, could quickly get the production moving.

It's a Matter of Size

Over the decades, Rodan's size has changed. Here are some vital stats from the various eras:

SHOWA ERA
Height – 164 feet   Weight – 15,000 tons
Wingspan – 394 feet

HEISEI ERA
Height – 230 feet   Weight – 16,000 tons
Wingspan – 492 feet

MILLENNIUM ERA
Height – 328 feet   Weight – 30,000 tons
Wingspan – 656 feet

MONSTERVERSE
Height – 154 feet   Weight – 39,000 tons
Wingspan – 871 feet

OPPOSITE:
The character poster featuring Rodan for 2019's *Godzilla: King of the Monsters.*

Rodan in his 1956 solo film.

Rodan in his solo debut in 1956.

Release date: December 26, 1956 (Japan), November 7, 1957 (US)

Lead actors: Kenji Sahara, Yumi Shirakawa, Akihiko Hirata, Akio Kobori, Yoshifumi Tajima, Minosuke Yamada, Ren Imaizumi, Fuyuki Murakami

Primary Rodan suit sctors: Haruo Nakajima, Katsumi Tezuka

▼

In the coal mines beneath Kitamatsu, Kyushu, an investigation is taking place due to a high number of brutal murders. It's soon discovered that a kaiju dragonfly species known as Meganulon is the cause of the murders, leading an engineer named Shigeru, along with the police and military, to explore the caverns. Underground, Shigeru sees Rodan hatch from his egg and begin to feast on Meganulon. Rodan escapes from the cave and begins a path of destruction all over the Far East, with his ability to create shockwaves, massive gusts of wind, and deadly gas. As the Japan Self-Defense Force battles Rodan, things turn from bad to worse as a second Rodan appears . . .

This film is the only time Rodan has the weaponized ability to shoot bursts of concentrated gas from his mouth. The American release of *Rodan* also marks the first professional acting job of George Takei (of *Star Trek* fame), who did three days of voiceover work. A prologue was created for the original American release featuring stock footage of the very first US nuclear bomb tests, as a way to link the creation/awakening of Rodan with the atomic bomb.

In Japan, the kaiju is known as Radon, but the name was adjusted to Rodan for the United States and United Kingdom to make sure there was no confusion with the chemical element. In a few of the original US releases, the name Radon was dubbed in before Toho requested the name change. Toho later trademarked the Rodan name.

Though he started out as an enemy of mankind, in later films Rodan served as an ally to Godzilla, kaiju, and humankind. The design originally paralleled more of a stocky, traditional pterosaur with small wings, but the final designs would turn Rodan into the large pterosaur that has flown across screens for close to seventy years.

▼▼ THE SHOWA ERA (1954–1975) ▼▼

☢ *Rodan* (1956)

Director: Ishirō Honda

Producer: Tomoyuki Tanaka

Writers: Kaoru Mabuchi, Takeo Murata, Ken Kuronuma

Alternate film titles: *Radon, Giant Monster of the Sky* (Japan), *Rodan! The Flying Monster!* (US), *Rodan: Bird of Death* (Poland), *Flying Monster Vulture* (Taiwan, China), *The Sons of the Volcano* (Spain)

KAIJU FACT

Rodan was Toho's first kaiju movie filmed in color.

RODAN'S CINEMATIC GUEST APPEARANCES

Though Rodan only has one movie of his own, he's appeared in a number of films through the decades, including:

- ▶ *Ghidorah, the Three-Headed Monster* (1964)
- ▶ *Invasion of Astro-Monster* (1965)
- ▶ *Destroy All Monsters* (1968)
- ▶ *Godzilla vs. Gigan* (1972), in footage from previous films
- ▶ *Godzilla vs. Megalon* (1973), in footage from previous films
- ▶ *Terror of Mechagodzilla* (1975), in footage from previous films
- ▶ *Bye-Bye Jupiter* (1984), in footage from previous films
- ▶ *Godzilla vs. Mechagodzilla II* (1993)
- ▶ *Godzilla: Final Wars* (2004)
- ▶ *Kong: Skull Island* (2017), in which he's seen in a cave painting
- ▶ *Godzilla: King of the Monsters* (2019)

TOP TO BOTTOM: Scenes from *Invasion of Astro-Monster* (1965), *Destroy All Monsters* (1968), and *Astro-Monster* again.

> **From the early planning stages with Mr. Tsuburaya, before the screenplay was written, the setting was an adventure set on a South Sea Island, where a mysterious giant creature is worshiped as a God. There's also a showman and beauty (in this case, little beauties), that causes a city to be rampaged. So yes, this is a Japanese version of King Kong. However, I wanted our final act to be a happy ending, and not like the denouement of Kong, which ended in tragedy.**
> **—Ishirō Honda on *Mothra* (1961)**

Birthed from the 1961 serialized story "The Luminous Fairies and Mothra" by Takehiko Fukunaga, Yoshie Hotta, and Shinichiro Nakamura, Mothra is one of Toho's most popular kaiju. According to David Kalat's *A Critical History and Filmography of Toho's Godzilla Series*, polls taken during the 1990s showed that Mothra was very popular with women. In that decade, women were also the biggest demographic of Japan's movie-watching audience. Toho honored Mothra by crowning her "Queen of Monsters."

Producer Tomoyuki Tanaka created Mothra so that Toho could make a kaiju movie that women might want to see, thus expanding their potential audience. Director Ishirō Honda, when discussing the beginnings of the film, said, "For Mothra, producer Tomoyuki Tanaka set up a plan to create a completely different monster movie from what we had previously produced. We asked three young novelists to create the original story, and Shin'ichi Sekizawa was responsible for the screenplay. During the screenplay development, Mr. Sekizawa coined the term *Shobijin* [little beauties] for the twin fairies."

For the first Mothra film, which features her caterpillar form, multiple versions of the suit were made, though the most notable was the suit built to 1/25th scale. It needed as many as six suit actors inside to move it. Legendary Godzilla suit performers Haruo Nakajima and Katsumi Tezuka were part of that caterpillar team. A hand-operated model was also used. For the adult/kaiju moth version of Mothra, three models were built for filming. The largest model was 1/100th in scale with a wingspan of eight feet. The mid-sized model had very flexible wings, which came in handy for

OPPOSITE:
The Japanese poster for *Mothra* (1961).

The title character in *Mothra* (1961).

A scene from *Mothra vs. Godzilla* (1964).

hatching scenes. The smallest model was used for long shots during filming, with a tiny motor inside that made the wings flap. The movie's special effects were led by Eiji Tsuburaya, and for the Shobijin (the tiny fairies played by Emi and Yumi Ito), Tsuburaya had them film all of their scenes in front of a blue screen with oversized sets. Their scenes were later composited into the film.

Mothra is typically depicted as a kind and benevolent being who only destroys while acting as a protector of the Earth, her followers on Infant Island, or her egg or children. She may also cause damage while defending Earth from a greater threat. Mothra is usually accompanied by the Shobijin, small priestesses or fairies who speak on her behalf. While she doesn't have a film catalog as extensive as Godzilla, Mothra has had many guest appearances in multiple Godzilla films and other projects.

▼▼ THE SHOWA ERA (1961–1980) ▼▼

☢ *Mothra* (1961)

Director: Ishirō Honda
Producer: Tomoyuki Tanaka
Writers: Shinichi Sekizawa (screenwriter), Takehiko Fukunaga, Yoshie Hotta, Shinichiro Nakamura (storywriters)
Alternate film titles: *The Invincible Wonder Beast*

OPPOSITE: Cover art featuring Mothra for *Ebirah, Horror of the Deep* (1966).

(Iceland), *Mothra Threatens the World* (Germany), *Mothra, The Wild Goddess* (Brazil), *Mothra the Indestructible* (Mexico)
Release date: July 30, 1961 (Japan), May 10, 1962 (US)
Lead actors: Frankie Sakai, Hiroshi Koizumi, Kyoko Kagawa, Ken Uehara, Jerry Ito, Takashi Shimura, Emi Ito, Yumi Ito

——— ▼ ———

A team of explorers from Japan and Rolisica (a fictional country that blends characteristics of both Russia and America) embark on a mission to Infant Island, which had been subjected to H-bomb testing by the Rolisican government. Despite the terrifying amounts of radiation present, the island still supports life. The team discovers two beautiful young fairies, known as the Shobijin, who are only a foot tall and serve as the guardians of Mothra's sacred egg. Nelson, a member of the Rolisican

KAIJU FACT

Actor Jerry Ito's name is listed as "Jelly Ito" in the American release of *Mothra* (1961).

QUEEN OF THE GUEST APPEARANCE

Although Mothra has her own film franchise, the Queen of the Monsters has also had some great guest appearances in multiple Godzilla films, including:

▶ *Ghidorah, the Three-Headed Monster* (1964)
If not for Mothra being able to convince Godzilla and Rodan to work together to defeat Ghidorah, the Earth would be property of the three-headed mega-dragon. Mothra has fantastic leadership skills.

▶ *Destroy All Monsters* (1968)
In one of the greatest team-up movies of all time, Mothra battles alongside Godzilla, Minilla, Rodan, Gorosaurus, Anguirus, Kumonga, Manda, Baragon, and Varan to put an end to King Ghidorah.

▶ *Godzilla, Mothra, and King Ghidorah: Giant Monsters All-Out Attack* (2001)
In this movie, the unexpected happens and Mothra and King Ghidorah have to team up to fight Godzilla, who has become a pure force of evil.

team, later returns to the island to kidnap the twins and plans to showcase them around the world. However, the egg hatches into a kaiju larva, which grows into an Imago, or kaiju moth, form that sets out to rescue its Shobijin.

In the book *Ishiro Honda: A Life in Film, from Godzilla to Kurosawa* by Steve Ryfle and Ed Godziszewski, the authors note that, according to Honda, *Mothra* portrays nuclear anxiety and a proxy relationship between America and Japan. They mention that the fictitious country of Rolisica is a "pushy capitalist superpower," interested in Nelson's money and thus allowing his crimes in Japan to go unpunished. They also note that the Rolisican atomic ray gun, which has the capability to fire atomic heat rays and was used to combat Mothra in the film, violates one of Japan's non-nuclear principles, banning the transport of nuclear weapons into the country. Honda's vision of understanding and cooperation is achieved through religion, which is evident in the religious iconography of Infant Island. However, the film's political satire "never gets too serious," from the author's observations. The film was a critical and commercial success, earning praise in both Japan and America, including high marks in the *New York*

Times. Hazel Flynn of the *Los Angeles Citizen News*
said, "The sight of the huge flying monster flapping
its wings is one of the most impressive special
effects I've ever encountered."

▼▼ THE HEISEI ERA (1995–1998) ▼▼

☢ *Rebirth of Mothra* (1996)

Director: Okihiro Yoneda
Producers: Shogo Tomiyama, Hiroaki Kitayama
Writer: Masumi Suetani
Alternate film titles: *Mothra's Rebirth* (Sweden), *Mothra:
The Seal of the Elias* (Germany)
Release date: December 14, 1996 (Japan), 2000 (US)
Lead actors: Sayaka Yamaguchi, Megumi Kobayashi, Aki
Hano, Kazuki Futami, Maya Fujisawa, Hitomi Takahashi,
Kenjiro Nashimoto

———— ▼ ————

When Toho decided to put Godzilla productions
on hold after *Godzilla vs. Destoroyah* (1995), they
pivoted to an all-new series of Mothra films.
Completely disconnected from the previous films
or appearances in the Showa Era, *Rebirth of Mothra*
(1996) is the final film that Tomoyuki Tanaka would
be involved in before passing away in 1997 at the
age of 86. In this movie, the Queen of Monsters
summons an egg to carry on her legacy after her
impending death. Later, a logging company in
Hokkaido unknowingly discovers the tomb of the
evil space monster Desghidorah, a demonic three-
headed dragon. Belvera, a fairy like her sisters, Moll
and Lora, and an Elias (or fairy priestess), detests
her younger sisters and is determined to destroy
mankind—and she intends to use Desghidorah
to do it. Belvera's sisters, Moll and Lora, with the
help of two children and their tiny divine moth
kaiju known as Fairy, call upon Mothra to stop
Desghidorah and ensure humanity's future. When
Mothra seems on the verge of defeat, her larval son,
Mothra Leo, hatches early and joins the battle.

Moll and Lora are the new priestesses in this
series of Mothra films, replacing the Shobijin. The
film was successful in Japan, grossing over 1.96
billion yen in Japan and earning a sequel.

☢ *Rebirth of Mothra II* (1997)

Director: Kunio Miyoshi
Producers: Shogo Tomiyama, Hiroaki Kitayama
Writer: Masumi Suetani
Alternate film titles: *Mothra 2: The Battle Under the
Deep Sea* (Japan), *Mothra 2: The Battle Under the Surface*
(Sweden), *Mothra: The Sunken Kingdom* (Germany)
Release date: December 13, 1997 (Japan), 2000 (US)
Lead actors: Megumi Kobayashi, Sayaka Yamaguchi, Aki
Hano, Hikari Mitsushima, Masanao Shimada, Masaki
Otake, Mizuho Yoshida

In this follow-up to *Return of Mothra* (1996), a massive sea monster named Dagahra appears near the coast of Okinawa, accompanied by a swarm of poisonous, starfish-like creatures known as Barem. Later, a group of kids stumbles upon a small, fluffy creature called Ghogo. Belvera believes that Ghogo is the key to unlocking the hidden treasure of the lost Nilai-Kanai civilization, once a society of powerful and intelligent beings that created Dagahra to remove pollution from their seas, though Dagahra proved too strong to control and wiped them out. The children decide to team up with Belvera's sisters Moll and Lora to find the hidden treasure before Belvera does. Meanwhile, Mothra Leo battles Dagahra, but even Leo finds himself struggling against the powerful sea monster. The treasure of the Nilai-Kanai civilization may give Leo and Japan the advantage they need.

Koichi Kawakita

Rebirth of Mothra II is the last tokusatsu or kaiju film with special effects led by Koichi Kawakita, a special effects director, optical photographer, and cinematographer who worked on tokusatsu television series and kaiju films for over 50 years. Notable films for which he served as special effects director include *Godzilla vs. Biollante* (1989), *Godzilla vs. King Ghidorah* (1991), *Godzilla vs. Mothra* (1992), *Godzilla vs. Mechagodzilla II* (1993), *Godzilla vs. SpaceGodzilla* (1994), *Godzilla vs. Destoroyah* (1995), and *Rebirth of Mothra* (1996).

A scene from *Rebirth of Mothra II* (1997).

OPPOSITE:
The Japanese
poster for *Mothra
vs. Godzilla* (1964).

Though the film did not meet Toho's expectations, garnering poor reviews from critics and making less money at the box office than previous films, they thankfully went on to complete the Mothra trilogy.

☢ *Rebirth of Mothra III* (1998)

Director: Okihiro Yoneda
Producer: Shogo Tomiyama
Writer: Masumi Suetani
Alternate film titles: *Mothra 3: Invasion of King Ghidorah* (Japan), *Mothra: King Ghidorah Returns* (Germany)
Release date: December 12, 1998 (Japan), 2014 (US)
Lead actors: Megumi Kobayashi, Misato Tate, Aki Hano, Atsushi Ohnita, Miyuki Matsuda, Takuma Yoshizawa, Kyohei Shinozaki, Tsutmo Kitigawa, Ayano Suzuki

Mothra takes on Gigan in *Godzilla: Final Wars* (2004).

When the terrifying three-headed space dragon kaiju King Ghidorah returns to Earth and begins to kidnap children so he can feed off their life force, Mothra Leo, along with Moll and Lora, tries to stop him, but the trio is no match for King Ghidorah's power. To save Mothra Leo, Moll sacrifices herself and sends him back to the Cretaceous Period, when King Ghidorah was not as powerful (even though he *did* almost wipe out the dinosaurs). But even with his adversary in a weaker state, Mothra must use all his strength to defeat one of the deadliest kaiju.

In this film, Mothra Leo (also known as Rainbow Mothra due to his colorful wings) has three additional forms: Light Speed Mothra (which can fly at speeds as fast as 186,000 miles per

Mothra Powers and Abilities

In her larval stage, Mothra can bite kaiju with her mandibles and spit silk streams to trap or confuse opponents. As a kaiju moth (Imago), Mothra can release yellow, poisonous scales from her wings that can weaken opposing kaiju or reflect attacks. The Monsterverse version of Mothra can spit streams of silk in Imago form.

THE FORMS OF MOTHRA OVER THE DECADES

▶ **LARVAL STAGE**
In her Larval Stage, Mothra can spray enemies with streams of silk to trap them. The larvae will also bite kaiju, preferably clinging their tails. Mothra Leo can change colors in his Larval Stage and can also fire a powerful beam from his chest cavity.

▶ **IMAGO STAGE**
Mothra's Imago Stage gives her the ability to scratch and carry kaiju. Her wings make gusts of wind strong enough to tear cities apart and send kaiju flying. She can also release poisonous scales, a powder-like substance from her wings that will kill her enemy. She only uses this attack when she knows that she will die, because the loss of her scales will prevent her from being able to fly.

Mothra Leo's Imago Stage allows him to fire beams of energy from his forehead, shoot lightning bolts from his wings, fire green energy beams from his chest, and charge himself with energy to attack enemy kaiju at speeds of Mach 85. He can also break apart into multiple tiny Mothras that explode upon contact with his enemies, and can release powder in a circle that will bring down a giant beam of energy from the sky upon his opponent.

▶ **FIRE MOTHRA**
After being set aflame by Gigan during a battle in Godzilla Final Wars, Mothra flew at high speed directly at Gigan, destroying both Gigan and herself.

▶ **ETERNAL MOTHRA**
Eternal form is the final form of Mothra Leo, with a power set similar to Armored Mothra, though without the armored shell. In this form, Mothra Leo's wings can slice and dice his enemies and his strength increases. He can also pass through enemies at blazing speeds to make them explode and fire a heat laser.

WHO ARE EMI AND YUMI ITO?

Emi Ito and Yumi Ito were identical-twin Japanese singers and actresses who performed as the singing duo the Peanuts from 1958 to 1975. They were the first successful J-pop (Japan Pop) group, selling over 10 million records worldwide. They appeared on *The Ed Sullivan Show* in 1966 and were also well-received in Germany and Austria. In the kaiju fandom, they are known for their roles as the Shobijin, the fairy-sized singing priestesses of Mothra in the kaiju's first 1961 film.

The Shobijin are featured in the Mothra films, and in most of them, they sing Mothra's Song, with Emi and Yumi's version being the most famous and catchy. The song is a way of calling for Mothra when they are in need of assistance or rescue, and of notifying Mothra of dangers.

While filming their roles as the Shobijin, the Ito twins had very little acting experience, but picked up the required skills very quickly, learning their lines without difficulty. Their acting career was quite brief, ending in 1964, though they continued to tour as the Peanuts until retiring in 1975. Emi passed away on June 15, 2012, and Yumi died on May 18, 2016. They starred as the Shobijin in *Mothra* (1961), *Mothra vs. Godzilla* (1964), and *Ghidorah, the Three-Headed Monster* (1964).

second), Aqua Mothra (able to swim underwater and fire multiple laser beams from his forehead and body), and Armored Mothra (an armored version of Mothra with sharp wings, increased strength, and heat lasers). Even though *Rebirth of Mothra III* is popular amongst Mothra and kaiju fans, it had the lowest box office numbers of the three films in the trilogy, putting a hold on future Mothra live-action films.

▾▾ MOTHRA IN RECENT YEARS ▾▾

Mothra appears in the following Millennium Series films:

- ☢ *Godzilla, Mothra, and King Ghidorah: Giant Monsters All-Out Attack* (2001)
- ☢ *Godzilla Against Mechagodzilla* (2002)
- ☢ *Godzilla: Tokyo SOS* (2003)
- ☢ *Godzilla: Final Wars* (2004)

Mothra appears in the following Monsterverse films:

- ☢ *Godzilla: King of the Monsters* (2019)

Although Mothra has no cinematic appearances in the Reiwa Era (. . . yet?), she was mentioned in the animated *Godzilla: City on the Edge of Battle*, and an astral projection of the unborn child of Mothra appeared in the animated *Godzilla: The Planet Eater*. In the anime *Godzilla Singular Point*, there are also small moths that bear an uncanny resemblance to Mothra.

OPPOSITE: Japanese poster art for *Godzilla, Mothra, and King Ghidorah: Giant Monsters All-Out Attack* (2001).

A statue of Mothra in Osaka, Japan, in 2024.

nspired by the Czechoslovakian monster movie *Le Golem* (1936), directed by Julien Duvivier, Daimajin was first created at the Daiei Motion Picture Company. But he wasn't meant to have his own film series—he was created to be one of Gamera's first rivals, and would've been called Uchu Hyojin, aka the Space Iceman. But as the creators continued to work on the character of Hyojin, he was refined into Daimajin and it was decided that the character would receive his own film. The studio created Barugon to battle Gamera in *Gamera vs. Barugon* (1966) and began production on the Daimajin trilogy.

All three films in the Daimajin trilogy have a very similar plot and structure but differ in style. This is perhaps because the movies were filmed simultaneously, each with a different director. The three films revolve around Japanese villages that are thrown into turmoil when tyrannical warlords overthrow the peaceful village leaders and enslave the citizens to work in poverty. The people's faith and belief in the wrathful god Majin, who resides within a towering stone shogun statue in their mountains, is the only thing that keeps them from losing hope. When the villains ignore the faith of the distressed and abused people, the Majin statue descends to the villages to inflict destructive

vengeance on the faithless enemies of their people as Daimajin.

Although the screenplays for all three films were written by Tetsuro Yoshida and the rapid production and release schedule meant the films were very similar, each film has its own unique mood. It is a violent and intense movie series that touches on themes of faith, loyalty, feudal oppression, retribution, and sacrilege.

A scene from the 1966 film.

OPPOSITE: Poster art for *Daimajin* (1966).

THE THREE FORMS OF DAIMAJIN

. . . .

DORMANT STATUE FORM
Daimajin is immobile and lifeless. He can hear the pleas of the people who approach him.

ACTIVE FORM
Daimajin comes to life, with footsteps so heavy they can cause earthquakes. His stone body cannot be harmed by any human weapon and he can instill fear in his enemies by filling their minds with images of ghosts and demons. Daimajin can also transform into a fireball and move quickly over large distances.

SPIRIT FORM
Daimajin can transform into a white sphere and travel swiftly. Additionally, he exhibits telekinetic powers, as demonstrated in *Return of Daimajin*, in which he parts a lake to reach a warlord's village. Daimajin can extinguish fires instantly by chopping with his hands, and while submerged, he can generate strong water currents at will. He can shoot fireballs or fire blasts from his hands and legs, cause thunderstorms, and emit electricity from his headdress.

▾▾ THE DAIMAJIN FILM SERIES ▾▾

☢ *Daimajin* (1966)
Director: Kimiyoshi Yasuda
Producer: Masaichi Nagata
Writer: Tetsuro Yoshida
Alternate film titles: *Majin, the Monster of Terror* (US), *Fury of the Mountain God* (Singapore), *Vengeance of the Monster* (Canada), *Daimajin, the Evil God* (Spain), *Majin* (France), *Daimajin – Frankenstein's Monster Awakens* (West Germany)
Release date: April 17, 1966 (Japan), 1967 (US—television release)
Lead actors: Miwa Takada, Yoshihiko Aoyama, Jun Fujimaki, Ryutaro Gomi, Ryuzo Shimada, Tatsuo Endo
Primary Daimajin suit actor: Chikara Hashimoto

——— ▼ ———

In Japan, a family of peasants is frightened by a series of earthquakes which they believe to be caused by Daimajin, a Yokai spirit trapped within the mountain. Meanwhile, Lord Hanabasa and his chamberlain, Samanosuke, are trying to take control of the region. During a visit to a shrine, Samanosuke and his men murder Hanabasa's family, though Hanabasa's son and daughter, Tadafumi and Kozasa, escape Samanosuke's wrath with the help of a samurai

┌─ KAIJU FACT ─┐

Daimajin suit actor Chikara "Riki" Hashimoto was a professional baseball player in Japan from 1953 to 1958 with the Mainichi Orions. When he had to retire early due to a career-ending injury, he became an actor. He was the suit actor for all three Daimajin films and is most known for playing Hiroshi Suzuki in *Fist of Fury* (1972) with Bruce Lee.

総天然色

大魔神
（だいまじん）

製作 永田雅一

少女の涙が魔神を動かした
大岩壁も城門も
その一撃で
木ッ葉みじん！

The Japanese poster for *Daimajin* (1966).

named Kogenta. The shrine becomes occupied by Samanosuke's men, who prohibit gatherings there. The priestess Shinobu tries to reason with Samanosuke, to no avail. She later finds Kogenta and the children and takes them to the top of the mountain where Daimajin, a stone idol, is located.

As Tadafumi and Kozasa grow up, Samanosuke has, in the ensuing years, enslaved their village. When the siblings attempt to free the town of Samanosuke's wrath, their efforts fail. They then decide to go to the mountain where Daimajin is located to seek help. Samanosuke's men follow them and attempt to destroy the idol. Kozasa pleads with Daimajin to save her brother.

In a 2014 review, critic Tim Brayton said, "*Daimajin* works splendidly enough as a straightforward drama about desperate people struggling for safety and security that it doesn't need anything else to justify it. Heck, it doesn't even need to throw a giant monster at its plot in order to be completely engaging, beautiful, and emotionally resonant, that's just a nice bonus." The Daimajin trilogy has a cult following in America, sparking discussion across kaiju review and fan-sites, as well as on many pop culture and movie review sites and blogs.

☢ *Return of Daimajin* (1966)

Director: Kenji Misumi

Producer: Masaichi Nagata

Writer: Tetsuro Yoshida

Alternate film titles: *Return of Giant Majin* (US), *Return of the Mountain God* (Singapore/Hong Kong, China)

Release date: August 13, 1966 (Japan), 1970 (US— television release)

Lead actors: Kojiro Hongo, Shiho Fujimura, Taro Marui, Jutaro Hojo, Koichi Uenoyama, Asao Uchida

Primary Daimajin suit actor: Chikara Hashimoto

— ▼ —

In this sequel to *Daimajin*, Daimajin is now located on a different island. Of the three villages on the island, two (Chigusa and Nagoshi) are lands of

Another piece of *Daimajin* (1966) poster art.

peace, and the third is ruled by a tyrant who decides to conquer the two villages during an annual festival. The other villagers are chased by the tyrant's army until they end up on an island where the Daimajin statue is located. The tyrant orders his army to destroy the statue, and its remains sink to the bottom of the lake. However, the statue's destruction awakens Daimajin, who is ready to unleash havoc.

The difference in tone between *Daimijin* and *The Return of Daimijin* is quickly noticeable. The sequel is well-lit and has more of a blockbuster feel at times. There are odes to Akira Kurosawa films like *The Hidden Fortress* (1958) and *Seven Samurai* (1954), and even a tiny nod to *The Ten Commandments* (1956). *Return of Daimajin* was directed by the legendary Kenji Misumi, creator of the *Lone Wolf and Cub* films, the first film in the Zatoichi series, and *Hanzo the Razor: Sword of Justice*.

☢ *Wrath of Daimajin* (1966)

Director: Kazuo Mori

Producers: Masaichi Nagata, Hisashi Okuda

Writer: Tetsuro Yoshida

Alternate film titles: *Mountain God Strikes Again* (Singapore), *Daimajin Strikes Again* (US)

Release date: December 10, 1966 (Japan)

OPPOSITE:
The Japanese poster for *Return of Daimajin* (1966).

DAIMAJIN KANON

In 2010, a TV drama brought back the concept of Daimajin for modern audiences. Set in present-day Tokyo, *Daimajin Kanon* features a woman named Kanon, who has moved to the city to become a pop singer, but instead suffers from heartbreak and betrayal when her boyfriend steals one of her songs. The stolen song was a personal song from Kanon's family, and it sends the boyfriend into superstardom.

But little does anyone know that demons and dark spirits are seeping and growing, preying on people's rage and fears. Kanon falls into a deep depression, then suddenly a spirit approaches her, revealing a dangerous secret. According to the spirit, Kanon and her family's song can summon an ancient guardian named Bujin (the name of Daimajin in this series). Bujin is the only thing that can defeat the coming onslaught of demons. However, there is a problem: the song is one of love and happiness, and the magic will only work if Kanon sings it with all her heart, honestly and truly.

While the previous movies in the franchise focused on the destructive wrath of the titular giant idol, the TV series delved into the true meaning and power of prayer, which here brings the Daimajin to life. It ran for 26 episodes during late nights, targeting an audience who enjoyed anime and manga and would appreciate the exploration of more mature themes.

Lead actors: Hideki Ninomiya, Masahide Iizuka, Shinji Hori, Muneyuki Nagatomo, Toru Abe, Takashi Nakamura
Primary Daimajin suit actor: Chikara Hashimoto

▼

In the third and final movie of the Daimajin trilogy, the Daimajin statue that appeared in the first two movies is seen on top of a mountain. An evil warlord, on the hunt for slave labor, abducts a group of fathers from a nearby village and forces them to work in labor camps. When four of the sons of the enslaved fathers decide to rescue their relatives, they must cross the treacherous terrain of Majin Mountain, where evil samurai and the angry Daimajin reside. The boys are smart enough to show respect to the statue when they pass it, so they don't provoke the Daimajin. Later, the warlord's men disrespect the statue, causing it to come to life; chaos ensues for those who have not shown Daimajin proper respect.

This film, though continuing the dark, grim mood of the previous two films in the series, is a child's journey akin to films like *The Goonies* (1985) and *The NeverEnding Story* (1984). Reviewer Tim Brayton, while pleased with the first two films, had mixed feelings about the last one, saying, "What's odd, actually, is that compared to *Daimajin* and *Return of Daimajin*, the third film arguably has the freshest plot, recycling elements from the original movie but not largely remaking it, as was generally true of the first sequel; and despite that, it feels far more stale."

KAIJU FACT

Wrath of Daimajin was the only film of the Daimajin trilogy not released in the United States by American International Pictures' television division. It was not dubbed for the US until 2012.

A statue of
Daimajin in
Kyoto Station in
September 1999.

12 ULTRAMAN

> Ultramen aren't here to save the humans.
> We're here to combine our powers with the humans,
> and to fight together.
> —Ultraman Taro

Created by special effects mastermind Eiji Tsuburaya and developed by Tsuburaya and head writer Tetsuo Kinjo, Ultraman came to life due to the popularity of another science-fiction TV series from Tsuburaya, *Ultra Q*. Ultraman and the other Ultra Series focus on an alien race of giant superheroes from the M78 Nebula who come to Earth to battle Ultra Kaiju or other extraterrestrial behemoths. Ultraman is also the pioneer of Kyodai Heroes, the first hero in that specific subgenre. Kyodai is a tokusatsu subgenre that features Japanese superheroes and/or mecha that can grow to massive heights to battle kaiju or monsters that can grow to kaiju size. In Japan, Kyodai is a mainstream superhero genre. A Kyodai hero is a protector of humanity.

The idea for Ultraman originated when Tsuburaya and Kinjo were working on three different concept pitches for the Tokyo Broadcasting System (TBS). Some of those pitches were eventually put together to create the first Ultraman. The popular manga *Astro Boy*, created by legendary Osamu Tezuka, significantly influenced Tsuburaya and Kinjo's decision to create their own live-action superhero series.

The first pitch was a *Doctor Who*-like series featuring a young girl and a funny-looking monster with big eyes. The second pitch, *Scientific Special Search Party: Bemular*, focused on the adventures of the Science Patrol, who disguised themselves as an art/photography team by day while actually working as monster and alien trackers by night. One of its members was able to transform into Bemular, a giant winged monster who could fight other monsters. But the idea of two giant monsters fighting each other was considered too visually cumbersome. Though the pitch was not greenlit, the Science Patrol would become the Scientific

What Is *Ultra Q*?

Ultra Q was the progenitor to the Ultraman/Ultra Hero series. It can be summed up as kaiju meets *The X-Files*, with a touch of *The Twilight Zone*. *Ultra Q* followed the journey of three investigators who take the initiative to study the sudden and mysterious surge in kaiju attacks and supernatural events in Japan. Each episode featured a new monster of the week. Many of the villainous kaiju that are featured in the original Ultraman series were repurposed kaiju suits from *Ultra Q*.

OPPOSITE:
Ultraman in 1972.

Gabora, the Uranium Monster, one of the Ultraman foes.

and atmosphere, Ultra Heroes can only fight for limited amounts of time before their energy is exhausted. Having a human host allows an Ultra Hero to better adapt to Earth's atmosphere. An Ultra Hero having a human host also gives both Ultra Hero and human host advanced healing properties. The First Generation of Ultra Heroes have red and silver uniforms with glowing eyes. The Second and Third Generation of Ultra Heroes break from this standard color palette and expand on the uniform and helmet designs.

The original design for Ultraman was created by artist and production designer Tohl Narita and Narita's assistant, Akira Sasaki. Narita also designed many of the kaiju and monsters for the original Ultraman series. Ultraman uses suitmation (an Eiji Tsuburaya concept developed for the Godzilla films) for its larger-than-life battles. Suit actor Haruo Nakajima, known for his work on the Showa Era of Godzilla films, provided choreography for the original Ultraman series, and the original Ultraman suit actor was Bin Furuya.

Special Search Party in the Ultraman series. Later, a third concept, called Redman, was developed. It featured a superhero who hunted down and killed evil aliens who destroyed his distant home planet.

While developing a fourth pitch for Ultraman, artist Toru "Tohl" Narita revamped his concept art of Redman and created a new hero, using red and silver for the now-iconic suit. This redesign became the Ultraman design that debuted in 1966. After seeing the final design, TBS executives felt that Ultraman could be marketable to Western audiences.

Shin Hyata in *Ultraman* (1966–1967).

Every Ultraman or Ultra Hero must have a human host to survive on Earth. They also have a light on the center of their chest that serves as a warning that an Ultra Hero is low on energy or is severely wounded. Because of Earth's pollution

host to transform into their respective Ultra Hero. The Transformation Items differ for every Ultra Hero. For example, the original Ultraman uses the Beta Capsule, a handheld silver and black cylinder with a red button. To transform into Ultraman, Shin Hayata holds the Beta Capsule up to the sky while pressing the red button in its center. Each Ultra Hero also has their own Signature Technique or ability that allows them to vanquish maniacal and vile Ultra Kaiju, such as the original Ultraman's Spacium Beam, a powerful beam that emits from his hand.

The popularity of Ultraman in Japan can be compared to Superman in America. Both characters are aliens from distant planets who have alter-egos (and special abilities) on Earth, and who are willing to protect humanity with all their might. Ultraman is also an international icon, having generated billions of dollars in merchandising. As the character approaches his sixtieth anniversary, Ultraman has spawned many renditions across multiple television series and specials, comics, manga, movies, animated projects, and games. We've covered some highlights here from across the generations, to pay respect to Japan's greatest superhero.

The eras of Ultraman over the decades are broken down into First, Second, and Third Generations, with each generation having its particular moods and themes. The First Generation, running from 1966's *Ultraman* to 1993's *Ultraman: The Ultimate Hero*, delves into the mysterious and bizarre and has a strong continuity across different Ultra series. The Second Generation tends to be a little more freewheeling with the ideas and concepts of what Ultraman should and can be, covering media from 1996's *Ultraman Tiga* to 2007's *Ultraman Mebius*. The Third Generation takes inspiration from the previous generations, with a focus on serialized plots and succinct continuity, and makes a push for the Ultra Heroes to build stronger relationships among themselves and humans. Starting with *Ultraman Ginga* in 2013, the Third Generation is still going strong. The most recent series was *Ultraman Blazar* in 2023, with more series to come.

Every Ultra Hero has a device called a Transformation Item, which allows their human

▼▼ FIRST-GENERATION ▼▼

☢ Ultraman (1966–1967)

Directors: Hajime Tsuburaya, Toshihiro Iijima, Samaji Nonagase, Kazuho Mitsuta, Akio Jissoji, Yuzo Higuchi
Producers: Eiji Tsuburaya
Writers: Tetsuo Kinjo, Shozo Uehara, Masahiro Yamada, Mamoru Sasaki, Keisuke Fujikawa, Taro Kaido, Ryu Minamikawa, Bunzo Wakatsuki, Mamoru Sasaki, Tatsuo Miyata, Kitao Senzoku, Shin'ichi Sekizawa
Release date: July 17, 1966–April 9, 1967
Total episodes: 40
Lead actors: Susumu Kurobe, Akiji Kobayashi, Hiroko Sakurai, Sandayu Dokumamushi, Masanari Nihei, Bin Furuya
Primary Ultraman suit actor: Bin Furuya

Ultraman was recognized by the Guinness World Records for "TV series with most number of spin-offs."

An Ultra Hero named Ultraman from the M78 Nebula arrives on Earth to pursue Ultra Kaiju. After merging with the dying Science Patrol officer Shin Hayata, he becomes Earth's first defender against extraterrestrial threats. The series revolves around the Science Patrol, an extraordinary scientific team dedicated to investigating and thwarting threats from aliens and kaiju. At the start of the series, the team doesn't know that Hayata can transform into Ultraman in times of peril.

Ultraman was a massive success in both Japan and America, with United Artists Television acquiring the rights to air the series in America no more than two months after it first aired in Japan.

The heroes of the 1975 series *Ultraman*.

Ultraman stayed in syndication in America until the mid- to late 1980s. Mark Schilling of *The Japan Times* called the series "a rite of passage for Japanese boys (and a few girls) and their families," adding, "the series is as much a part of the national fabric as furikake (rice topping) and chopsticks."

☢ *Ultraseven* (1967)

Directors: Hajime Tsuburaya, Samaji Nonagase, Kazuho Mitsuta, Akio Jissoji, Toshitsugu Suzuki, Toshihiro Iijima, Tatsumi Ando

Producer: Eiji Tsuburaya

Writers: Tetsuo Kinjo, Masahiro Yamada, Akihiko Sugano, Bunzo Wakatsuki, Shozo Uehara, Mamoru Sasaki, Shin'ichi Sekizawa, Keisuke Fujikawa, Ryu Minamikawa, Onisuke Akai, Hiroyasu Yamaura, Takashi Kawasaki

Alternate title: *Ultra7* (Cinar English Dubbed Version)

Release date: October 1, 1967–September 8, 1968

Total episodes: 49

Lead actors: Kohji Moritsugu, Shōji Nakayama, Yuriko Hishimi, Sandayū Dokumamushi, Bin Furuya, Shinsuke Achiwa

Primary Ultraseven suit actors: Koji Uenishi, Eichi Kikuchi

The Banned *Ultraseven* Episode

The twelfth episode of *Ultraseven*, "From Another Planet with Love," features a character called Alien Spell, who is covered in bizarre scars. Alien Spell is labeled a *Hibaku Seijin* (meaning "A-Bomb Survivor Alien"), a term derived from the word *hibakusha*, which refers to survivors of the atomic bombings of Hiroshima and Nagasaki. The episode was banned in Japan as of 1970, as it was seen as offensive to survivors, and it has not aired in Japan since. It accidentally aired in the United States in the dubbed version of *Ultraseven* produced by CINAR, titled "Crystalized Corpuscles."

In the near future, Earth is frequently attacked by extraterrestrial threats. To combat these threats, the Terrestrial Defense Force creates the Ultra Guard, a team of six highly skilled combat specialists who use advanced vehicles and weapons. The TDF also has a new member on their team, an enigmatic figure named Dan Moroboshi. Moroboshi is actually an alien from the Land of Light in Nebula M78 and can transform into the heroic giant superhero Ultraseven.

After the success of shows such as *Ultraman* and Japanese-dubbed episodes of *Lost in Space*, the Tokyo Broadcasting System approached Tsuburaya Productions to produce another sci-fi series. The result was *Ultraseven*, a show that was so popular that the Tokyo Broadcasting System ordered an additional ten episodes while it was still in production. *Ultraseven* was also a major merchandise seller in Japan.

OTHER FIRST-GENERATION ULTRA HERO SERIES

. . . .

Return of Ultraman (1971–1972): Hideki Gô, a car racer turned Monster Attack Team patrol member, merges with another Ultraman to combat a range of monsters.

Ultraman Ace (1972–1973): After being severely injured in a monster attack, Seiji Hokuto and Yuko Minami are revived and given two Ultra Rings, which they use to unite into a new Ultra being, Ultraman Ace.

Ultraman Taro (1973–1974): After being killed during a monster attack, Kotarô Higashi is transformed by the entire Ultra Family into Ultraman Taro, a powerful new Ultra-being.

Ultraman Leo (1974–1975): After being injured by evil aliens, Dan Moroboshi (also known as Ultra Seven) takes a young Ultra-like being from L77 under his wing and names him "Ultraman Leo" to continue his mission of defending Earth.

Ultraman 80 (1980–1981): Mild-mannered schoolteacher Takeshi Yamato becomes Ultraman 80 and defends the Earth against giant monsters created from people's anger and negative energy.

An *Ultraman* poster from the 1980s.

A statue for
Ultraman Tiga
(1996).

▾▾ SECOND-GENERATION ▾▾

☢ *Ultraman Tiga* (1996)

Directors: Shingo Matsubara, Hirochika Muraishi, Kyōta Kawasaki, Yasushi Okada, Shin'ichi Kamisawa, Tōdō Fuyuki, Tsugumi Kitaura, Masaki Harada, Teruyoshi Ishii, Akio Jissoji, Kyōta Kawasaki, Kazuho Mitsuta,

Writers: Chiaki J. Konaka, Keiichi Hasegawa, Masakazu Migita, Shōzō Uehara, Ai Ōta, Akio Satsukawa, Shinsuke Onishi, Akio Satsukawa, Hideyuki Kawakami, Kazunori Saito, Kyōta Kawasaki, Yasushi Hirano, Junki Takegami, Hidenori Miyazawa, Shinichi Kamisawa, Kazuyoshi Nakazaki, Hirochika Muraishi, Minoru Kawasaki, Nobuhisa Kodama

Release date: September 7, 1996–August 30, 1997

Total episodes: 52

Lead actors: Hiroshi Nagano, Takami Yoshimoto, Akitoshi Ohtaki, Shigeki Kagemaru, Yukio Masuda, Yoichi Furuya, Mio Takaki

Primary Ultraman Tiga suit actors: Shunsuke Gondo, Koji Nakamura (Evil Tiga)

───── ▾ ─────

Sculptures of Ultraman Tiga, Ultraman Dyna, and Ultraman Gaia in Shanghai, China, in 2023.

After a fifteen-year hiatus, Ultraman returns in *Ultraman Tiga*, a series set in an alternate universe that is separate from the First Generation of Ultra Heroes. This Ultra Hero is the first to have multiple colors on their uniform instead of the traditional red and silver.

In this series, Ultraman Tiga, also known as the giant of light, protected ancient human civilization 30 million years ago. After that civilization perished, Tiga turned into a stone statue. In the twenty-first century, Tiga is resurrected by merging with pilot Daigo from the Global Unlimited Task Squad (GUTS) defense team, who unknowingly has Ultra DNA in his body from his ancestors. The Earth faces threats from space and other dimensions by invading forces, and it's up to the newest Ultra Hero to keep humanity safe from harm.

Because of Tiga's immense popularity in Japan, the character had the most exposure and airtime of the other Second-Generation Ultraman. This popularity led to a tribute series called *Ultraman Trigger: New Generation Tiga*. It was released on TV Tokyo from July 10, 2021, to January 22, 2022, to commemorate *Ultraman Tiga*'s twenty-fifth anniversary. *Trigger* was a modern retelling of *Tiga*.

OTHER SECOND-GENERATION ULTRA HERO SERIES

Ultraman Dyna (1997–1998): As humanity begins to colonize other planets, GUTS' newest member, Shin Asuka, bonds with Ultraman Dyna to protect the colony.

Ultraman Gaia (1998–1999): Gamu Takayama, a member of Alchemy Stars, gains powers from Ultraman Gaia after falling through a portal of light when a monster known as C.O.V. attacks Earth.

Ultraman Cosmos (2001–2002): A group of light particles called Chaos Header comes to Earth and takes control of monsters to use them to destroy the planet. Earth's salvation comes when Ultraman Cosmos unites with Musashi Haruno.

Fans dressed as their favorite Ultraman heroes.

An Ultraman Mebius costume.

Ultraman Nexus (2004–2005): The First Ultraman series meant for adults, *Ultraman Nexus* features six human hosts, all members of the Terrestrial Liberation Trust, a global organization that battles space beasts, who become Ultraman over the course of the season.

Ultraman Max (2005–2006): A young man named Toma becomes the human host to Ultraman Max.

Ultraman Mebius (2006–2007): Mirai Hibino, also known as Mebius, is a rookie Ultraman who disguises himself as a member of the monster defense force called Guards for Utility Situation (GUYS) to defend Earth.

Ultraseven X (2007): In this reimagining of *Ultraseven* (1967), Jin, who suffers from amnesia, transforms into a giant hero to battle aliens and protect the world.

▾▾ THIRD-GENERATION ▾▾

☢ *Ultraman Blazar* (2023)

Directors: Kiyotaka Taguchi, Takanori Tsujimoto, Kazuhiro Nakagawa, Tomonobu Koshi, Masayoshi Takesue, Ryuta Miyazaki

Writers: Keigo Koyanagi, Jun Tsugita, Taiki Yamazaki, Sumio Uetake, Junichiro Ashiki, Takao Nakano, Toshizo Nemoto

Distributors: Tsuburaya Productions (Japan)

Release date: July 8, 2023–January 20, 2024

Total episodes: 25

Lead actors: Tomoya Warabino, Himena Tsukimiya, Hayate Kajihara, Konomi Naito, Yuki Ito, Masaya Kato, Hideyoshi Iwata

Primary Ultraman Blazar suit actor: Hideyoshi Iwata

—— ▼ ——

Ultraman Blazar was the thirty-fifth Ultra Hero series and part of Tsuburaya Productions' sixtieth anniversary. As Earth's temperature continues to rise due to climate change, a special unit of the Global Guardian Force (GGF), a multi-national organization created to battle kaiju and alien threats, led by Gento Hiruma, faces a dangerous situation when their cleanup operation at an experimental factory goes wrong. However, an Ultraman comes to their rescue. Later, Gento is transferred to lead the newly formed Special Kaiju Reaction Detachment, a covert team that uses the Earth Garon mecha to combat kaiju attacks. Gento must become the host of Ultraman Blazar to lead the Special Kaiju Reaction Detachment against the kaiju while also trying to understand the meaning of his visions of another galaxy.

Ultraman Blazar takes Ultraman in a new, exciting direction, and is an incredible series with stunning production and designs. The Blazar suit is adorned with glowing blue crystals and vibrant electric lines, giving it an almost skeletal appearance. The transformation stones and weapons have raw, sharp-edged facets that are striking and memorable. Overall, *Blazar* is a fantastic-looking series that focuses on characters and storytelling, and will leave a lasting impression.

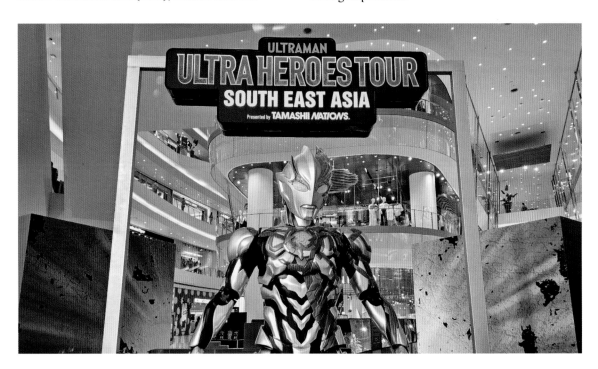

A promotional display for *Ultraman Blazar* (2023) in Thailand.

OTHER THIRD-GENERATION ULTRA HERO SERIES

Ultraman Ginga (2013): All the Ultra Heroes and monsters in the universe have been transformed into small figures called Spark Dolls and scattered across the universe. A young man named Hikaru Raido discovers the Ginga Spark, which grants him the power to transform into Ultraman Ginga. With the help of the Ginga Spark, Hikaru can connect with the Spark Dolls and restore them to their original size, merging with them to become one.

Ultraman Ginga S (2014): Hikaru reunites with the Ginga Spark and joins the defense team known as the Ultra Party Guardians. As Ultraman Ginga, he continues to battle kaiju that want to destroy the universe.

Ultraman X (2015): When an Ultra Warrior bonds with Daichi Oozora, a member of the science military unit Xeno Invasion Outcutters, Daichi uses his Transformation Item, the X Devizer, to turn into Ultraman X.

Ultraman Orb (2016): Using his Orb Ring to access the power of two previous Ultra Heroes, Gai Kurenai fuses into Ultraman Orb as he battles the sinister Lord Monster.

Ultraman Geed (2017): After escaping a kaiju attack, Riku Asakura and his partner Pega stumble upon a secret underground base. There, Re.M (an artificial intelligence named Remote Management) gives Riku the Geed Riser and Ultra Capsules and Riku transforms into the hero Ultraman Geed.

Ultraman R/B (2018): When Katsumi and Isami Minato, two brothers with clashing personalities, obtain incredible powers, they begin to work on overcoming their differences to defend Earth as Ultraman Rosso and Ultraman Blu.

Ultraman Taiga (2019): Hiroyuki Kudo joins E.G.I.S. (Enterprise of Guard and Investigation Services), a private security organization that handles cases related to aliens, and works tirelessly as Ultraman Taiga to keep the peace.

Ultraman Z (2020): Ultraman Zett, disciple of Ultraman Zero, joins the Inter Galactic Defense Force and carries on his mentor's legacy by fighting new threats.

Ultraman Trigger: New Generation Tiga (2021–2022): This modern retelling of *Ultraman Tiga* (1996), produced to commemorate Ultraman Tiga's twenty-fifth anniversary, follows Kengo Manaka, a member of a special forces unit located on a colonized Mars, who has an encounter with the Giant of Light and becomes Ultraman Tiga.

Ultraman Decker (2022): An unknown swarm of floating space objects called Sphere launches an attack on Earth, causing the planet to lose contact with the rest of the universe. The invasion disrupts the peaceful life of Kanata Asumi, who discovers a hidden power within himself—the Light—and transforms into Ultraman Decker to fight the invasion.

▼▼ OTHER ULTRAMAN PRODUCTIONS ▼▼

☢ Ultraman: Towards the Future (1992)

Director: Andrew Prowse

Producers: Kiyoshi Suzuki, Sue Wild

Writer: Terry Larsen

Release date: January 4, 1992–March 28, 1992 (US), July 8, 1995–September 30, 1995 (Japan)

Total episodes: 13

Alternate title: *Ultraman Great* (Japan)

Lead actors: Dore Kraus, Ralph Cotterill, Gia Carides, Rick Adams, Lloyd Morris, Grace Parr, Robert Simper, Steve Apps

Primary Ultraman suit actors: Steve Apps, Robert Simper

———— ▼ ————

Jack Shindo and Stanley Haggard are crew members of the first space mission to Mars. While exploring the red planet they encounter a gigantic slug-like creature called Gudis. Suddenly, Ultraman Great, an alien hero, appears to fight Gudis. During the fight, a rockslide pins Shindo, and Haggard tries to escape in their starship, but Gudis destroys it. As Gudis is about to win the fight with Ultraman Great, it transforms into a virus and travels to Earth to corrupt all life, mutating other creatures into monsters and awakening existing ones. But to survive on Earth, Gudis needs a human host. Ultraman Great then merges with Jack, allowing him to become the colossal Ultra Hero when all seems lost. Jack then joins the Universal Multipurpose Agency (UMA) to help them fight against the monsters.

A Japanese-Australian co-production between Tsuburaya Productions and the South Australian Film Corporation, *Ultraman: Towards The Future* was an attempt to create a new Ultraman series that could bring the Ultra Hero to mainstream American audiences. Even though it was filmed in Australia, the series never aired there. Sachs Family Entertainment distributed the series in the United States to Fox Kids, where it aired on Saturdays. It was later redubbed and aired in Japan. This series

also marked the first time that an Ultraman suit was made of spandex, instead of the traditional rubber suits used in previous Tsuburaya-produced Ultra Hero series. The series was not successful in the United States, likely due to the lack of easy, consistent access to Ultraman content for American audiences. This was the last Ultraman series to air on American television until the English-dubbed version of *Ultraman Tiga* aired on the Fox Box Saturday lineup in 2002.

☢ Ultraman Powered (1993)

Director: King Wilder

Producers: Juliet Avola, Shigeru Watanabe, King Wilder

Writers: Walter Doty, John Douglas, Todd Gilbert, Kazunori Ito, Stephen Karandy, Tim Lennane, Bud Robertson, King Wilder, Hiroshi Yamaguchi

Release date: April 8, 1995–July 1, 1995 (Japan)

Total episodes: 13

Alternate title: *Ultraman: The Ultimate Hero* (US)

Lead actors: Kane Kosugi, Harrison Page, Sandra Guibord, Robyn Bliley, Rob Roy Fitzgerald, Scott Rogers

Primary Ultraman suit actor: Scott Rogers

———— ▼ ————

The Worldwide Investigation Network Response, also known as WINR (pronounced as "Winner"), is a team that springs into action when an aggressive alien race called the Baltans invade Earth. But it is only when Ultraman Powered, a heroic alien, teams up with WINR member Kenichi Kai, that they can successfully fight off the Baltans. Ultraman

An Ultraman sculpture at the world's first Ultraman theme park, located in Shanghai.

OPPOSITE LEFT: Action figure of Ultraman Tiga.

OPPOSITE RIGHT: An Ultraman Ginga costume.

ULTRAMAN'S TRANSFORMATION ITEMS

A group of Ultraman cosplayers, illustrating the character's lasting legacy.

Ultraman Transformation Items are pieces of technology from the Land of Light, such as the Beta Capsule, the Ultra Eye, or the Ultra's home world. They allow the human host to become Ultraman. The devices vary for each Ultra, from a pair of glasses to a badge. Several take the form of bracers and bracelets that appear at will. The most common form is that of a stick, a throwback to the original Beta Capsule.

Here is a sample of some of the Transformation Items used in certain Ultra Hero series.

▶ *Ultraman* – BETA CAPSULE: To transform into Ultraman, Shin Hayata holds the handheld cylinder-style Beta Capsule up to the sky while pressing the red button in its center.

▶ *Ultraseven* – ULTRA EYE: A thin pair of red and sliver glasses; this Transformation Item is used by Dan Moroboshi to turn into Ultraseven. Dan simply places the Ultra Eye onto his eyes, causing him to transform into Ultraseven.

▶ *Ultraman Tiga* – SPARKLENCE: Daigo Madoka raises the Sparklence, an item that looks something like a sword hilt with gold trim and a marble handle, then presses the gold button. The top opens, engulfing Daigo in a bright flash of light, transforming him into Tiga.

▶ *Ultraman Blazar* – BLAZAR BRACE: A jagged wrist brace, Gento Hiruma inserts a Blazar Stone (a crystal of condensed energy) into the slot and presses on the other end of the device to initiate the transformation into Blazar.

Powered grants Kenichi the power to transform into Ultraman during moments of danger caused by all kinds of kaiju menaces.

Ultraman Powered was an American-Japanese co-production between Tsuburaya Productions and Major Havoc Entertainment. Produced and filmed in America, the goal of *Ultraman Powered* was to yet again attempt to push Ultraman from a cult following in America to a mainstream phenomenon. All thirteen episodes were produced and filmed in America and featured a predominately American cast. Unfortunately, Tsuburaya Productions and Major Havoc Entertainment were not able to find syndication or distribution in the United States, so it was never broadcast there. However, in Japan it was released on home video and aired on the Tokyo Broadcasting System. The costumes and designs of Ultraman and the evil kaiju in this series are great, but the suits were so fragile that the battles had to be very soft with minimal physical activity.

After this series failed to air in America, Tsuburaya made the decision to focus future Ultraman projects in Japan.

KAIJU FACT

Ultraman Powered is the first Ultra Hero to have blue eyes.

A NETFLIX ORIGINAL SERIES

ULTRAMAN

A poster for
Netflix's *Ultraman*
(2019–2023).

1013 OJTHEAR JAPANEASE KAIJU

> **The tragedy of the Mysterians is a good example for us!
> Don't use science in the wrong way!**
> **—Akihiko Hirata as Ryoichi Shiraishi
> in _The Mysterians_ (1957)**

A scene from _The Mysterians_ (1957).

Toho and other Japanese movie studios created many other kaiju films beyond franchise series like Godzilla, Gamera, and Mothra. Like the original _Godzilla_ (1954), some of the films dared to delve deeper than a person in a suit destroying stuff. But, of course, there were also plenty of films that were the standard "creature feature" fare. Films ranged across genres, from space fantasy to science fiction, from mythology to something just downright bizarre. Viewers can't deny that filmmakers during this period certainly took risks, some of which paid off—like the choice to make Frankenstein's monster into a kaiju.

Eagle-eyed readers will notice that director Ishirō Honda's name is mentioned a lot in this chapter. He directed forty-six films in his fifty-year career, leaving his valuable and cherished mark on the kaiju genre and inspiring future generations of filmmakers and special-effects creators.

▾▾ FILMS ▾▾

The Mysterians (1957)

Director: Ishirō Honda
Producer: Tomoyuki Tanaka
Writers: Takeshi Kimura, Jojiro Okami, Shigeru Kayama (story and adaption)

Alternate film titles: _The Earth Defense Force_ (Japan), _The Barbarians Invade Earth_ (Brazil), _Prisoners of the Martians_ (France), _Space Beasts_ (West Germany), _Invasion of the Moon_ (Greece), _Earth is Under Attack_ (Sweden)
Release date: December 28, 1957 (Japan), May 27, 1959 (US)
Lead actors: Kenji Sahara, Yumi Shirakawa, Momoko Kochi, Akihiko Hirata, Takashi Shimura, Susumu Fujita, Hisaya Ito
Primary suit actor: Haruo Nakajima

——— ▾ ———

A forest near Mount Fuji is suddenly engulfed in a raging fire, followed by a violent landslide that destroys an entire village. While investigating

OPPOSITE:
A scene from _The Last Dinosaur_ (1977).

The poster for *The Mysterians* (1957).

these incidents, authorities are attacked by a giant extraterrestrial robot called Moguera. The robot advances toward another town but is eventually stopped by the Japan Self-Defense Force (JSDF). Upon closer inspection, the robot turns out to be of alien origin, and it's not long before a vast, domed base emerges from the ground near Fuji. The dome's inhabitants, the Mysterians, claim to come in peace and that they only wish to obtain a small tract of land and the capability to wed Earth women. However, humanity soon realizes that the Mysterians are mobilizing to wipe out human civilization. In response, all the planet's militaries band together to form the Earth Defense Force and launch a desperate war against the Mysterians.

The Mysterians gained positive reviews in the United States upon its release. *Variety* called it "well-produced," and said the "special effects involving sliding land, quaking earth and melting mortars are realistically accomplished, proving the facility with which the Japanese filmmakers deal in miniatures."

A climactic scene from *The Mysterians* (1957).

Christopher Stewardson, a reviewer for *ourculture* magazine, said, "Lying beneath its visual prowess is a set of questions, themes, and ideas that elevate *The Mysterians* as one of the decade's most fascinating films. It asserts a warning for humanity: don't misuse science. For 1957, in the midst of a spiraling nuclear arms race between the United States and the Soviet Union, the film is chilling. When examined through the lens of 2020, *The Mysterians* is arguably even more frightening today."

The Birth of Japan (1959)

Director: Hiroshi Inagaki
Producers: Sanezumi Fujimoto, Tomoyuki Tanaka
Writers: Ryuzo Kikushima, Toshio Yasumi
Alternate film titles: *The Age of the Gods* (Brazil), *Three Treasures* (Spain)
Release date: November 1, 1959 (Japan), December 20, 1960 (US)
Lead actors: Toshiro Mifune, Yoko Tsukasa, Akihiko Hirata, Kyoko Kagawa, Takashi Shimura, Setsuko Hara, Kumi Mizuno, Misa Uehara, Kinuyo Tanaka, Akira Kubo, Akira Takarada

— ▼ —

The Birth of Japan retells the Yamata no Orochi legend, in which Susanoo embarks on a grand adventure to fight the legendary serpent Orochi. His mission is to rescue the maidens of a village in the newly-formed country of Japan. Meanwhile, Ouso, the son of Emperor Keikoh, is expected to succeed his father on the throne. However, Otomo, the emperor's vassal, favors Ouso's stepbrother, Waka, and plans to get rid of Ouso by sending him on a dangerous mission.

Despite the danger, Ouso successfully completes the mission and returns to his father's castle under a new name: Prince Yamato Takeru. Otomo then plots to send the prince on an even more perilous mission. However, Otomo is unaware that the gods have blessed the prince, and the outcome is far from what they had expected.

KAIJU FACT

Legendary actor Toshiro Mifune (who played Ouso/Prince Yamato in 1959's *The Birth of Japan*) turned down the role of Obi-Wan Kenobi in *Star Wars*.

Matango (1963)

Director: Ishirō Honda
Producer: Tomoyuki Tanaka
Writers: Takeshi Kimura, Shin'ichi Hoshi, Masami Fukushima
Alternate film titles: *Matango, The Island of Death* (Brazil), *Attack of the Mushroom People* (US), *Matango, the Monster* (Italy), *Matango, Fungus of Terror* (UK)
Release date: August 11, 1963 (Japan), 1965 (US)
Lead actors: Akira Kubo, Kumi Mizuno, Hiroshi Koizumi, Kenji Sahara, Hiroshi Tachikawa, Yoshio Tsuchiya, Miki Yashiro
Primary Matango suit actors: Haruo Nakajima, Tokio Okawa, Koji Uruki, Masaki Shinohara, Kuniyoshi Kashima, Toku Ihara

— ▼ —

Loosely based off the short story "The Voice in the Night" by William Hope Hodgson, *Matango* follows seven affluent friends from Tokyo who end up stranded on an uninhabited island in the Ogasawara chain after their yacht sinks in a storm.

The Japanese poster for *Matango* (1963).

On the island, they come across a deserted ship and discover that the crew of that ship was researching the effects of nuclear testing on the island. The crew vanished after consuming strange mushrooms known as "Matango," which grow on the island. As resources become scarce, the survivors begin to turn on each other, and, one by one, they fall under the influence of the deadly Matango. Ian Berriman of *SFX Magazine* called *Matango* "a surprisingly downbeat example of Japanese horror, with an extremely cynical view of human nature."

KAIJU FACT

Toho reached out to American horror/science-fiction director John Carpenter to direct a *Matango* remake, but Carpenter declined.

☢ *Ominous Star Gorath* (1962)

Director: Ishirō Honda
Producer: Tomoyuki Tanaka
Writers: Takeshi Kimura, Jojiro Okami
Alternate film title: *UFOs Destroy the Earth* (West Germany)
Release date: March 21, 1962 (Japan), November 27, 1963 (US–exclusive showing)
Lead actors: Ryo Ikebe, Yumi Shirakawa, Akira Kubo, Kumi Mizuno, Hiroshi Tachikawa
Primary suit actor: Katsumi Tezuka (as Maguma)

——— ▼ ———

In 1976, the JX-1 Hayabusa, Japan's most famous rocket, is launched with a crew of 30 men from the Interstellar Exploration Agency's rocket launch site at Mt. Fuji to investigate the planet Saturn. After the nine-month journey, mission control informs the crew that a small, runaway, rogue collapsed star called Gorath by the international scientific community has entered Earth's solar system. The crew of the JX-1 Hayabusa tries to find a way to move Earth out of its orbit to avoid a collision with the runaway star but fails. Then it's up to the crew of the JX-2 to prevent the destruction of Earth.

In Donald Willis' 1985 book *Variety's Complete Science Fiction Reviews*, it's said that *Variety* called this film "generally a first-class endeavor," noting that "particular credit goes to Eiji Tsuburaya for his special effects." *Variety* also noted that actor Ryo Ikebe was a highlight of the cast.

He rolled THE SEVEN WONDERS OF THE WORLD into ONE!

Poster art for *Frankenstein vs. Baragon* (1965).

☢ *Frankenstein vs. Baragon* (1965)

Director: Ishirō Honda
Producers: Tomoyuki Tanaka, Reuben Bercovitch, Henry Saperstein, Samuel Arkoff
Writer: Kaoru Mabuchi
Alternate film titles: *Frankenstein vs. the Subterranean Monster* (Japan), *Frankenstein Conquers the World* (US/UK), *Frankenstein Against the World* (Brazil), *Frankenstein to the Conquest of Earth* (Italy), *Frankenstein: The Horror with the Ape Face* (West Germany)
Release date: August 8, 1965 (Japan), July 8, 1966 (US)
Lead actors: Tadao Takashima, Nick Adams, Kumi Mizuno, Yoshio Tsuchiya, Koji Furuhata, Jun Tazaki
Primary suit actor: Koji Furuhata (as Frankenstein), Haruo Nakajima (as Baragon)

—————— ▼ ——————

In this bizarre kaiju film, the Nazis have secured Frankenstein's monster's immortal heart during World War II and given it to the Japanese. The heart is kept in a military hospital in Hiroshima, until the atomic bomb destroys the city. Fifteen years later, Dr. James Bowen, Sueko Togami, and Kenichiro Kawaji discover a wild boy, who they realize has regenerated from the irradiated heart of Frankenstein's monster. The boy grows to a gigantic size as they continue to feed him.

The boy—Frankenstein—manages to escape and is soon blamed for several disasters throughout Japan. However, Togami and Bowen believe these disasters were caused by a separate creature, the subterranean monster Baragon. The scientists work to prove Frankenstein's innocence while Frankenstein fights to save them from Baragon.

After two previous aborted attempts, *Frankenstein vs. Baragon* is the first appearance of Frankenstein's monster in a Toho film. The film also introduces the kaiju Baragon, who would go on to become a recurring character in the Godzilla series. In the alternate ending of the film's international release, after Frankenstein beats Baragon, a

The title characters face off in *Frankenstein vs. Baragon* (1965).

kaiju octopus emerges from a lake and drags Frankenstein under the water. For contrast, in the original, Frankenstein and Baragon are swallowed by the Earth as the ground collapses beneath them.

Tim Brayton of AlternateEnding.com said the film "has absolutely no interest in allegory," depicting a nuclear bombing mushroom cloud in the prologue and making continuous references to the bombing of Hiroshima in the first hour of the film.

☢ Frankenstein's Monsters: Sanda vs. Gaira (1966)

Director: Ishirō Honda
Producers: Tomoyuki Tanaka, Kenichiro Tsunoda, Henry G. Saperstein, Reuben Bercovitch
Writers: Kaoru Mabuchi, Ishirō Honda, Reuben Bercovitch

Alternate film titles: *The War of the Gargantuas* (US), *Frankenstein: Duel of the Giants* (West Germany), *Katango* (Italy), *The War of the Gorillas* (Mexico), *King Kong Wars* (Sweden)
Release date: July 31, 1966 (Japan), July 29, 1970 (US)
Lead actors: Kenji Sahara, Kumi Mizuno, Russ Tamblyn, Jun Tazaki
Primary suit actor: Haruo Nakajima as Gaira, Hiroshi Sekita as Sanda

—— ▼ ——

In this very loose sequel to *Frankenstein vs. Baragon* (1965), director Ishirō Honda felt that it would be better to have the follow-up be a standalone story. At the start of the film, Japan's Self-Defense Force has deployed its newly developed Type 66 Maser Cannons to take down Frankenstein, but another

A battle of the Gargantuas in *Frankenstein's Monster: Sanda vs. Gaira* (1966).

kaiju arrives to rescue him. Dr. Paul Stewart, a scientist, realizes that the savage Green Gargantua, Gaira, has regenerated from severed tissue left behind by Sanda, the kaiju Brown Gargantua. Sanda finds out about his brother's habit of eating humans and attacks him, and the kaiju battle in Tokyo, even as Sanda tries to stop his brother's rampage without using force.

Giant Space Monster Dogora (1964)

Director: Ishirō Honda
Producers: Tomoyuki Tanaka, Yasuyoshi Tajitsu
Writers: Shin'ichi Sekizawa (screenplay), Jojiro Okami (story)
Alternate film titles: *Dagora, the Space Monster* (US), *Dogora: The Monster from the Great Swamp* (Italy), *Dogora, The Space Invader* (Brazil), *Dogora: Monster Octopus* (Turkey)
Release date: August 11, 1964 (Japan), 1965 (US)
Lead actors: Yosuke Natsuki, Yoko Fujiyama, Hiroshi Koizumi, Akiko Wakabayashi, Nobuo Nakamura, Seizaburo Kawazu, Robert Dunham

——— ▼ ———

Dogora, a giant alien creature resembling a jellyfish, arrives on Earth and consumes all the coal in the Tokyo area. In response, a scientist, a diamond broker, and a police inspector team up to find a way to kill it, as missiles and shells prove to be ineffective. After several failed attempts, the protagonists discover that wasp venom can hopefully destroy the beast.

Dogora's design was inspired by a 3D illustration created by artist Shigeru Komatsuzaki for the Shogakukan publication *Weekly Shōnen Sunday*. Protozoa served as a reference for creating the monster's design.

☢ Gezora, Ganimes, Kamoebas: Battle! Giant Monsters of the South Seas (1970)

Director: Ishirō Honda
Producers: Tomoyuki Tanaka, Yasuyoshi Tajitsu
Writer: Ei Ogawa
Alternate film titles: *Space Amoeba* (US), *Yog, Monster From Space* (US), *The Challenge of the Monsters* (Brazil), *The Danger Came From Space* (Netherlands), *Space Monster* (Turkey), *Monsters of Horror Attack* (West Germany)
Release date: August 1, 1970 (Japan), June 9, 1971 (US)
Lead actors: Akira Kubo, Atsuko Takahashi, Yukiko Kobayashi, Kenji Sahara, Yoshio Tsuchiya, Tetsu Nakamura
Primary suit actor: Haruo Nakajima as Gezora/Ganimes, Haruyoshi Nakamura as Kamoebas

——— ▼ ———

After taking over the unmanned probe Helios 7, a mysterious alien life form lands near a South Pacific Island called Sergio. It mutates a cuttlefish, two

A US poster for *Gezora, Ganimes, Kamoebas: Battles! Giant Monsters of the South Seas* (1970).

stone crabs, and a Mata turtle into giant monsters, which begin attacking the island's inhabitants and a group of Japanese visitors. The visitors must work together with the islanders to stop the Space Amoeba before it can escape Sergio and take over the Earth.

Eiji Tsuburaya, who was Toho's special effects director for a long time despite his failing health, expressed his desire to be involved in the movie's production and was named the film's special effects supervisor. His former apprentice, Sadamasa Arikawa, was the director of special effects. Unfortunately, Tsuburaya died just two days after filming started, on January 25, 1970, and is only credited in the early promotional materials for the film.

KAIJU FACT

Although Godzilla does not appear in *Gezora, Ganimes, Kamoebas: Battle! Giant Monsters of the South Seas* (1970), it does take place in the same universe, as confirmed in *Godzilla: Tokyo SOS* (2003).

☢ *Great Desperate Monster Battle: Daigoro vs. Goliath* (1972)
Director: Toshihiro Ijima
Producer: Hajime Tsuburaya
Writer: Kitao Senzoku
Release date: December 17, 1972 (Japan)
Lead actors: Hiroshi Inuzuka, Shinsuke Minami, Kazuya Kosaka, Akiji Kobayashi, Tomonori Yazaki, Hachiro Misumi
Primary suit actors: Tetsuo Yamamura (as Daigoro), Hisashi Kato (as Goliath)

— ▼ —

In this Toho Studio/Tsuburaya co-production, produced to celebrate the tenth anniversary of Tsuburaya Productions, Daigoro begins as an infant

kaiju orphaned after his mother died while trying to defend her child from the military. An inventor who goes by the name Uncle decides to take care of the orphaned Daigoro and bring him to Japan, where he raises him as his own. Daigoro eventually becomes too big for Uncle to care for, so he decides to promote Daigoro as a spectacle and feed him with the earnings. When a monster named Goliath crashes to Earth, the two monsters engage in a fierce battle.

☢ *Yamato Takeru* (1994)
Director: Takao Okawara
Producer: Shogo Tomiyama
Writer: Wataru Mimura
Alternate film title: *Orochi, the Eight-Headed Dragon* (US—home video)
Release date: July 9, 1994 (Japan)
Lead actors: Masahiro Takashima, Yasuko Sawaguchi, Akaji Maro, Saburo Shinoda, Keaki Mori, Yuki Meguro, Hiroshi Abe, Hiroshi Fujioka, Nobuko Miyamoto
Primary suit actors: "Hurricane" Ryu Hariken (as Kumasogami), Kenpachiro Satsuma (as Yamata no Orochi), Wataru Fukuda (as Utsuno Ikusagami), Yuij Saeki (as Kaishin Muba)

— ▼ —

This fantasy-filled spectacular was originally supposed to be a remake of *The Birth of Japan* (1959), but director Takao Okawara decided to make it a futuristic-style drama instead of a period piece. The emperor of the House of Yamato has twin boys, Ousu and Oto, but he strongly dislikes Ousu and believes that he is fated to be killed by the shaman Tsukinowa. However, Amano Shiratori, the White Bird of the Heavens, intervenes and saves Ousu, and the emperor's sister takes Ousu under her wing. Years later, Ousu is finally allowed to return to the castle, but soon after, his biological mother becomes ill and dies under mysterious circumstances. Ousu's brother, Oto, attacks him in a fit of anger, and Ousu kills his own twin in self-defense. The emperor banishes Ousu until he can successfully deal with

An illustration of Yamato no Orochi, the eight-headed dragon featured in *Yamato Takeru* (1994).

the barbarians living in the Kumaso domain. Ousu does eventually succeed, only to still be rejected by his father, so he changes his name to Yamato Takeru. Yamato's aunt warns him of a looming threat, as the evil god Tsukuyomi plans to return and endanger the Earth. Yamato Takeru must now prepare himself for battle against the eight-headed dragon Yamata no Orochi.

In a 2019 review, Robert Firsching of AllMovie.com gave *Yamato Takeru* three-and-a-half stars out of five, praising it as "a refreshing throwback and a great way to spend a Saturday afternoon."

☢ *The Beastman Snowman* (1955)
Director: Ishirō Honda
Producer: Tomoyuki Tanaka

Writers: Takeo Murata, Shigeru Kayama
Alternate film titles: *The Snowman* (US)
Release date: August 14, 1955 (Japan), February 1956 (US–Toho Subtitled Limited Release), May 17, 1957 (Distributors Corporation of America Dubbed Release)
Lead actors: Akira Takarada, Akemi Negishi, Momoko Kochi, Nobuo Nakamura, Sachio Sakai
Primary suit actor: Fuminori Ohashi (as Snowman), Takashi Ito (as Snowman's child)

——— ▼ ———

Told in flashbacks, a group of five friends who traveled to the Japanese Alps in Nagano recall their time on holiday and the horrors of the Beastman Snowman, as they are asked questions by a reporter who's trying to make sense out of the bizarre and deadly ordeal.

Richard Boone as Masten Thrust in *The Last Dinosaur* (1977).

goes awry, the lone survivor of a Tyrannosaurus rex attack is a geologist named Chuck Wade, who has discovered a hidden world filled with dinosaurs and other prehistoric creatures. Thrust, wanting to see these dinosaurs for himself, leads an expedition back to the drill site, but once Thrust and the others enter the land lost to time, they are hunted by the Tyrannosaurus rex as they try to survive and find a way back home.

The Last Dinosaur was the first of three Japanese/American co-productions between Tsuburaya Studios and Rankin/Bass Productions with the goal of a United States theatrical release. The film acquired international distribution, but failed to find a distributor in the US, and so ended up a TV movie for ABC. It was such a success that ABC agreed to two more films from Tsuburaya Studios and Rankin/Bass Productions.

☢ *The Bermuda Depths* (1978)

Director: Tsugunobu Kotani (credited as Tom Kotani)
Producers: Authur Rankin Jr., Jules Bass, Benni Korzen
Writers: William Overgard, Aruthur Rankin Jr.
Release date: 1978 (Japan), January 27, 1978 (US)
Lead actors: Carl Weathers, Leigh McCloskey, Burl Ives, Connie Sellecca, Julie Woodson

——— ▼ ———

In the second film of the Tsuburaya Studios and Rankin/Bass Productions partnership, Magnus is looking for closure twenty years after the death of his parents in Bermuda when he runs into an old friend, Eric, now a marine biologist who is working alongside Dr. Paulus. Paulus is looking for giant creatures in the depths of the sea. When a woman named Jennie, who Magnus hasn't seen since their childhood days in Bermuda, comes back into Magnus' life, a mystery unfolds as the turtle that they found as children is now a kaiju-sized threat that must be stopped.

The slow-paced *The Bermuda Depths* is a kaiju movie that tries to be multiple things, shifting from science fiction to fantasy to romance. The

☢ *The Last Dinosaur* (1977)

Directors: Tsugunobu Kotani (credited as Tom Kotani), Alexander Grasshoff
Producers: Noboru Tsuburaya, Arthur Rankin Jr., Jules Bass, Kazuyoshi Kasai, Benni Korzen, Kinshiro Ohkubo, Masaki Izuka
Writer: William Overgard
Release date: 1977 (Japan), February 11, 1977 (US—television release)
Lead actors: Richard Boone, Joan Van Ark, Steven Keats, Masumi Sekiya
Primary Tyrannosaurus suit actor: Toru Kawai

——— ▼ ———

Wealthy and extravagant game hunter Masten Thrust owns an oil-drilling company and a special manned-craft laser drill called the Polar Borer. When a drilling expedition in the polar ice caps that Thrust ordered final act of the film is heavily influenced by Steven Spielberg's *Jaws*, to the point that Dr. Paulus even says that they need "a bigger boat" when trying to hunt the kaiju turtle.

🔘 *The Ivory Ape* (1980)

Director: Tsugunobu Kotani (credited as Tom Kotani)
Producers: Arthur Rankin Jr., Benni Korzen, Masaki Îzuka
Writers: Arthur Rankin Jr., William Overgard
Release date: 1980 (Japan), April 18, 1980 (US)
Lead actors: Jack Palance, Steven Keats, Cindy Pickett, Céline Lomez, Earle Hyman

———— ▼ ————

In the final film of the Tsuburaya and Rankin/Bass partnership, a rare albino gorilla is running loose in Bermuda after escaping from evil game hunter Marc Kazarian. Special government agents Baxter and Lil want to find the ape before Kazarian does and protect it, but Kazarian has told the people in Bermuda that the ape is a killer and must be taken at all costs, living or dead.

Jack Palance chews up the scenery in his every moment on screen as the big game hunter known as Kazarian, and everyone in the film is massively overdramatic. The gentle ape is normal-sized, but there is still the possibility that it could grow up to be something massive or mysterious. Tsuburaya's visual effects are fantastic, and the ape suit is very striking for its time.

The titular kaiju in *The Last Dinosaur* (1977).

GLOBAL DOMINATION

Jaegers in
*Pacific Rim:
Uprising* (2018).

> **❝**————————————————————
>
> **Today we face the monsters that are at our door, and bring the fight to them. Today, we are canceling the apocalypse!**
> **—Idris Elba as Marshal Stacker Pentecost**
> **in _Pacific Rim_ (2013)**
>
> ————————————————————**❞**

There are many films that feature monsters, creatures, or humans that are kaiju-sized, inspired by Godzilla and other classic kaiju franchises. Some of the films discussed in this chapter were prevalent during the "Creature Feature" era in American cinema in the 1950s, when theaters would have double-billings of monster B-movies on weekends. There are also many internationally produced films that wanted to cash in on the sensations of _King Kong_ and _Godzilla_.

From the 1980s to the present, there have been film characters that could loosely be classified as kaiju. We'll give an honorable mention to the Stay Puft Marshmallow Man in _Ghostbusters_ (1984); the burrowing Graboids that terrorize the citizens of Perfection, Nevada in the film _Tremors_ (1990); the genetically created dinosaurs of the _Jurassic Park_ and _Jurassic World_ franchises, including a corny nod to Godzilla in the final act of _The Lost World: Jurassic Park_ (1997); and even appearances in Marvel properties, from the large monsters and supernatural giants featured in the _Guardians of the Galaxy_ films to the size-changing hero Ant-Man.

The films that you are about to read about range from serious to deadly and absurd. Some were produced to capitalize on the successes of Godzilla and King Kong; others attempted to reinvent the genre. Every decade has had some form of monster movie, regardless of their success or failure, because there has always been an audience for them, both mainstream and cult.

▼▼ *AMERICAN FILMS* ▼▼

☢ *Mighty Joe Young* (1949)

Directors: Merian C. Cooper, Ernest B. Schoedsack
Producers: Merian C. Cooper, John Ford
Writers: Ruth Rose, Merian C. Cooper
Release date: July 27, 1949 (US)
Lead actors: Terry Moore, Ben Johnson, Robert Armstrong, Frank McHugh

OPPOSITE:
Poster for *Yongary, Monster from the Deep* (1967).

A scene from *Mighty Joe Young* (1949).

In Africa, a young child named Jill Young purchases a baby gorilla, even though her father explicitly told her not to do so. Jill names the baby gorilla Joe and the two have a strong connection; she even sings to him to soothe him and keep him calm.

A decade later, nightclub owner Max O'Hara and his business partner, a cowboy named Gregg, want to retrieve lions from Africa for their outlandish Hollywood nightclub. While in Africa, Joe frees the animals that Max and Gregg have captured, and Jill orders them to leave her land. Max convinces Jill that she and Joe will make for the ultimate attraction in his Hollywood nightclub, and Jill and Joe accept. After a few performances, Jill realizes that bringing Joe to America was the wrong choice and must find a way to get him home, no matter the cost.

A warning to viewers that even though this film was made in the late 1940s, there are some

scenes in which animals actually get hurt or are used in unsafe stunts, not to mention the colonialist themes. But the great thing about *Mighty Joe Young* is the stop-motion animation created by Willis O'Brien and a young Ray Harryhausen. In fact, this film marks the first credited feature-length film work for Harryhausen, who would go on to put his trademark stop-motion effects in popular films such as *The 7th Voyage of Sinbad* (1958), *Jason and the Argonauts* (1963), and *Clash of the Titans* (1981). The way that they're able to portray the emotion, movement, and energy of the larger-than-life gorilla is amazing, and a major upgrade from *King Kong*, the film that inspired young Harryhausen to enter the world of special effects.

A poster for *Mighty Joe Young* (1949).

☢ The Beast from 20,000 Fathoms (1953)

Director: Eugène Lourié
Producers: Jack Dietz, Hal E. Chester
Writers: Fred Freiberger, Eugène Lourié, Louis Morheim, Robert Smith
Alternate film titles: *Panic in New York* (West Germany), *The Awakening of the Dinosaur* (Italy), *The Atomic Monster Appears* (Japan), *The Monster of the Sea* (Brazil), *The Monster of Lost Time* (Portugal), *The Monster of Remote Times* (Spain)
Release date: June 13, 1953 (US), December 22, 1954 (Japan)
Lead actors: Paul Christian, Paula Raymond, Cecil Kellaway, Kenneth Tobey, Lee Van Cleef

to life after a century-long slumber due to an American atomic bomb test at the Arctic Circle. The angry Rhedosaurus beats a path of destruction and death all the way to New York City, where one of the surviving physicists, Thomas Nesbitt, along with paleontologist Thurgood Elson and assistant Lee Hunter, must attempt to find a way to take down the dinosaur before it's too late.

This is the film that served as a major inspiration for *Godzilla*, preceding

Loosely based on the short story "The Foghorn" by renowned science-fiction author Ray Bradbury, *The Beast from 20,000 Fathoms* features a massive dinosaur known as the Rhedosaurus that comes

the King of the Monsters' 1954 debut by one year and four months. It is also the film on which Ray Harryhausen, who oversaw *The Beast*'s special effects, officially created his "Dynamation" stop-motion animation method for the Rhedosaurus. Dynamation is the process that allows the actors in a movie to interact with and appear alongside stop-motion animation models. On a budget of just $200,000, *The Beast From 20,000 Fathoms* grossed over $5 million at the box office, making it a massive success.

☢ *Them!* (1954)

Director: Gordon Douglas
Producer: David Weisbart
Writers: Ted Sherdeman, Russell S. Hughes
Alternate film title: *The Spiders* (Sweden)
Release date: June 16, 1954 (New York Premiere), June 18, 1954 (US)
Lead actors: James Whitmore, Edmund Gwenn, Joan Weldon, James Arness

——— ▼ ———

Nominated for an Academy Award for Best Effects and Special Effects, *Them!* was Warner Bros.' most

One of *Them!* (1954).

full-sized ant models for the film. The models were operated with pulleys and ropes during filming. For other scenes that required the kaiju ants, smaller models were made. Real ants were also used. The film was originally to be filmed in 3D and in color, but when the camera technology failed, producers opted for a widescreen, black-and-white film, with only the title graphic having color.

☢ *Tarantula* (1955)

Director: Jack Arnold
Producer: William Alland
Writers: Robert M. Fresco, Martin Berkeley, Jack Arnold
Release date: November 23, 1955 (Los Angeles premiere), December 23, 1955 (US)
Lead actors: John Agar, Mara Corday, Leo G. Carroll, Nestor Paiva

▼

Sheriff Jack Andrews requests that Dr. Hastings inspect the body of a dead scientist who worked with biologist Dr. Gerald Deemer. Unbeknownst

successful film of 1954 and built on the themes of the dawning of the nuclear age. FBI Agent Graham and Dr. Harold Medford are investigating a murder in New Mexico when they stumble upon giant ants that are terrorizing a town. If Graham and Medford don't stop "them," they could wipe out all of mankind.

Them! has a great cast and is a beautiful balance of horror and action, with some light jokes every now and then to cut the tension. Dick Smith, a studio technician for Warner Bros., built the two

KAIJU FACT

Leonard Nimoy (*Star Trek*, *Mission: Impossible*) has an uncredited part in *Them!* (1954) as an army staff sergeant.

Poster art for *Tarantula* (1955).

Another beast, this one from *Hollow Mountain* (1956).

to Hastings, Deemer, who is using his scientific knowledge to end world hunger, has been injecting test animals with a special formula. And when one of those animals, a tarantula, comes into contact with radioactive energy, it becomes a twenty-story behemoth hell-bent on destruction and terror.

Tarantula was the first of Universal-International Pictures' many monster-attack films. John Agar, who plays Dr. Hastings, starred in a slew of B-movies and creature features in his career; he is very one note, but the rest of the cast is fantastic. Clifford Stine, who handled the visual effects, used a live tarantula anytime the kaiju-sized spider was moving in the film. Forced perspective was used to make the real spider seem larger than it actually was, and a giant mock-up of the spider was built for closer, intimate scenes. Miniatures were used for close-ups.

The Beast of Hollow Mountain (1956)

Directors: Edward Nassour, Ismael Rodriguez
Producers: William Nassour, Edward Nassour
Writers: Robert Hill, Jack DeWitt, Willis O'Brien
Release date: August 1956 (US)
Lead actors: Guy Madison, Patricia Medina, Carlos Rivas, Edward Noriega

▼

In one of the first cowboy versus dinosaur movies, American cowboy Jimmy Ryan is trying to figure out why his struggling ranch in northern Mexico has so many missing cattle. He and his partner Felipe discover the carcass of one of the dead cattle stuck in a swamp of quicksand, and Jimmy believes that his rival rancher Enrique Rios is responsible for it. But little do they know that in Hollow Mountain, a monster has awakened.

Though the cultural insensitivities of the time sometimes show through, *The Beast of Hollow Mountain* is an entertaining film, as long as you don't expect to see the beast until near the end of the film. The movie sometimes feels like a telenovela meets a Western via *Jurassic Park*, all on a Roger Corman budget. The titular beast—a green-scaled allosaurus—was filmed using a technique patented by Edward Nassour called "Nassour Regiscope," which controlled miniatures that were shot inches from the camera.

The poster for *The Amazing Colossal Man* (1957).

🔘 *The Amazing Colossal Man* (1957)

Director: Bert I. Gordon
Producers: James H. Nicholson, Samuel Z. Arkoff
Writers: Mark Hanna, Bert I. Gordon
Release date: August 28, 1957 (US)
Lead actors: Glenn Langan, Cathy Downs, William Hudson

— ▼ —

When Lieutenant Colonel Glenn Manning gets caught in a plutonium atomic bomb test in Nevada, he grows to over sixty feet tall. His fiancée, Carol Forrest, despairs once Dr. Paul Lindstrom explains that the plutonium blast has caused new cells to generate at an alarming rate, which means Glenn will continue to grow to a point at which his heart will no longer be able to support his body. Glenn, no longer wanting to be a "freak" for military and science studies, escapes and heads for Las Vegas in a confused and destructive state, as Carol and Paul try to find a way to prevent Glenn from causing harm to himself and others.

This film is one of many B-movie features from director Bert I. Gordon, who directed sixteen sci-fi and creature feature films from 1955 to 1977. Most of the scenes where the enlarged Glenn is sitting in a room or other environments were done using forced perspective and miniature props. You don't watch this movie for the acting.

GROWING...!
GROWING...!
GROWING...!
to a GIANT...!
to a MONSTER...!

WHEN WILL IT STOP?

THE AMAZING COLOSSAL MAN

Produced & Directed by **BERT I. GORDON** · Screenplay by **MARK HANNA** and **BERT I. GORDON**
A JAMES NICHOLSON-SAMUEL Z. ARKOFF PRODUCTION
AN AMERICAN-INTERNATIONAL PICTURE

Glenn Manning, the colossal man, lifts a military truck with ease.

🔘 *The Giant Claw* (1957)

Director: Fred F. Sears
Producer: Sam Katzman
Writers: Samuel Newman, Paul Gangelin
Release date: June 1957 (US)
Lead actors: Jeff Morrow, Mara Corday

— ▼ —

Mitch MacAfee, an engineer at a radar facility, spots what he thinks is an unidentified flying object, prompting the Air Force to investigate. When three pilots are sent to investigate, one of the pilots tragically loses his life and the military blames Mitch for spreading unfounded rumors—until a commercial flight disappears moments after the pilot of the flight reports a UFO sighting. With the

FLYING BEAST OUT OF PREHISTORIC SKIES!

THE GIANT CLAW

JEFF MARA
MORROW · CORDAY   SAMUEL NEWMAN · PAUL GANGELIN   RALPH HAMMERAS · GEORGE TEAGUE
SAM KATZMAN   FRED F. SEARS · OLIVIER   COLUMBIA

help of scientist Sally Caldwell, Mitch must find out what deadly monster is causing havoc in the skies.

Though influenced by *Rodan*, *The Giant Claw* has possibly one of the most poorly produced kaiju ever put on screen, even though Sears and Katzman normally had better budgets than most B-movie filmmakers. The Claw is supposed to be a massive, dangerous bird but it looks like a low-rate puppet and takes you out of the film as soon as you see it.

☢ The Deadly Mantis (1957)

Director: Nathan Juran
Producer: William Alland
Writer: Martin Berkeley
Release date: May 1, 1957 (Los Angeles, CA), May 26, 1957 (US)
Lead actors: Craig Stevens, William Hopper, Alix Talton, Donald Randolph

——— ▼ ———

When a volcano explodes in the South Seas, it causes a major shift in the North Pole's icebergs, which in turn releases an enormous praying mantis that had been trapped in the ice for millennia. After the mantis destroys a radar station in the Canadian Arctic, Colonel Joe Parkman investigates and finds

a large spur in the snow, which he takes to General Ford and the high-level scientists Ford requests to identify the spur. Once Dr. Nedrick realizes that the spur is that of a giant praying mantis, he, Parkman, and photographer and magazine editor Marge Blaine set out to end the mantis' reign of terror.

Four different Mantis were used during the production of the film. A one-foot model and a six-foot model were built for flying and walking scenes, and a real praying mantis climbed a miniature model of the Washington Monument in one of the climactic kaiju scenes. The fourth model was a two-hundred-foot-long and forty-foot-high papier-mâché mantis, fitted with a hydraulic system to make its legs, claws, and head move. It had a wingspan of one hundred and fifty feet. The film was critically panned upon its original release but has since amassed a cult following, even being featured in an episode of *Mystery Science Theater 3000*.

☢ Beginning of the End (1957)

Director: Bert I. Gordon
Producer: Bert I. Gordon
Writers: Fred Freiberger, Lester Gorn
Release date: June 28, 1957 (US)
Lead actors: Peter Graves, Peggie Castle, Morris Ankrum, Than Wyenn

——— ▼ ———

Audrey Aimes, a photojournalist looking for her next big story, comes across a small town in Illinois

A giant locust attacks in *Beginning of the End* (1957).

that was destroyed in the middle of the night. Army personnel are on the scene, but withholding information about what took place. Looking for answers, Aimes connects with a nearby Department of Agricultural farm run by Dr. Ed Wainwright that's experimenting with radiation to grow large fruits and vegetables to put an end to world hunger. It turns out a group of locusts has eaten massive quantities of Wainwright's radioactive wheat, turning them into gigantic creatures rampaging across Illinois toward Chicago. It will take Wainwright, Aimes, and the Army to end the plague.

KAIJU FACT

The week *Beginning of the End* premiered, Bert I. Gordon began directing *The Amazing Colossal Man* for American International Pictures.

Beginning of the End was the first film from AB-PT Studio, a merger of the American Broadcasting Company and United Paramount theaters. Seeing the success of the giant-insect movie craze following films like *Them!*, AB-PT sought to create low-budget feature films to put in its own theaters. *Beginning of the End* was the only film the studio ever released.

Director Bert I. Gordon handled the special effects for the film. When animated grasshoppers were deemed too expensive, Gordon used real grasshoppers via rear projection (an in-camera effect in which actors are placed in front of a screen with their supposed background projected onto it) and static matte work (which allows filmmakers to merge a foreground image, such as actors, with a background image of a landscape or other environment). There's even a scene where grasshoppers are simply placed on a large photo cutout of a high-rise building in Chicago. The movie has its charms, but it falls short as it tries to convey concerns about pesticides and invasive species during the 1950s.

☢ *Attack of the 50 Foot Woman* (1958)
Director: Nathan Juran
Producers: Jacques Marquette, Bernard Woolner
Writer: Mark Hanna
Release date: May 19, 1958 (US)
Lead actors: Allison Hayes, William Hudson, Yvette Vickers, Roy Gordon

▼

In this low-budget cult classic, heiress Nancy Archer has yet another fight with her deceitful husband Harry and decides to take a drive to figure out her feelings. Nancy almost crashes head-on into a mysterious orb in the California desert. Nancy and Harry eventually return to the scene, so Nancy can prove her story is true, but while there, Nancy is abducted by a giant from the UFO. Days later, Nancy is found on the roof of her pool house with strange radiation gashes and burns which make her grow fifty feet tall. At that height, she is no longer the easy-to-control woman that society expects her to be, and she is able to enact revenge on Harry and others who have wronged her.

Of course, this film was released during an era when women were fighting for their very rights, so to have a character like Nancy who can do what she pleases by sheer force alone was very empowering—even if it was delivered in the form of B-movie. In a 2024 article in *The Times*, Kevin Maher says, "Yes,

A lobby card for *Attack of the 50 Foot Woman* (1958).

the effects are risible. And yes, the B-list director Nathan Hertz squeezes every possible second of screen time from a giant rubber hand and lots of screaming extras. But in the cultural moment when Barbie has been revamped as a totem of female empowerment, this can only be seen as the original feminist doll movie." The theatrical version of *Attack of the 50 Foot Woman* suffers from a very short runtime, but Allison Hayes (the titular 50-Foot Woman) is fantastic and chews up the scenery anytime she's on the screen.

☢ *The Giant Gila Monster* (1959)
Director: Ray Kellogg
Producers: Gordon McLendon, Ken Curtis
Writers: Ray Kellogg, Jay Simms
Release date: June 25, 1959 (US)
Lead actors: Don Sullivan, Fred Graham, Lisa Simone, George Fisher

▼

Two teens are killed when their car is knocked into a ravine and the citizens of a small Texas town try to figure out what happened. It is only once the kaiju Gila monster attempts to destroy a locomotive that the town understands this monster has a taste for blood and destruction as it makes its way to the local sock hop.

Harry (William Hudson) about to get scooped up by the 50 Foot Woman.

McLendon-Radio Pictures allowed Ray Kellogg to direct the film in exchange for him also overseeing the special effects, which were handled by Ralph Hammeras and Wee Risser. Rear-projection techniques were used to place the Gila monster into the film.

☢ *The Giant Spider Invasion* (1975)

Director: Bill Rebane
Producers: William W. Gillett Jr., Richard L. Huff, Bill Rebane
Writers: Robert Easton, Richard L. Huff
Release date: October 24, 1975 (US)
Lead actors: Steve Brodie, Barbara Hale, Alan Hale, Robert Easton

—— ▼ ——

In a small town in northern Wisconsin, a meteor blazes across the sky and makes impact near a farm, causing an explosion. When a drunk and seedy farmer and his wife investigate the meteor on their land, they find geodes that they think are valuable diamonds. But they actually contain spiders from another world that grow into giants after hatching. The spiders run amok, and it's up to NASA doctor J.R. Vance, Dr. Jenny Langer, and the local sheriff to end the deadly menace.

The Giant Spider Invasion was a major success in 1975, grossing over $22 million on a $250,000–$300,000-budget. It was filmed in just six weeks, with a cast featuring B-movie legend Steve Brodie, *Perry Mason* actress Barbara Hale, and the Skipper from *Gilligan's Island*, Alan Hale. It's a wonder they were able to afford all three of these actors, who all do a fantastic job with the material they're given.

The filming was not without its problems. A large prop spider exploded in a tree, injuring crew members and starting multiple brush fires. For a scene in which a giant spider crushes a house, a manned spider prop was dropped onto a house via a crane as a bulldozer pulled the house down. The people inside the spider were almost impaled by the broken wood from the torn-down house.

A scene from *The Giant Spider Invasion* (1975).

Zarkorr! The Invader (1996)

Directors: Aaron Osborne, Michael Deak

Producers: Albert Band, Charles Band, Rob Martin, Steve Sechrest

Writer: Benjamin Carr (also known as Neal Marshall Stevens)

Release date: April 1996 (US)

Lead actors: Ryhs Pugh, De'Prise Grossman, Mark Hamilton, Torie Lynch

— ▼ —

Aliens that have been observing and studying Earth decide to test humanity by unleashing a kaiju named Zarkorr to destroy the world with its laser eyes and destructive claws. When an average postal worker discovers a hologram of a pixie teenage alien, she tells him that he is the chosen one who will save the world and destroy Zarkorr.

Zarkorr feels out of sorts—perhaps because Michael Deak filmed all the Zarkorr scenes before the script was even written (likely because the filmmakers hoped to build an inexpensive film around a few well-done kaiju scenes). The film comes from Full Moon Entertainment, one of the longest-running low-budget B- and Z-movie studios in America. The principal photography for this movie lasted only one week, and it shows. But the red, horned, heavily-ribbed Zarkorr costume—an amalgamation of Godzilla and Tolkien's Smaug the Dragon—looks great, especially for a film of this caliber. The costume was one of the earlier works of Jodi Zimelman, who would later handle costuming for thirty years' of popular TV, including *Jesse*, *Spin City*, *Still Standing*, *'Til Death*, *Hot In Cleveland*, and *Abbott Elementary*.

A poster for *Zarkorr! The Invader* (1996).

KAIJU FACT

Zarkorr's roar comes from the roar of the Tyrannosaurus rex in *Jurassic Park*.

Anaconda (1997)

Director: Luis Llosa

Producers: Verna Harrah, Leonard Rabinowitz, Carole Little

Writers: Hans Bauer, Jim Cash, Jack Epps Jr.

Release date: April 11, 1997 (US)

Lead actors: Jennifer Lopez, Ice Cube, Jon Voight, Eric Stoltz, Jonathan Hyde, Owen Wilson, Danny Trejo, Kari Wuhrer

— ▼ —

Filmmaker Terri Flores and anthropologist Steven Cale take a production crew to the Amazon to film a documentary about a long-lost Indigenous

Jonathan Hyde meets the monster in *Anaconda* (1997).

tribe known as the Shirishamas. While boating on the Amazon River, they assist the seedy Paul Serone, who promises he can help them find the Shirishamas if they let him come along with him. But Serone is actually a snake hunter who is trying to capture a giant anaconda, even if it means putting everyone's life in danger.

Anaconda was a massive success, taking in close to $140 million at the box office. The giant anacondas in the film were a mix of CGI and practical animatronic snakes. The animatronic queen snake was a forty-foot-long model that weighed over two tons, and the other animatronic snake was twenty-five feet long and weighed close to 1,500 pounds. Due to the high price tag on high-quality CGI in the 1990s, it cost $100,000 per second to put the CGI snake on the screen. The forty-foot model has resided at the California Academy of Sciences in San Francisco ever since.

☢ *Eight Legged Freaks* (2002)
Director: Ellory Elkayem
Producers: Dean Devlin, Bruce Berman
Writers: Jesse Alexander, Ellory Elkayem, Randy Kornfield
Release date: July 17, 2002 (US), August 15, 2002 (Germany), September 26, 2002 (Australia)
Lead actors: David Arquette, Kari Wuhrer, Scott Terra, Doug E. Doug, Scarlett Johansson

The poster for *Eight Legged Freaks* (2002).

What happens when you combine *The Giant Spider Invasion* and *Beginning of the End* and put that mix on a steroid regimen? You get the funny and sometimes creepy *Eight Legged Freaks*.

In the small mining town of Prosperity, Arizona, a barrel of toxic wastelands in a pond and begins to leak. The crickets at the pond are exposed to toxic waste, unbeknownst to a local spider farmer who collects the crickets to feed his collection. Once the spiders eat the contaminated crickets, they grow to massive sizes and attack the town.

One great thing about this film is that it never takes itself too seriously. The CGI spiders can look outdated when compared to today's special effects, but it doesn't take away from the movie. The late Roger Ebert enjoyed the film for just that reason,

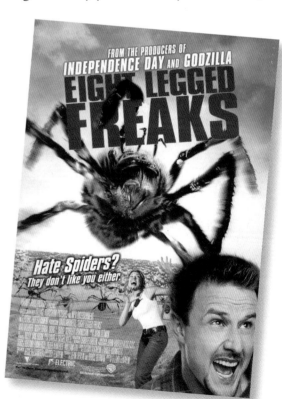

giving it three out of four stars and saying it has "laughs, thrills, wit and scary monsters, and is one of those goofy movies like *Critters* that kids itself and gets away with it." The idea to make the film came from director Ellory Elkayem's 1997 short film, *Larger Than Life*, which involved people fighting spiders. *Eight Legged Freaks* earned over $45 million at the box office.

☢ *Cloverfield* (2008)

Director: Matt Reeves
Producers: J.J. Abrams, Bryan Burk
Writer: Drew Goddard
Release date: January 18, 2008 (US)
Lead actors: Lizzy Caplan, Jessica Lucas, T.J. Miller, Michael Stahl-David, Mike Vogel, Odette Yustman

——— ▼ ———

In this found-footage film, Rob Hawkins is at a farewell party in Manhattan, hosted by his brother Jason and his brother's girlfriend, Lily Ford, to send Rob off to his new job in Japan. Hud Platt, Rob's best friend, is recruited by Jason to film the party with a camcorder. An earthquake knocks out the city's power, an oil tanker gets damaged near Liberty Island, and fiery debris flies nearby. As Rob and the others attempt to flee to safety, destruction creeps closer to Manhattan. The head of the Statue of Liberty rolls down the street and, moments later, the menace appears, as a giant behemoth destroys the Woolworth Building. As the military arrives, the monster (known as Clover or the Large-Scale Aggressor) releases parasite-like creatures from its body to wreak additional chaos, death, and destruction.

Cloverfield built a massive following by launching a teaser trailer using footage from the preparation stage of the film, ending with the severed head of the Statue of Liberty rolling down the street. There was no film title on the teaser,

KAIJU FACT

Neville Page, a concept artist and creature designer on films such as *TRON: Legacy*, *Avatar*, *Star Trek* (2009), and *Prometheus*, designed the monster for Cloverfield.

Promotional art for *Cloverfield* (2008).

which fueled online speculation and made it a viral success before it made its way to theaters. Clover is truly one of the ugliest monsters ever seen on film, which only enhances its fright factor. The film was a massive success, generating over $170 million dollars at the box office and spawning two sequels.

☢ *Pacific Rim* (2013)

Director: Guillermo del Toro
Producers: Guillermo del Toro, Thomas Tull, Jon Jashni, Mary Parent
Writers: Guillermo del Toro, Travis Beacham, Neil Cross (uncredited), Patrick Melton (uncredited), Drew Pearce (uncredited), Marcus Dunstan (uncredited)

A poster for *Pacific Rim* (2013).

Release date: July 12, 2013 (US), July 1, 2013 (Mexico City)
Lead actors: Charlie Hunnam, Idris Elba, Rinko Kikuchi, Charlie Day, Rob Kazinsky, Ron Perlman

——— ▼ ———

In 2013, deadly giant alien creatures known as kaiju appeared on Earth from an interdimensional portal at the bottom of the Pacific Ocean known as the Breach. To defend Earth, society begins to build giant mecha called Jaegers. The Jaegers are co-piloted by two people using a process called drifting, which uses a neural bridge to create a mental link between the pilots to alleviate the mental stress of piloting the massive mecha. In 2025, world leaders end the Jaeger program to alleviate costs and instead build coastal walls to keep the kaiju out. The walls, of course, are ineffective. Marshal Stacker Pentecost, who has the remaining Jaegers, pilots, mechanics, and scientists in a Hong Kong military base, plans a mission to use a nuclear weapon to destroy the Breach. He recruits a traumatized pilot named Raleigh Becket and trainee Mako Mori to pilot the legendary American Jaeger Gispy Danger, the last hope against the kaiju apocalypse.

Not only is *Pacific Rim* visually stunning and full of fantastic performances. The film also grapples with themes of personal loss, survivor's guilt, learning how to move forward, and learning how to build trust. Becket and Mori's story is not a love story, but one about two damaged people who

KAIJU FACT

One hundred kaiju and Jaegers were designed for *Pacific Rim* (2013), but only a fraction of them made it to the final cut.

must face and overcome their suppressed pain and trauma to work together effectively. The Jaeger and kaiju designs are original, organic, and incredible. The film's 2018 sequel, *Pacific Rim: Uprising*, is an entertaining follow-up full of fantastic Jaeger/kaiju battles that performed well overseas, but it didn't fare as well in the US, ending the possibility of more movies.

☢ *Colossal* (2016)

Director: Nacho Vigalondo
Producers: Nahikari Ipiña, Russell Levine, Nicolas Chartier, Zev Foreman, Dominic Rustam
Writer: Nacho Vigalondo
Release date: September 9, 2016 (TIFF), April 7, 2017 (US)
Lead actors: Anne Hathaway, Jason Sudeikis, Dan Stevens, Austin Stowell, Time Blake Nelson

——— ▼ ———

When Gloria, an alcoholic, unemployed party girl is kicked out of the apartment that she shares with her then-boyfriend, Tim, she must leave the life she once had in New York and move back to her family home in Mainhead, New Hampshire. Back home, she reunites with one of her good friends from her childhood, Oscar. One night, when the

news reports of a giant monster destroying Seoul, South Korea, Gloria realizes that she has a mental link to the kaiju and can control it with her body movements. Gloria must discover why her life is now connected with this monster, and how her actions, relationships, friendships, and personal decisions can either make things better or cause a path of severe destruction.

This is not your typical kaiju film; it's more of a somber dark comedy with a solid cast. The film isn't about kaiju as much as it's about abuse, alcoholism, and the dangers of toxic relationships.

☢ *The Meg* (2018)

Director: Jon Turteltaub
Producers: Lorenzo di Bonaventura, Belle Avery, Colin Wilson
Writers: Dean Georgaris, Jon Hoeber, Erich Hoeber
Release date: August 10, 2018 (US)
Lead actors: Jason Statham, Li Bingbing, Rainn Wilson, Ruby Rose, Winston Chao, Cliff Curtis, Jessica McNamee

A poster for *The Meg* (2018).

Based on the 1997 novel *Meg* by Steve Alten, *The Meg* follows Jonas Taylor, an experienced deep sea rescue diver, who is brought in by expert oceanographer Zhang to rescue a submersible crew from the Mariana Trench. Jonas' ex-wife, Lori, is part of the endangered crew. What they don't know is that a prehistoric 75-foot-long shark known as the Megalodon, a monster Jonas has faced before, has caused the submersible to require rescue.

The Meg lived in "development hell" for over a decade, hopping from Disney's Hollywood Pictures division to New Line Cinema, and finally landing at Warner Bros. in 2013, with principal filming starting in October 2016. An American and Chinese co-production, *The Meg* was a worldwide success at the box office, grossing over $530 million. A 2023 sequel, loosely based on another Alten novel called *The Trench*, features even larger, prehistoric apex predators and creatures of the deep. It also had a successful run at the box office, leaving room for yet another sequel.

☢ *Rampage* (2018)

Director: Brad Peyton
Producers: Brad Peyton, Beau Flynn, Hiram Garcia, John Rickard
Writer: Ryan Engle
Release date: April 13, 2018 (US)
Lead actors: Dwayne Johnson, Naomie Harris, Malin Akerman, Jake Lacy, Jeffrey Dean Morgan

——— ▼ ———

Former special forces officer turned primatologist Davis Okoye works for the San Diego Wildlife Sanctuary as a member of their anti-poaching unit. He has a close bond with a rare albino gorilla named George whom he saved from poachers. When George, a wolf, and a crocodile come into contact with a treacherous and experimental pathogen from debris from an exploded space station, the animals grow into giant, raging beasts. Davis teams with Kate Caldwell, a disgraced genetic engineer, to find an antidote to turn the kaiju-sized animals back to normal and prevent Earth's destruction.

Rampage has as much destruction and action as the Midway Games video game it's based on. Dwayne "The Rock" Johnson is probably one of the last great action stars of cinema (along with *The Meg*'s Jason Statham), and serves the film well.

☢ *Love and Monsters* (2020)

Director: Michael Matthews
Producer: Shawn Levy
Writers: Brian Duffield, Matthew Robinson
Release date: October 16, 2020 (US)
Lead actors: Dylan O'Brien, Jessica Henwick, Dan Ewing, Michael Rooker

——— ▼ ———

An asteroid heading toward Earth causes an apocalyptic fallout, which mutates cold-blooded animals into giant monsters that devastate the Earth and slaughter most of mankind. Joel Dawson is separated from his girlfriend, Aimee, during an evacuation but promises that he will find her. Several years later, Joel lives in an underground bunker city where survivors have paired up in relationships so that they won't be alone as they battle kaiju and search for supplies. Because Joel has frozen in previous situations dealing with kaiju, he is relegated to the kitchen. After kaiju ants invade the bunker, Joel decides to leave to try to find Aimee because he doesn't want to end up alone.

Love and Monsters was supposed to have a wide theatrical release in early 2020, but due to

the COVID-19 pandemic, Paramount decided to release the film digitally and have a minimal screen release in the States. It was released internationally by Netflix the following year. The special effects are done well for a film that had a budget of only $30 million. It has a "coming-of-age" feel to it and there are subtle odes to films such as *Tremors*, *Stand by Me*, and *I Am Legend*.

Monster Hunter (2020)

Director: Paul W. S. Anderson
Producers: Jeremy Bolt, Paul W. S. Anderson, Dennis Berardi, Robert Kulzer, Martin Moszkowicz
Writer: Paul W. S. Anderson
Release date: December 18, 2020 (US), December 3, 2020 (Netherlands), December 4, 2020 (China), March 26, 2021 (Japan)
Lead actors: Milla Jovovich, Tony Jaa, Clifford "T.I" Harris, Meagan Good, Jin Au-Yeung, Ron Perlman, Josh Helman

——— ▼ ———

Based on the Capcom video game series, *Monster Hunter* follows the journey of US Army Ranger Natalie Artemis and her team as they search the desert for a group of missing soldiers. A bizarre storm sucks them into a portal to the New World, where gigantic, dangerous, and powerful monsters roam free. Artemis teams with Hunter, a survivor of the New World who knows how to combat the monsters, to survive the monsters, and, hopefully for Artemis, find a way back home.

Ariana Greenblatt (left) and Michael Rooker in *Love and Monsters* (2020).

▾▾ *INTERNATIONAL FILMS* ▾▾

☢ *Gorgo* (1961)

Director: Eugène Lourié
Producer: Wilfred Eades
Writers: John Loring, Daniel Hyatt
Release date: December 24, 1960 (Hong Kong), February 10, 1961 (Philadelphia, PA), March 16, 1961 (Los Angeles, CA), March 29, 1961 (New York, NY), October 27, 1961 (United Kingdom)
Lead actors: Bill Travers, William Sylvester, Vincent Winter, Christopher Rhodes

———— ▼ ————

In this British kaiju film, boat captain Joe Ryan, his crew, a local fisherman, and an orphaned village boy named Sean capture an enormous sea monster and

Gorgo (1961) is one of the UK's entries into the kaiju canon.

decide to take it to London to put it on display. This causes the monster's mother to invade London in search of her child, destroying everything in her path.

This B-movie was originally set in Japan, as an homage to Godzilla, but the producers changed their minds on locations multiple times before settling on Ireland and England. Like the first thirty years of Godzilla films, the Gorgo kaiju was brought to life using suitmation. Even though the film was unrated in the United States and other countries, meaning that anyone could see the movie, British censors decided to give the film an X rating in the UK, meaning that children under the age of sixteen were not allowed to view it.

☢ *Reptilicus* (1961)

Directors: Poul Bang (Danish version), Sidney W. Pink (US version)
Producers: Sidney Pink, J. H. Zalabery
Writers: Ib Melchior, Sidney Pink, Poul Bang, Bob Ramsing
Release date: February 20, 1961 (Denmark), November 1962 (US)
Lead actors: Carl Ottosen, Ann Smyrner, Mimi Heinrich, Dirch Passer, Bodil Miller, Marla Behrens

———— ▼ ————

In this Danish-American kaiju movie, a mining operation discovers a giant reptile's tail while drilling and takes it to Copenhagen to be preserved and studied in a low-temperature room at the Denmark Aquarium. When the entry to the room is left open, the tail begins to thaw and regenerate like a starfish, and soon it is a fully grown reptile that begins to terrorize Copenhagen.

Reptilicus is one of the most poorly constructed kaiju in the history of cinema. Sci-fi film critic Glenn Erickson called the monster "a wiggly marionette that moved like something from *Kukla, Fran, and Ollie*

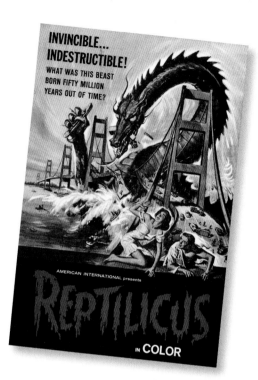

INVINCIBLE...
INDESTRUCTIBLE!
WHAT WAS THIS BEAST
BORN FIFTY MILLION
YEARS OUT OF TIME?

AMERICAN INTERNATIONAL presents

REPTILICUS

IN COLOR

(a kid's puppet TV show from the 1950s)," and said the film's "dubbing was terrible and the optical effects so distractingly bad that I couldn't help but roll my eyes."

☢ *Bulgasari* (1962)

Director: Kim Myeong-je
Producer: Cho Yong-jin
Writers: Woo Beom, Yun Beom
Release date: December 1, 1962
Lead actors: Choi Moo-ryong, Um Aing-ran, Gang Mi-ae, Kim Dong-won

——— ▼ ———

When Nam Hyeong, a skilled martial artist is brutally murdered, the hatred that remains in his

soul resurrects him into a revenge-seeking, iron-eating kaiju known as Bulgasari.

Bulgasari was the first kaiju film made in South Korea, and the first Korean film to implement special effects. Even though Bulgasari is a major part of South Korea's cinematic history, it is considered as a lost film, with no prints of the film seen in decades.

☢ *Yongary, Monster from the Deep* (1967)

Director: Kim Ki-duk
Producer: Cha Tae-jin
Writers: Kim Ki-duk, Seo Yun-sung
Release date: August 13, 1967 (South Korea), 1969 (US—television release)
Lead actors: Oh Yeong-il, Nam Jeong-im

——— ▼ ———

In this South Korean-Japanese co-production, a kaiju reptile awakens due to an earthquake caused by a nuclear bomb test and runs amok in Seoul.

Yongary is one of the better *Godzilla* clones of its time. The original Korean film prints have been lost for almost 50 years, but the English print remains available.

Poster art for *Reptilicus* (1961).

A scene from *Yongary, Monster from the Deep* (1967).

KAIJU FACT

Although the original *Bulgasari* (1962) is lost to time, its screenplay is preserved at the Korean Film Archive. Unfortunately, it is not available for public viewing.

KAIJU FACT

Gamera monster suit
maker Masao Yagi helped
design the Yongary suit.

☢ *Queen Kong* (1976)
Director: Frank Agrama
Producers: Keith Cavele, Virgilio De Blasi
Writers: Ron Dobrin, Fabio Piccioni, Frank Agrama
Release date: December 10, 1976 (Germany)
Lead actors: Robin Askwith, Rula Lenska, Roger
Hammond, Jon Rees

— ▼ —

In this British-German sophomoric parody of *King
Kong*, the roles of the male and female characters
are reversed, with Ray Fay as the damsel in distress,
trying to escape the wrath of Queen Kong and film
director Luce Habit.

A scene from
Queen Kong
(1976).

Queen Kong never made it to the theaters in the
United States—or most of the rest of the world—in
1976 due to a lawsuit by movie producer Dino De
Laurentiis, who was producing the remake of King
Kong at the time, and RKO Radio Pictures, who
were the copyright holders of *King Kong*. The film
had a limited release in Germany and Italy and
wasn't available for viewing elsewhere until thirty
years after its initial release.

☢ *The Mighty Peking Man* (1977)
Director: Ho Meng-hua
Producer: Runme Shaw
Writer: Kuang Ni
Alternate film title: *Goliathon* (US)
Release date: August 11, 1977 (Hong Kong, China), March
1980 (US), March 4, 1978 (Japan), December 9, 1983
(Canada)
Lead actors: Danny Lee, Evelyne Kraft, Hsiao Yao, Ku Feng,
Lin Wei-fu ——— ▼ ———

From the internationally renowned Shaw
Brothers Studio of Hong Kong comes a *King Kong*

When Johnny Feng takes a trip to the Himalayan mountains to talk to the natives about a mysterious phenomenon, he is introduced to the giant gorilla known as Utam, the Mighty Peking Man. Like in *King Kong*, Utam is taken from his home to be exhibited, and chaos eventually reigns.

LEFT: The poster for *The MIghty Peking Man* (1977).

RIGHT: THe poster for *Tentacles* (1977).

Tentacles was yet another film attempting to cash in on the *Jaws* phenomenon, joining an illustrious list that includes *Mako: The Jaws of Death* (1976), *Orca* (1977), *Alligator* (1980), *The Last Shark* (1981), and *Devil Fish—aka Devouring Waves* (1984). It has a cast of Hollywood legends but there is very little entertainment in this movie.

☢ *Pulgasari* (1985)

Director: Shin Sang-ok
Producers: Kim Jong Il, Shin Sang-ok
Writer: Kim Se Ryun
Release date: 1985 (North Korea), July 4, 1998 (Japan), July 22, 2000 (South Korea)
Lead actors: Kenpachiro Satsuma, Chang Son Hui, Ham Gi Sop, Jong-uk Ri

———— ▼ ————

Loosely based on the lost South Korean film *Bulgasari*, this North Korean kaiju movie features a creature that devours metal. Pulgasari also shares a blood bond with the daughter of an activist blacksmith who fights on behalf of the people who are suffering in feudal Korea. The kaiju becomes an

☢ *Tentacles* (1977)

Director: Ovidio G. Assonitis
Producer: Enzo Doria
Writer: Steven W. Carabatsos
Release date: February 25, 1977 (Italy), 1977 (US)
Lead actors: John Huston, Shelley Winters, Bo Hopkins, Henry Fonda, Claude Akins

———— ▼ ————

In this Italian-produced film, a slew of people go missing at a seaside resort and journalist Ned Turner finds out that a giant octopus is wreaking havoc along the coast due to unregulated drilling.

ally to the peasants, but his never-ending hunger for metal and minerals could mean the downfall of civilization.

South-Korean director Shin Sang-ok was ordered to direct *Pulgasari* by North Korean supreme leader Kim Jong II. Both Shin and his wife, actress Choi Eun-hee, were kidnapped by North Korea Special Forces in 1978 to make fantasy and propaganda movies for the North Korean government. After many years of captivity, Shin and Choi managed to escape during a film festival in Austria and came to the United States in 1986.

☢ *Yonggary* (1999)

Director: Shim Hyung-rae
Producers: Shim Hyung-rae, Yang Jae-hyeok, Lee Yeong-ho
Writer: Park Hui-jun
Release date: July 17, 1999 (South Korea)
Lead actors: Harrison Young, Donna Phillipson, Richard B. Livingston, Briant Wells, Brad Sergi, Dan Cashman, Bruce Cornwell

——— ▼ ———

This reimagining of the 1967 film features a cast of predominantly American character actors in an attempt to land distribution from an

A poster for *Yonggary* (1999).

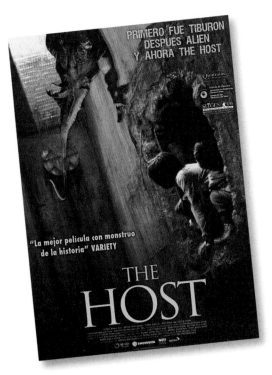

A poster for *The Host* (2006).

American movie studio. In this version, Yonggary is a massive dinosaur that lived 200 million years ago and is around fifty times the size of a Tyrannosaurus rex. The creature is brought back to life by an extraterrestrial species called the Galaxions, who plan to conquer the Earth with the reanimated dinosaur.

The kaiju suits took over six months to design, and they were then scanned for 3D digital effects and CGI. Suit actors were used during filming and replaced with CGI versions of the kaiju in post-production. When *Yonggary* premiered, it was the most expensive film produced in South Korean history.

☢ *The Host* (2006)

Director: Bong Joon-ho
Producer: Choi Yong-bae
Writers: Bong Joon-ho, Ha Joon-won, Baek Chul-hyun
Release date: July 27, 2006 (South Korea)
Lead actors: Song Kang-ho, Byun Hee-bong, Park Hae-il, Bae Doona, Ko Ah-sung

——— ▼ ———

In the year 2000, an American pathologist working for the military orders a Korean assistant to take over 200 bottles of formaldehyde and dump them down

A scene from *The Host* (2006).

a drain, which leads into the Han River. As the years pass, the fish in the river continue to die off and people start to report sightings of a strange creature roaming the river. The creature eventually attacks the city, kidnapping the daughter of Park Gang-du, who runs a snack bar at the park. Park makes it his mission to find his daughter at all costs, even as the government and the military stand in his way.

The creature in this film is unlike any kaiju seen before, a deformed, walking fish that is fully visible at almost every given chance on screen. The creature was created by Chin Wei-chen, modeled by the Weta Workshop, with animatronics provided by John Cox's Australian special-effects creature workshop. On a budget of just $10–11 million, *The Host* made over $90 million worldwide and received much critical praise. In 2009, Quentin Tarantino listed *The Host* as one of the top twenty films to exist since 1992, the year he started directing.

Monsters (2010)

Director: Gareth Edwards
Producers: Allan Niblo, James Richardson
Writer: Gareth Edwards
Release date: March 13, 2010 (SXSW Festival), October 29, 2010 (US), December 3, 2010 (UK)
Lead actors: Scoot McNairy, Whitney Able

▼

NASA sends a space probe to search for extraterrestrial life in the universe, which takes

samples from Europa, one of Jupiter's moons, for research. The probe crashes in Mexico, with the exposed samples creating giant, alien creatures near the Mexico/US border. A large border wall is built to keep the US safe from harm. Photojournalist Andrew Kaulder is ordered by his employer to find the news agency owner's daughter, Samantha, in Mexico and bring her back to the US. Samantha and Andrew must then make their way through the dangerous monster zone to get home.

Gareth Edward's directorial debut is a low-budget, postmodern, satirical sci-fi film, in which the monsters and special effects don't command your attention as much as the story. A sequel, *Monsters: Dark Continent,* debuted on May 1, 2015. Ironically, Gareth Edwards was already committed to directing Legendary Pictures' *Godzilla* (2014), so it was directed by British television director Tom Green.

KAIJU FACT

Director Gareth Edwards built all the visual effects for *Monsters* (2010) using personal software on his computer. He created 250 visual effects shots in only five months.

<blockquote>
" ... in the 1970s [Godzilla] was uniformly characterized as a hero who cooperated with humans. The Hanna-Barbera show took it to an extreme, sure, but it wasn't out of line with what Toho was up to.
—Mark Pellegrini, *AIPT*
"
</blockquote>

The immense world of kaiju and Kyodai Heroes is not just limited to live-action cinema. From classics like Hanna-Barbera's Grape Ape to a modern take like Ginormica in *Monsters vs. Aliens*, and spanning original animated stories and adaptations of popular manga, comics, and live-action films, there are a good number of animated films and series that add to the lore of Godzilla, King Kong, and Ultraman. There are also other films and series that have their followings, be they small or massive, and differ from their kaiju and Kyodai colleagues. This is not a complete list of animated projects that involve kaiju, but rather serves to highlight the diversity of work that has been produced.

▼▼ ANIMATED FILMS ▼▼

☢ *Godzilla: Planet of the Monsters* (2017)
Directors: Kobun Shizuno, Hiroyuki Seshita
Producer: Keiji Ota
Writer: Gen Urobuchi
Voice actors: Mamoru Miyano, Takahiro Sakurai, Kana Hanazawa
Release date: November 17, 2017 (Japan), January 17, 2018 (Netflix—Worldwide)

Humanity has no choice but to abandon Earth due to it being overrun with kaiju, including the king of all monsters, Godzilla. In the year 2048, the emigration starship known as the Aratrum seeks an inhabitable planet for humankind. When they finally reach their destination in the Cetus constellation, 11.9 light years away from Earth, they discover that the planet is uninhabitable. Captain Haruo Sakaki, who blames Godzilla for the death of his parents when he was a child, sets a course to return to Earth with a special brigade to destroy Godzilla and reclaim Earth from the monsters. But due to all the light-year travel, they return to Earth 20,000 years later and find a planet now built around kaiju.

Co-director Kobun Shizuno was pleased with the production of the film because Toho gave the

A scene from *Pacific Rim: The Black* (2021–2022).

OPPOSITE: The King of the Monsters on top of the Empire State Building in *Godzilla: The Series* (1998–2000).

filmmakers the chance to make their own Godzilla story without worrying about fitting it into the continuity of decades of Godzilla movies. While the film is beautiful to watch, it crawls at a snail's pace, and I had a hard time feeling any sympathy for the main characters in the story. Brian Ashcraft of *Kotaku* said that the "anime version of Godzilla is surprisingly effective and frightening" and that the film is "not a perfect picture, but it was a powerful proof of concept: Godzilla works as an anime."

☢ *Godzilla: City on the Edge of Battle* (2018)

Directors: Kobun Shizuno, Hiroyuki Seshita
Producer: Keiji Ota
Writers: Tetsuya Yamada, Gen Urobuchi
Voice actors: Mamoru Miyano, Takahiro Sakurai, Kana Hanazawa
Release date: May 18, 2018 (Japan), July 18, 2018 (Netflix—Worldwide)

Godzilla's design in *Godzilla: The Planet Eater* (2018).

In the sequel to *Godzilla: Planet of Monsters*, Captain Sakaki and those who survived the Godzilla attack are now captives of the Indigenous people of Earth, known as the Houtua. Since the Houtua are a peaceful people, they let Sakaki and his crew leave, but warn them of the dangers of pursuing battle with Godzilla. When Sakai finds out that Nanometal (what was once used to build Mechagodzilla) is still available on Earth, he and his crew go to Mechagodzilla City, built over the former construction site of the original robot kaiju. Sakai feels that the city gives them the best chance to take down Godzilla once and for all, but the Houtua warn Hauro that the Nanometal may not be the salvation they think it will be.

The concept and premise of this film have promise, but the execution is lacking. The characters, in particular, come off extremely dry, even though the film is heavily character

Sakaki from
Godzilla: The Planet Eater (2018).

driven. *IGN*'s Naoya Fujita rated the film 4.5 out of 10, saying, "*Godzilla: City on the Edge of Battle* takes some promising ingredients but cooks them into an unpalatable meal. We never really understand what the protagonists are fighting for, and there's not even a satisfying scene of urban destruction (a Godzilla staple). It fails both emotionally and viscerally."

☢ *Godzilla: The Planet Eater* (2018)
Directors: Kobun Shizuno, Hiroyuki Seshita
Producer: Keiji Ota
Writer: Gen Urobuchi
Voice actors: Mamoru Miyano, Takahiro Sakurai, Kana Hanazawa
Release date: November 3, 2018 (Tokyo International Film Festival), November 9, 2018 (Japan), January 9, 2019 (Netflix—Worldwide)

▼

In the final installment of the trilogy of animated Godzilla films from Toho Animation and Polygon Pictures, Earth is out of options following the destruction of Mechagodzilla City. But an archbishop named Metphies claims that God can

be summoned to destroy Godzilla. Unfortunately, Sakai and the others discover that the god that Metphies speaks of is Ghidorah, the three-headed supernatural entity that destroyed Metphies's home world many years ago. Sakaki now must confront Metphies to prevent him from calling forth Ghidorah, who may destroy not just Godzilla, but the entire Earth.

Patrick Galvan, a critic from *Syfy Wire*, regarded this movie as the best of the trilogy. According to him, the movie "has a few things going for it that its two predecessors lacked, but it nonetheless fails— just as they did—to rise above the wall of mediocrity which has rendered this three-film saga the single dullest stretch in the history of the Godzilla franchise to date."

☢ *The Mighty Kong* (1998)
Director: Art Scott
Producers: Denis deVallance, Lyn Henderson
Writer: William J. Keenan
Voice actors: Dudley Moore, Jodi Benson, Randy Hamilton, William Sage, Jason Gray-Stanford, Richard Newman
Release date: June 16, 1998 (US)

This musical adaptation of *King Kong* is based on the public domain novelization written by Delos W. Lovelace in 1932, to avoid paying licensing fees, although it does contain some similarities to the 1976 live-action remake. In the animated film, the musical number "Dolly of Pa Pali" has the character Ann Darrow imagining herself dancing with animals from the sea, which may be a nod to *The Little Mermaid*, as Jodi Benson voiced both Ann Darrow in *The Mighty Kong* and Ariel in *The Little Mermaid*.

☢ Kong: King of Atlantis (2005)

Director: Patrick Archibald
Producer: Allen Bohbot
Writer: Sean Catherine Derek
Voice actors: Kirby Morrow, Scott McNeil, Saffron Henderson, Daphne Goldrick, Paul Dobson, Pauline Newstone
Release date: November 22, 2005 (US)

——— ▼ ———

This direct-to-video animated movie is a continuation of *Kong: The Animated Series*, which ended in 2001 (more on page 194 about the series). In *Kong: King of Atlantis*, King Kong is convinced that his family lineage is linked to Atlantis, so he ventures to the mythical kingdom and ends up helping to defend it from the evil rule of Queen Reptilla.

The film was made to cash in on Peter Jackson's *King Kong*, with the DVD of this film being released just one month before Jackson's film. Todd Douglass Jr. of DVDtalk.com said, "The story behind *Kong: King of Atlantis* is pretty bad and not very well thought out or executed," adding, "In addition to some poor storytelling, concepts, and characters, the folks behind this project thought it would be a good idea to include cheesy musical numbers."

OPPOSITE:
A poster for
Monsters vs. Aliens
(2009).

☢ Kong: Return to the Jungle (2007)

Director: Stuart Evans
Producers: Allen Bohbot, Rick Ungar
Writers: Rick Ungar, Sean Catherine Derek
Voice actors: Kirby Morrow, Scott McNeil, Saffron Henderson, Kathy Morse, Paul Dobson, David Kaye, Richard Newman
Release date: 2007 (US)

——— ▼ ———

In this standalone, direct-to-video animated sequel to *Kong: King of Atlantis*, a blue-hued Kong and other beasts are captured by hunters and are transported from Kong Island to New York. Once there, they escape into the city, and chaos ensues. It was the first 3D/CGI animated Kong film, and the animation style is quite crude.

KAIJU FACT

Kong: Return to the Jungle was released on DVD shortly after Peter Jackson's *King Kong* extended edition hit theaters, to capitalize on the movie's popularity.

☢ Monsters vs. Aliens (2009)

Director: Conrad Vernon, Rob Letterman
Producer: Lisa Stewart
Writers: Maya Forbes, Wally Wolodarsky, Rob Letterman, Jonathan Aibel, Glenn Berger, Conrad Vernon
Voice actors: Reese Witherspoon, Seth Rogen, Hugh Laurie, Will Arnett, Kiefer Sutherland, Rainn Wilson, Paul Rudd, Stephen Colbert
Release date: March 27, 2009 (US)

——— ▼ ———

In this feature-length animated action/sci-fi/comedy, Susan Murphy gets hit by a radioactive meteorite that contains quantonium, which causes her to grow fifty feet tall on her wedding day. She's taken captive, renamed "Ginormica," cut off from her family and friends, and placed in a secret

Ultraman has been animated many times over the decades, including in the recent Netflix series (2019–2023).

government facility, where she's introduced to other misfit monsters. The hope is that these monsters will become a team of heroes to save the Earth from an impending alien threat.

☢ *Ultraman: The Adventure Begins* (1987)

Directors: Mitsuo Kusakabe (Director), Ray Patterson (Supervising Director)
Producer: Noboru Tsuburaya
Writer: John Eric Seward
Voice actors: Michael Lembeck, Chad Everett, Adrienne Barbeau, Stacy Keach Sr., Lorna Patterson (US Voices) Toru Furuya, Shinji Ogawa, Hiromi Tsuru, Kōhei Miyauchi, Rihoko Yoshida (Japan Voices)
Alternate titles: *Ultraman USA* (Japan)
Release date: October 12, 1987 (US), April 29, 1989 (Japan)

——— ▼ ———

When a stunt pilot trio known as the Flying Angels encounters a bizarre pulse of light during one of their performances, pilots Scott Masterson, Chuck Gavin, and Beth O'Brien crash, yet they survive,

completely unharmed. A special agent from outer space contacts the trio to let them know that they have become the human hosts of three alien warriors who will save the Earth from a group of monsters from the planet Sorkin. The trio become the Ultra Force, able to transform into giant Ultra Heroes, assisted by their robotic companions Ulysses, Samson, and Andy, and a fleet of sleek fighter ships.

Ultraman: The Adventure Begins was a Japanese-American co-production between legendary animation studio Hanna-Barbera and Tsuburaya Productions, the owners of the Ultraman franchise. The animation services were outsourced to anime studios Ashi Productions (*Machine Robo*, *Macross 7*, *Blue Seed*) and Studio Sign (*Demon Slayer*, *Boruto: Naruto Next Generations*, *Naruto Shippuden*). The hope with this film was to bring Ultraman into the American mainstream, and, if successful, produce an animated series, but the film, unfortunately, was not successful in the US.

OPPOSITE:
A statue of *Attack on Titan* (2013–2023) protagonist Eren Yeager at Universal Studios Japan.

▾▾ ANIMATED SERIES ▾▾

☢ *Attack on Titan* (2013–2023)

Creator: Hajime Isayama

Directors: Tetsurō Araki (Seasons 1–3), Masashi Koizuka (Seasons 2–3), Yuichiro Hayashi (Season 4), Jun Shishido (Season 4)

Producers: Over 12 producers

Writers: Yasuko Kobayashi (Seasons 1–3), Hiroshi Seko (Season 4)

Voice actors: Bryce Papenbrook, Trina Nishimura, Jessie James Grelle (US Voices), Yūki Kaji, Yui Ishikawa, Marina Inoue (Japanese Voices)

▬▬▬ ▼ ▬▬▬

Based on the popular manga series of the same name, *Attack on Titan* is a dark fantasy anime set in post-apocalyptic times. Citizens reside in cities surrounded by giant walls to protect them from the "Titans," a race of kaiju-sized humanoids that eat humans. The series focuses on the adventures of Eren Yeager and his friends, Armin Arlert and Mikasa Ackerman. Their hometown is attacked and destroyed by Titans, who eat Eren's mother in the process. In the aftermath, Eren and his friends join an elite unit of soldiers known as the Scout Regiment, seeking revenge and to take back their world from the Titans.

KAIJU FACT

A live-action film adaptation of *Attack on Titan* was released in multiple parts in 2015. The film was criticized for deviating from the source material, but the special effects and Titan designs were praised.

The entrance
to Attack on Titan:
Race for Survival
at Universal
Studios Japan.

Attack on Titan is without question one of today's most popular anime. *Esquire* called is the Best Anime Series of 2023, and Lauren Orsini of *Forbes* had *Titan* on her list of the Best Anime Series of the Decade. Phelim O'Neill of the *Guardian* called the series "spellbinding . . . It's all wonderfully acrobatic and intense." *Attack on Titan* even set a Guinness World Record for being the most in-demand anime TV show.

☢ *Gamera: Rebirth* (2023–)

Creator: Kadokawa/Polygon Studios
Director: Hiroyuki Seshita
Producers: Sho Tanaka, Haruki Satomi, Yukio Haruyama
Writers: Kenta Ihara, Hiroshi Seko, Tetsuya Yamada, Hiroyuki Seshita
Voice actors: Ryan Bartley, Robbie Daymond, Abby Trott, Sean Chiplock (US Voices), Hisako Kanemoto, Yoshitsugu Matsuoka, Aki Toyosaki, Subaru Kimura (Japanese Voices)

—— ▼ ——

In the summer of 1989, best friends Boco, Joe, and Junichi are enjoying their final summer vacation before entering middle school. As the trio confront a bully named Brody who stole their money, a crisis breaks out and deadly kaiju appear. All four kids are saved by Gamera, and they band together as they watch Gamera take on multiple kaiju and protect Tokyo.

Kayleigh Dray, writing for *The A.V. Club*, pointed out several flaws in *Gamera: Rebirth*, and compared it to *Stranger Things*. While she acknowledged the effort put into developing the characters and the themes of friendship, she criticized the animation for feeling clunky and likened the look of the admittedly likeable characters to PlayStation 2 animations.

☢ *Godzilla* (1978–1979)

Directors: Ray Patterson, Carl Urbano (Season 1), Oscar Dufau, George Gordon (Season 2)
Producers: Doug Wildey, Iwao Takamoto
Writers: Herb Armstrong, Don Heckman, Bob Johnson, Duane Poole, Dick Robbins, Sam Roeca, George Shea, Bob Stitzel, Tom Swale, David Villaire
Voice actors: Ted Cassidy, Don Messick, Jeff David, Al Eisenmann, Hilly Hicks, Brenda Thompson

Produced by Hanna-Barbera, this particular version of Godzilla was faced with many challenges during its production. Joseph Barbera wanted the series to be a one-to-one match with the Godzilla movies from Toho, but American cartoons had many restrictions in the 1970s.

In *Japan's Favorite Mon-Star: The Unauthorized Biography of "The Big G"* by Steve Ryfle, Barbera said in an interview, "When they start telling you in Standards and Practices, 'Don't shoot any flame at anybody, don't step on any buildings or cars,' then pretty soon, they've taken away all the stuff he [Godzilla] represents. That became the problem, to maintain a feeling of Godzilla and at the same time cut down everything that he did."

The series originally aired on NBC Saturday mornings. It centered on Godzilla, his young and goofy cousin Godzooky, and a team of marine scientists. Every kaiju that Godzilla battles in this series is an original creation, as Hanna-Barbera did not have the rights from Toho for the other kaiju in Godzilla's universe. In this series, the King of the Monsters is always portrayed as a protector of good. Due to Standards and Practices restrictions, Godzilla's atomic breath is replaced with fire, and he can also shoot laser beams from his eyes.

KAIJU FACT

Godzilla is voiced by actor Ted Cassidy in the 1978–1979 series, who played Lurch in the original *Addams Family* TV series.

Hanna-Barbera's interpretation of the King of the Monsters in the late 1970s.

☢ *Godzilla: The Series* (1998–2000)

Writers: Over thirty writers were featured in this series, including notable comic book writers Marv Wolfman and Len Wein, and animation writers such as Robert Skir (*X-Men*, *Gargoyles*, *Batman: The Animated Series*), Craig Miller, and Lara Runnels (*Extreme Ghostbusters*, *90210*)

Producers: Richard Raynis, Dean Devlin, Roland Emmerich, Audu Paden

Voice actors: Frank Welker, Ian Ziering, Malcolm Danare, Rino Romano, Charity James, Brigitte Bako, Tom Kenny, Kevin Dunn, Paget Brewster, Joe Pantoliano, Clancy Brown, Roddy McDowall, Ronny Cox, Michael Chiklis, Susan Eisenberg, Dennis Haysbert, Ron Perlman

———— ▼ ————

Picking up where the Sony *Godzilla* left off, Dr. Nick Tatopoulos, the leader of the Humanitarian

The Great Grape Ape and friends in his 1975 series.

Environmental Analysis Team (H.E.A.T.), gets permission to investigate the remains of Madison Square Garden to make sure that none of Godzilla's eggs in the stadium survived. While searching, Nick stumbles across one untouched egg. The egg hatches to reveal a baby Godzilla, who automatically imprints on Nick. As the monster quickly grows to kaiju size, it continues to protect Nick and be an ally to H.E.A.T. as they protect the world from the sudden rise of deadly kaiju appearing all over the globe. Actors Kevin Dunn, Michael Lerner, Malcolm Danare, and Frank Welker (the voice of Godzilla) all reprise their roles.

The animated series succeeds in ways the source film could only dream of. The stories are fun, full of risk, and have a tone similar to some of the Godzilla films of the Showa Era, and the characters have an admirable amount of depth for a kids' show. This version of Godzilla better parallels his Toho counterpart, having atomic breath, incredible strength, and a lot of personality. The three-part "Monster Wars" mini-series in the first season is an homage to *Destroy All Monsters*, and all the kaiju Godzilla faces here are original concepts created specifically for the series. The series received more positive reviews from critics and fans than Sony's *Godzilla*, as it was considered more faithful to the source material.

Some of Marv Wolfman's most popular comics as a writer were *The New Teen Titans* and *Crisis on Infinite Earths,* which was the first major event limited series in DC Comics history. Len Wein not only co-created Swamp Thing for DC, but also revived the X-Men comics for Marvel in the 1970s, and co-created X-Men characters Wolverine, Nightcrawler, Storm, and Colossus.

☢ *The Great Grape Ape Show* (1975–1978)
Creators: William Hanna and Joseph Barbera
Director: Charles Nichols
Producers: William Hanna, Joseph Barbera, Iwao Takamoto
Writers: Dick Robbins, Duane Poole, Ray Parker, Jack Mendelsohn, Tom Dagenais, Joel Kane
Voice actors: Marty Ingels, Bob Holt

Meet Grape Ape, the friendly and caring forty-foot-tall purple gorilla who wears a green jacket, baseball cap, and bowtie. He and his best friend, an anthropomorphic dog named Beegle Beagle, roam America in Beagle's van (which Grape Ape rides on top of), getting into all types of adventures in this comical cartoon.

Of course, Grape Ape isn't a dangerous, violent monster like some of the other beasts discussed in this book, which sets him apart. Any violence that occurs on-screen fit the lighthearted tone of the show, and the point is not to frighten viewers or leave them awestruck. Even if the adults on the show often flee at the sight of Grape Ape, children are seldomly, if ever, scared of him. He certainly exists more in the realm of Joe Young, rather than King Kong!

Inhumanoids (1986)

Creator: Flint Dille
Director: Ray Lee
Producers: Margaret Loesch, Tom Griffin, Jules Bacal, Lee Gunther, Stephanie Graziano, Flint Dille, Chris Pelzer
Writers: Flint Dille, Buzz Dixon, Richard Merwin, Larry Parr
Voice actors: Michael Bell, Susan Silo, Ed Gilbert, Chris Latta, William Callaway, Neil Ross, Richard Sanders

▼

When evil monsters Metlar, Tendril, and D'Compose come back to life from their geological prisons and wreak havoc, it's up to the Earth

Corps—a team of science heroes with special armor and high-tech gear—to put this evil back where it belongs. Alongside their geological allies known as the Mutors, Earth Corps will fight these menacing monsters known as the Inhumanoids.

Based on the toy line by Hasbro, the short-lived *Inhumanoids* was unique for its ongoing plotlines, something that wasn't done a lot in the more episodic American animation of the 1980s. The cartoon could also get moody and dark. For example, the monster D'Compose had an exposed chest cavity with a gated ribcage that opened so he could imprison people inside his body. D'Compose could also turn humans into giant undead creatures with a single touch of his claw, and the cartoon would show those vivid and mildly graphic transformations.

The King Kong Show (1966–1967)

Writers: Bernard Cowan, Lew Lewis, Ron Levy
Producers: Arthur Rankin Jr., Jules Bass, William J. Keenan, Larry Roemer
Voice actors: Susan Conway, John Drainie, Carl Banas, Billie Mae Richards, Bernard Cowan

▼

In this American-Japanese co-production from Rankin/Bass and Toei Animation, King Kong saves young Bobby Bond from being eaten by a Tyrannosaurus rex. Kong then follows Bobby and his scientific team on their adventures around the world.

The King Kong Show was one of the first animated series that was produced in Japan specifically for an American production company. In the book *Comics Gone Ape! The Missing Link to Primates in Comics*, comics and pop culture historian Michael Eury writes, "The Rankin/Bass *King Kong* was an early case of identity theft, where the Kong name was appropriated (fully under license) to describe a new character that, at best, only remotely resembled his namesake. This was Kong done wrong."

KAIJU FACT

Earth Corps member Bradley Armbruster (codename Saber Jet) was also a member of G.I. Joe. As a member of the Joes, he was a fighter pilot named Ace.

Kong: The Animated Series (2000–2001)

Directors: Marc Boréal, Stéphane Roux, Chuck Patton, Joe Pearson

Producers: Allen Bohbot, Denis deVallance

Writers: Romain van Liemt, Sean Catherine Derek, Jean-Christophe Derrien, Eric Rondeaux, plus 22 additional writers

Voice actors: Kirby Morrow, Scott McNeil, Saffron Henderson, Daphne Goldrick, David Kaye, Pauline Newstone

— ▼ —

When the sinister Dr. Ramone De La Porte steals the Primal Stones from Kong Island, it's up to the clone of the original King Kong, Dr. Lorna Jenkins (who created the Kong clone), her archeologist and martial artist grandson Jason Jenkins, Jason's his best friend Eric "Tann" Tannenbaum, and Lua, the shaman of Kong Island, to recover the Primal Stones while also battling the evil forces of the fire-demon known as Chiros.

Kong leans heavily on science-fiction elements to gain viewers who also watched *Godzilla: The Series*. Because Dr. Jenkins created the Kong clone using the DNA of the original Kong and Jason's DNA, Jason and Kong share a strong bond. They can even fuse together using a "Cyber-Link," allowing Jason to merge into Kong and making Kong grow larger, but for only a short period.

Kong: King of the Apes (2016–2018)

Directors: Makoto Sato, Satoru Yanigawa, Hiroshi Uchibori, Kensuke Suzuki

Producers: Avi Arad, Allen Bohbot, Alexandra Bland, Jenn Rogan, Bernard Edlington

Writers: Ken Pontac, Andy Briggs, Dennis Haley, Marcy Brown, Sean Catherine Derek

Voice actors: Lee Tockar, Alessandro Juliani, Giles Panton, Kathleen Barr, Vincent Tong, Viv Leacock, Shannon Chan-Kent, Samuel Vincent, Tabitha St. Germain

— ▼ —

In the year 2050, Kong is framed for the destruction of natural history sites. Three kids—Lukas Remy, Doug Jones, and Francisca—help Kong clear his name and, along the way, encounter Lukas' evil brother, Richard Remy, and his vicious robotic dinosaurs known as Bionobots.

Distributed by Netflix, this series is extremely kid-friendly and is meant for a very young audience. The animation improves in Season Two, but it may not be enough for viewers to continue watching.

Kong in *Kong: King of the Apes* (2016–2018).

Moon Girl and Devil Dinosaur (2023–)

Directors: Ben Juwono, Samantha Suyi Lee, Trey Buongiorno, Christine Liu, Rodney Clouden

Writers: Jeffrey M. Howard, Liz Hara, Taylor Vaughn Lasley, Kate Kondell, Halima Lucas, Maggie Rose, Lisa Muse Bryant

A Los Angeles billboard for *Moon Girl and Devil Dinosaur* (2023–).

Producers: Steve Loter, Laurence Fishburne, Helen Sugland, Rafael Chaidez, Pilar Flynn, Rodney Clouden, Kate Kondell, Laura Bullen, Alexia Gates-Foale, Jeffery M. Howard, Barbara Stephen, Claudio Jimenez, Debbie Steer
Voice actors: Diamond White, Alfre Woodard, Fred Tatasciore, Laurence Fishburne, Sasheer Zamata, Jermaine Fowler, Gary Anthony Williams, Libe Barer

—— ▼ ——

Teenage savant Lunella Lafayette tries to help the family business stay afloat after blackouts in New York's Lower East Side by building a generator so powerful that it summons a red Tyrannosaurus rex (Devil Dinosaur) that imprints on her. When it is discovered that an evil supervillain is causing the blackouts, Lunella decides to become a superhero known as Moon Girl.

KAIJU FACT

Devil Dinosaur weighs ten tons and loves hot dogs.

Based on the Marvel Comic, Moon Girl and Devil Dinosaur made their way into the world of animation when Laurence Fishburne was shown the comic and began a push to get the series pitched and eventually created. The animation is vivid and crisp, and every episode is filled with fun, action, and excitement. Both Moon Girl and Devil Dinosaur have so much personality, and the supporting cast is funny and endearing. It also has appearances from classic Marvel Comics characters such as The Beyonder and Bill Foster (Black Goliath) (both voiced by Laurence Fishburne), Molecule Man (voiced by Edward James Olmos), and Maria Hill of S.H.I.E.L.D. (with Cobie Smulders reprising her role from live-action MCU films).

☢ *Pacific Rim: The Black* (2021–2022)

Directors: Hiroyuki Hayashi, Jae Hong Kim, Masayuki Uemoto, Susumu Sugai, Takeshi Iwata
Producers: Shuzo John Shiota, Craig Kyle, Greg Johnson, Ken Duer, Jack Liang, Bill E. Miller
Writers: Greg Johnson, Craig Kyle, Nicole Dubuc, Paul Giacoppo
Voice actors: Gideon Adlon, Calum Worthy, Erica Lindbeck, Victoria Grace, Allie MacDonald, Jason Spisak, Andy McPhee

—— ▼ ——

When Australia is overrun by kaiju and the Jaegers fail to stop them, everyone must abandon the

A scene from
*Pacific Rim:
The Black*
(2021–2022).

continent. Years later, teenagers Haley and Taylor Travis, who were left behind when their parents went to battle the kaiju, find an abandoned Jaeger, the Atlas Destroyer, and begin a quest to find their family. Along the way, they battle kaiju, as well as others who want the Atlas Destroyer for themselves.

Pacific Rim: The Black is a continuation of the Pacific Rim franchise, taking place many years after *Pacific Rim: Uprising*. It is a darker take than the films. The Jaegers in the series were designed by Jūki Izumo.

KAIJU FACT

The kaiju designs for *Pacific Rim: The Black* (2021–2022) were created by concept artist Yuuki Morita, who worked with animators to meld realistic designs with vibrant color tones for anime.

☢ *Skull Island* (2023–)

Directors: Willis Bulliner, Amanda Sitareh B., Daniel Araya, Julie Olson
Producers: Brad Graeber, Jen Chambers, Thomas Tull, Jacob Robinson, Brian Duffield, Jason Williams
Writer: Brian Duffield
Voice actors: Mae Whitman, Nicolas Cantu, Benjamin Bratt, Darren Barnet, Betty Gilpin, Phil LaMarr, John DiMaggio

— ▼ —

Thirty years ago, expeditioners Cap and Hiro, along with their sons Charlie and Mike, are traveling in the South Pacific in search of cryptids when they spot a girl, Annie, floating in the ocean. After rescuing her, Annie tells them that she escaped from another ship that was ransacked by mercenaries. When those same mercenaries sneak aboard the boat to capture Annie, a giant Kraken attacks the boat, destroying it and killing Hiro. Charlie, Mike, Annie, and Cap wash up on the shores of Skull Island, a place filled with terrifying monsters and the ruler of those monsters: Kong.

leaves the space station to head back to Earth to join the Science Guard, he encounters the alien Ultraman Joneus, who warns Hikari that danger is coming. To defend the planet, Joneus must merge with a human to help mankind. Hikari agrees to merge with Joneus, and when deadly kaiju aliens appear on Earth, he can now turn into the 130-foot-tall hero known as Ultraman Joneus.

The Ultraman series did not fully air in the United States during its original run, but instead was released as two movies made from cobbled together episodes and dubbed into English. *The Adventures of Ultraman* was released in 1981, and *Ultraman II* was released on VHS for American audiences in 1983.

☢ *Ultraman* (2019–2023)

Creators: Tsuburaya Productions, Production I.G, Sola Digital Arts
Directors: Kenji Kamiyama, Shinji Aramaki, Jeff Nimoy
Writers: Eiichi Shimizu, Jeff Nimoy, Ardwight Chamberlain
Producers: Joseph Chou, Mitsuhisa Ishikawa, Jamie Simone
Voice actors: Ryohei Kimura, Hideyuki Tanaka, Takuya Eguchi, Megumi Han, Sumire Morohoshi, Ken Uo, Shigeru Ushiyama, Ryota Takeuchi (Japanese Voices) Josh Hutcherson, Fred Tatasciore, Liam O'Brien, Gunnar Sizemore, Tara Jayne Sands, Brian Palerma, D.C. Douglas, Robbie Daymond (US Voices)

—— ▼ ——

Decades have passed since Ultraman was last seen, with many believing he went back to his planet of origin after defeating the many deadly kaiju aliens that once invaded Earth. The son of Shin Hayata (the original Ultraman), Shinjiro, discovers that he has what is known as the "Ultraman Factor," the Ultra DNA that gives one superhuman abilities. Shinjiro discovers his father was once Ultraman and picks up the mantle of the legendary hero as a new wave of aliens invades the Earth.

This series aired over three seasons on Netflix worldwide and Japanese television networks.

Exclusively produced for Netflix, this series is a continuation of the MonsterVerse King Kong films and shows.

☢ *The Ultraman* (1979–1980)

Creators: Tsuburaya Productions, Nippon Sunrise
Directors: Takeyuki Kanda, Hisayuki Toriumi
Producers: Noboru Tsuburaya, Kazuho Mitsuta, Masaru Tadakuma
Writers: Sōji Yoshikawa, Keiichi Abe, Bunzo Wakatsuki, Hiroyuki Hoshiyama, Keisuke Fujikawa, Yoshihisa Araki, Yasushi Hirano, Kiyoshi Miyata
Voice actors: Kei Tomiyama, Kinya Morikawa, Hidekatsu Shibata, Sumi Shimamoto, Masanari Nihei, Shingo Kanemoto

—— ▼ ——

The first Ultraman series to be animated and technically the eighth variation of the Ultraman series, *The Ultraman* debuted four years after the end of the live-action *Ultraman Leo*. The Earth Defense Forces (EDF) create the Science Guard to investigate glowing objects all over the skies around the world, and when EDF officer Choichiro Hikari

16
COMIC BOOKS, MANGA, AND PROSE

The world of comic books, graphic novels, and manga has also seen its fair share of kaiju stories. Once considered taboo or unsellable, kaiju have also planted a firm foot in the world of novels, with titles meant to appeal to everyone from kids to adults. Because these protagonists and antagonists can be seen as metaphors for war, peace, and the concern of taking up space in a crowded world, they make for fantastic stories in any artistic medium.

During the 1970s, Marvel Comics began to heavily invest in intellectual properties from film and television, making comics for hit films and TV series such as *Star Wars*, *2001: A Space Odyssey*, *Battlestar Galactica*, and *Star Trek*. When Godzilla's popularity in the United States began to grow again in the 1970s due to the Showa Era movies being played heavily on television, Marvel capitalized on the opportunity to create a comic starring the King of the Monsters and placed him in the Marvel universe. The big green machine met the likes of the Agents of S.H.I.E.L.D., the Fantastic Four, and the Avengers.

Still, the popularity of kaiju-centric comics, manga, and novels doesn't stem only from Godzilla. Many of the projects discussed in this chapter put their own unique twist on the genre, even creating their own monsters and worlds to tackle new social and cultural issues of the day.

▼▼ *COMIC BOOKS* ▼▼

☢ *Strange Tales* (1951–1968)

Publisher: Marvel Comics
Writers: Jack Kirby, Stan Lee, Steve Ditko, Dick Ayers, Larry Lieber, Bill Everett, Carl Wessler, Jim Steranko, Bob Powell, Marie Severin
Penciled artwork: Steve Ditko, Jack Kirby, Dick Ayers, Bill Everett, Paul Reinman, Don Heck, Joe Maneely, Carl Burgos, Sol Brodksy, Joe Sinnott, Jim Steranko, John Forte, Bob Powell, Ed Winiarski, George Roussos, Gene Colan, Marie Severin
Inkers: Steve Ditko, Jack Kirby, Dick Ayers, Bill Everett, Paul Reinman, Don Heck, Joe Maneely, Carl Burgos, Sol Brodksy, Joe Sinnott, Jim Steranko, John Forte, Bob Powell, Ed Winiarski, George Roussos, Gene Colan, Marie Severin
Colorists: Stan Goldberg, Jim Steranko, Marie Severin
Letterers: Artie Simek, Dick Ayers, Sam Rosen, Ray Holloway, Joe Letterese, Bill Everett, Morrie Kuramoto, Jim Steranko

——— ▼ ———

Strange Tales was a horror/science fiction anthology series that featured both comics and prose. Though there weren't giant monsters in every issue, there

OPPOSITE:
Cover detail
from an issue
of *Godzilla:
Kingdom of
Monsters*
(2011–2012).

Stan Lee.

were many that made their presence felt when they appeared, such as the giant Scarecrow, Fing Fang Foom, Orrgo: The Unconquerable, and Zzutak. Around issue #101, the series changed from its horror/science-fiction roots and became a superhero comic, featuring heroes from the Marvel universe. After issue #168, the series title was changed to *Doctor Strange*, as the titular magician had been a featured character in *Strange Tales* since 1964.

Where Monsters Dwell (1970–1975)

Publisher: Marvel Comics
Writers: Stan Lee, Larry Lieber, Carl Wessler, Bill Everett, Jack Oleck, Gerry Conway, Mimi Gold
Penciled artwork: Steve Ditko, Jack Kirby, Dick Ayers, Bill Everett, Marie Severin, and various artists
Inkers: Steve Ditko, Jack Kirby, Dick Ayers, Bill Everett, Marie Severin, and various inkers
Colorists: Marie Severin and various colorists
Letterers: Artie Simek, Ray Holloway, and various letterers

——— ▼ ———

Where Monsters Dwell takes Marvel Comics back to its *Strange Tales* roots, presenting an anthology of standalone stories featuring giant monsters like the Cyclops, Sporr, Grottu, Taboo, Rommbu, and Orogo. Most of these monsters were never seen again in the Marvel universe. But the series is probably best known for the introduction of the now-popular character, Groot, who debuted in *Where Monsters Dwell #6*.

Godzilla (1977–1979)

Publisher: Marvel Comics
Writer: Doug Moench
Penciled artwork: Herb Trimpe, Marie Severin, Tom Sutton, Jim Mooney, Dave Cockrum, Ernie Chan
Inkers: Herb Trimpe, Bob Wiacek, George Tuska, Marie Severin, Joe Rubenstein, Jim Mooney, Bob McLeod, Bob Layton, Fred Kida, Klaus Janson, Dan Green, Frank Giacoia, Tony DeZuniga, Ernie Chan, Jack Abel
Colorists: Don Warfield, Mary Titus, Mario Sen, George

Colorists: Petra Goldberg, George Roussos
Letterers: Danny Crespi, John Costanza, Jim Novak, Gaspar Saladino

An Italian cover of an issue of *Godzilla* (2010–).

The titular character, a crimson-red dinosaur, and his primate friend Moon Boy try to survive in a place known as Dinosaur World, an alternate Earth where primitive humans, dinosaurs, aliens, and other prehistoric creatures live. Devil Dinosaur and Moon Boy were created by timeless artist and creator Jack Kirby, who developed the characters during his third run at Marvel from 1975 to 1978.

Jack Kirby.

Roussos, Phil Rachelson, Francoise Mouly, Barry Grossman, Janice Cohen
Letterers: John Costanza, Danny Crespi, Elaine Heinl, Shelly Leferman, Jim Novak, Rick Parker, Bruce Patterson, Clem Robins, Joe Rosen, Gaspar Saladino, Glenn Simek, Jean Simek, Irv Watanabe, Denise Wohl

From 1977 to 1979, Godzilla was part of the Marvel universe, battling deadly kaiju such as Batragon and Yetrigar (which were both created by Doug Moench and Herb Trimpe). During Godzilla's adventures, the King of the Monsters ran into the Fantastic Four, the Avengers, and S.H.I.E.L.D.'s secret weapon, the mecha Red Ronin.

☢ *Devil Dinosaur* (1978)

Publisher: Marvel Comics
Writer/Creator: Jack Kirby
Penciled artwork: Jack Kirby
Inkers: Mike Royer, Joe Sinnott, Walter Simonson, Steve Leialoha, Frank Giacoia, John Byrne

Cover and interior art from assorted Godzilla comics, on display as part of Comic-Con International 2013.

☢ *Shogun Warriors* (1979–1980)

Publisher: Marvel Comics

Writers: Doug Moench, Roger Stern, Steven Grant

Penciled artwork: Herb Trimpe, Mike Vosburg, Walt Simonson, Marie Severin, Al Milgrom, Terry Austin

Inkers: Herb Trimpe, Mike Esposito, Al Milgrom, Jack Abel, Dan Green, Walt Simonson, Marie Severin, Bruce Patterson, Steve Mitchell, Terry Austin

Colorists: Carl Gafford, Andy Yanchus, Roger Slifer, Bob Sharen, Marie Severin, George Roussos, Barry Grossman

Letterers: Jim Novak, John Costanza, Irv Watanabe, Gaspar Saladino, Joe Rosen, Mark Rogan, Rick Parker, Tom Orzechowski, Diana Albers

———— ▼ ————

The *Shogun Warriors* were mecha, kaiju, and vehicle toys that Mattel imported from Japan and Americanized. Due to the success of the Godzilla comic (which also had a Shogun Warriors toy), Marvel and Mattel decided to create a Shogun Warriors comic series set in the Marvel universe.

Only three mecha from the Shogun Warriors toy line were used for the comics; Raydeen (known as Brave Raydeen in Japan), Dangard Ace (known as Wakusei Robo Danguard Ace in Japan), and Combatra (known as Chōdenji Robo Combattler V in Japan). All other characters and monsters were created for the series.

☢ *Godzilla: King of the Monsters* (1995–1996)

Publisher: Dark Horse Comics

Writers: Alex Cox, Arthur Adams, Kevin Maguire, Bob Eggleton, Kate Worley, Randy Stradley, Eric Fein, Ryder T. Windham

Penciled artwork: Brandon McKinney, Bob Eggleton, Kevin Maguire, Arthur Adams, Daniel Rivera, Francisco Solano López, Tatsuya Ishida, Chris Scalf, Bobby Rubio, Gordon Purcell, Mike Wolfer, Scott Kolins, Rich Suchy,

Inkers: Bob Eggleton, Andrew Pepoy, Arthur Adams, Daniel Rivera, Brian Garvey, Justin Bloomer, Chris Scalf, Keith Aiken, Barb Kaalberg, Jasen Rodriguez

Colorists: Bob Eggleton, Perry McNamee, Albert Deschesne, Cary Porter, Arthur Adams, Tom Roberts, Dave Nestelle, Chris Scalf, James Sinclair, Matt Hollingsworth, Perry MacNamee, Art Knight
Letterers: Clem Robbins, Pat Brosseau, Scott Reed, Pat Owsley, Tracey Hampton-Munsey, Mike DeLepine

——— ▼ ———

The most well-known Godzilla series from Dark Horse Comics, this series also featured Godzilla battling all-new kaiju created specifically for this comic series. In one arc, a villain who wanted to frame Godzilla for a number of tragic world events send Godzilla hurtling through time to tragedies from the sinking of the Titanic to the San Francisco Earthquake of 1906. He even gets thrown into the prehistoric era, right before the dinosaurs were wiped off the Earth.

☢ *Giant Monster* (2005)
Publisher: BOOM! Studios
Writer: Steve Niles
Penciled artwork: Nat Jones

Inker: Nat Jones
Colorist: Jay Fotos
Letterer: Ed Dukeshire

——— ▼ ———

While on his first-ever solo space flight, astronaut Don Maggert faces outer space horrors that transform him into a giant menace upon returning to Earth, making him a danger to not only himself but the entire world. This exhilarating and bloody tale features an antihero who rampages through cities, devouring anyone in his path, and the military will try to fight the monstrous beast, even though he seems to be unstoppable.

Giant Monster is an action-packed and suspenseful comic featuring a creature similar to Godzilla, but faster and with a much greater appetite for destruction. Please note that due to its violent content, this book may not be suitable for all readers. It is truly an explicit B-movie in comic book form, akin to films such *The Amazing Colossal Man* and *Giant Monster From Space*— on steroids.

Steve Niles, the writer of *Giant Monster* (2005).

A Godzilla action figure on display at Midtown Comics in New York City.

Toho-licensed kaiju and released *Godzilla: Kingdom of Monsters*, the first installment of a trilogy that also includes the stories *History's Greatest Monsters* and *Rulers of Earth*. The series reintroduces Godzilla to contemporary Japan with a deeper, darker tone and political commentary. There are also series such as *Godzilla: Legends*, an anthology series featuring iconic Toho monsters such as Heodorah, Anguirus, Rodan, Kumonga, and Titanosaurus.

A personal favorite from IDW's run is the miniseries *Godzilla: Cataclysm*, which depicts a world destroyed by monsters. Fans of the Heisei Era will be delighted to see the return of Biollante and Destoroyah in this series' pages. And then there's *Godzilla In Hell*—the title says it all.

☢ *Enormous* (2012, 2014–2016)

Publisher: Image Comics/215 INK (Invader Comics)
Writer: Tim Daniel
Penciled artwork: Mehdi Cheggour
Inker: Mehdi Cheggour
Colorist: Mehdi Cheggour
Letterer: Johnny Lowe

—— ▼ ——

In a world where resources are scarce, an environmental disaster gives rise to gigantic creatures called the Enormous. Humans fight to survive in this harsh new world, with everyone forced to hunt or be hunted. Originally a one-shot graphic novel published by Image in 2012, *Enormous* was followed by a twelve-issue mini-series published by 215 INK (now known as Invader Comics). *Enormous* also had a complimentary live-action web series. In this series about survival, even though the comic offers up plenty of fantastic (and deadly) kaiju, the bigger issue in the series is the fact that humankind has become just as monstrous and desperate since the Enormous arrived.

In a 2012 interview with CBR.com, writer Tim Daniel said, "I have a lifelong appreciation of

☢ *Godzilla* (2010–)

Publisher: IDW Publishing
Writers: Jonathan Vankin, Bobby Curnow, James Stokoe, Brandon Seifert, Jay Fotos, Chris Mowry, Joshua Hale Fialkov, Eric Powell, Tracy Marsh, John Layman, Cullen Bunn, and Duane Swierczynski, and additional writers.
Artwork: Simon Gane, Dean Haspiel, James Stokoe, Ibrahim Moustafa, Jeff Zornow, Matt Frank, Jeff Zornow, Brian Churilla, Victor Santos, Alberto Ponticelli, Dave Wachter, Simon Gane, and additional artists

—— ▼ ——

Godzilla has had a wild ride at IDW, the company that has published multiple mini-series and monthly series which also feature both original kaiju and kaiju from Toho Studios. IDW acquired the rights to Godzilla and several giant monster films, so as far as inspiration, it is quite a long list dating back to obvious childhood favorites like *Godzilla*, *King Kong*, *Gamera*, *The Blob*, *The Invasion of the Body Snatchers*, and so on. More recently, films like *Cloverfield*, *The Mist*, *The Host*, *Monsters*, and *Troll Hunter* have all had repeated viewings in our household. *Enormous* does a fair job of paying respect to both classic and modern monster tales from both film and literature while attempting to find some new ground to stomp around on."

☢ *Pacific Rim: Tales from Year Zero* (2013)
Publisher: Legendary Comics
Writer: Travis Beacham
Penciled artwork: Sean Chen, Yvel Guichet, Pericles Junior, Chris Batista
Inkers: Steven Bird, Geoff Shaw, Mark McKenna, Matt Banning
Colorists: Guy Major, Tom Chu, Dom Regan
Letterer: Patrick Brosseau

Tales From Year Zero takes place one year before the events of the first Pacific Rim film. It centers around the story of a reporter named Naomi Sokolov. Naomi is working on a retrospective article about the history of the Jaeger Program and the Kaiju War. She seeks the viewpoint of three eyewitnesses in the Jaeger Program: Tendo Choi, Jasper Schoenfeld, and Stacker Pentecost. A major part of the story deals with the Pan Pacific Defense Corps attempting to put an end to the Jaeger program so they can foolishly build anti-kaiju walls around major cities instead.

The additional stories deal with the growth, failures, sacrifices, and successes of getting the Jaegar program off the ground and show the reader more about Marshal Stacker Pentecost, who believes that the Jaeger program is Earth's only hope and salvation. Some kaiju battles take place, with Jaeger's battling a thick-clawed crustacean kaiju named Onibaba, and a lanky, yet deadly spine-appendaged kaiju named Karloff.

Travis Beacham, the writer of *Pacific Rim: Tales from Year Zero* (2013).

A display of Godzilla comics from an exhibit at San Diego Comic-Con 2013.

☢ *Godzilla* (2014–2021)

Publisher: Legendary Comics

Writers: Max Borenstein, Greg Borenstein, Arvid Nelson, Greg Keyes

Penciled artwork: Eric Battle, Yvel Guichet, Alan Quah, Drew Edward Johnson

Inker: Drew Edward Johnson

Colorists: Lee Loughridge, Allen Passalaqua

Letterers: Patrick Brosseau, John Roshell, Jimmy Betancourt, Sarah Jacobs, Comicraft, Richard Starkings, Jimmy Betancourt

— ▼ —

Legendary Comics (a subdivision of the movie studio Legendary Pictures) published three graphic novels that served as prequels to the Monsterverse Godzilla films. *Godzilla: Awakening* takes place before the 2014 Godzilla film, *Godzilla: Aftershock* takes place before the events of *Godzilla: King of the Monsters* (2019), and *Godzilla: Dominion* takes place before *Godzilla vs. Kong* (2021). Some of the characters from the *Awakening* graphic novel were later put into the live action *Monarch: Legacy of Monsters* (2023) streaming series.

☢ *Moon Girl and Devil Dinosaur* (2015–2023)

Publisher: Marvel Comics

Writers: Amy Reeder, Brandon Montclare, Jordan Ifueko

Penciled artwork: Natacha Bustos, Marco Failla, Brandon Montclare, Ray-Anthony Height, Felipe Smith, Dominike "Domo" Stanton, Alitha Martinez, Gustavo Duarte, Alba Glez

Inkers: various

Colorists: Tamara Bonvillain and various colorists

Letterers: various

— ▼ —

Despite being fearful of the monstrous Inhuman genes that she has, Lunella Lafayette is a genius preteen who aspires to make a difference. However, she realizes that intellect alone is not enough to achieve her goal. Her life takes an unexpected turn when a savage, red Tyrannosaurus rex is transported from the prehistoric past to the modern day.

Together, they form an incredible team that works wonders across the Marvel Universe. Moon Girl and Devil Dinosaur have had two series: one forty-seven-issue series that ran from 2015 to 2019 and a five-issue mini-series that ran from 2022 to 2023.

☢ *Kaijumax* (2015–2022)

Publisher: Oni Press
Writer: Zander Cannon
Penciled artwork: Zander Cannon
Inker: Zander Cannon
Colorist: Zander Cannon

—— ▼ ——

Godzilla meets *Orange Is The New Black* in this series, which explores a hidden island in the South Pacific called Kaijumax that serves as a maximum security prison for kaiju. A kaiju named Electrogor tries to survive with his family amongst prison corruption and other dangers. *Kaijumax* was published in seasons (five overall), with each season being a six-issue mini-series. In an interview with Bleeding Cool, creator Zander Cannon said, "All the monsters we see in this book are more the C- and D-Listers, the ones that were maybe in an episode of *Ultraman* but never had their own movie or faced Godzilla. I always liked to think of Monster Island (in the *Godzilla* film series) as kind of where the lame, off-brand monsters hung out."

☢ *Project Nemesis* (2015–2016)

Publisher: American Gothic Press
Writer: Jeremy Robinson
Penciled artwork: Matt Frank, Bob Eggleton
Inker: Matt Frank
Colorists: Diego Rodriguez, Matt Frank
Letterer: Marshall Dillon

—— ▼ ——

Based on the Nemesis Book Saga from author Jeremy Robinson, *Project Nemesis* follows the adventures of Jon Hudson, the lead investigator of Fusion Center-P of the Department of Homeland Security. Hudson, who has dealt with more false alarms and supposed Sasquatch sightings than most would believe, finds himself finally dealing with an actual threat: a growing monster called Nemesis.

☢ *Kill All Monsters* (2017)

Publisher: Dark Horse Comics
Writer: Michael May
Penciled artwork: Jason Copland
Inker: Jason Copland
Colorist: Jason Copland

—— ▼ ——

Giant, devastating monsters rule Earth, but it's up to a batch of pilots from different backgrounds and lives to pilot towering mecha to defeat the monsters. *Kill All Monsters* is a graphic novel that features some fantastic monster-on-robot fight scenes. What makes it stand out is the human touch and character depth given to the mech pilots, which makes them relatable to the reader. The story takes place in a world where a war between monsters and humans has been raging for decades, and mankind is on the brink of extinction. The fate of humanity rests on the shoulders of a few pilots and their mecha.

The kaiju in the graphic novel are highly diverse in design. As the story progresses, more types of monsters are introduced. These could easily be villains that Ultraman or Godzilla fought at some point in their lives. The monsters range from giant beetles to deformed, floating squid beasts, each with a unique appearance and abilities.

☢ *Monsters Unleashed* (2017–2018)

Publisher: Marvel Comics
Writers: Cullen Bunn, Justin Jordan, Robbie Thompson
Penciled artwork: Francesco Gaston, Sebastian Carrillo, Alberto Alburquerque, Alex Areizmendi, Andrea Broccardo, David Baldeon, Ramon F. Bachs
Inkers: Jay Leisten and various inkers
Colorists: various
Letterers: Travis Lanham and various letterers

In this twelve-issue mini-series, the heroic kaiju Aegia, Slizzik, Scragg, Hi-Vo, and Mekara are led by the monster hunter Elsa Bloodstone and Kid Kaiju into battle against massive monsters. The mini-series was collected in two volumes. From 1973 to 1975, Marvel published *Monsters Unleashed* as a black-and-white anthology series that featured monsters like Man-Thing and the giant dragon Fing Fang Foom.

☢ *Ultramega* (2021)
Publisher: Image Comics
Writer: James Harren
Penciled artwork: James Harren
Inker: James Harren
Colorist: Dave Stewart
Letterer: Andres Juarez

▼

A cosmic plague has broken out, turning ordinary people into monstrous kaiju. Only three powerful individuals, known as the Ultramega, stand in the way of this frenzy. However, their battles are so intense that entire cities get destroyed, and the aftermath is equally horrific. The Ultramega will eventually face their final showdown even as they ponder if this is a fight they can actually win in this mini-series.

The fights in the series are intense and bloody, as giant humanoid warriors battle titanic monsters. The comic leans heavily into body horror, emphasizing the human cost of these battles. The Ultramega are depicted as musclebound giant superheroes, similar to Ultraman. However, the comic stresses that they are made of flesh and bone, and the wounds they sustain are real. These wounds carry over when they return to their human form.

☢ *Jenny Zero* (2021–2022)
Publisher: Dark Horse Comics
Writers: Dave Dwonch, Brockton McKinney
Penciled artwork: Magenta King
Inker: Magenta King
Colorists: Megan Huang, Arnaldo Robles

Jenny can grow to kaiju-size to fight her monstrous opponents, but has failed as a superhero for the military. Struggling to live up to her late father's reputation as a superhero, she becomes an alcoholic who lives with her best friend, an heiress to a hotel fortune. But strange creatures, clandestine societies, and her having to walk within her father's legacy make her question whether she can become sober and focus on saving the world. In a review, Jake Palermo of MonkeysFightingRobots.com said, "*Jenny Zero* hooks readers in with an all-too-human story about workplace troubles. Because with a job as stressful as Jenny's, looking at it while intoxicated might make it easier."

☢ *Godzilla vs. the Mighty Morphin Power Rangers* (2022)
Publisher: IDW Publishing/BOOM! Studios
Writer: Cullen Bunn
Penciled artwork: Nikolas Draper-Ivey, Alex Sanchez, Freddie Williams II
Inkers: Nikolas Draper-Ivey, Alex Sanchez, Freddie Williams II
Colorists: Andrew Dalhouse, Nikolas Draper-Ivey, Alex Sanchez
Letterers: Johanna Nattlie, Nathan Widick

▼

When the Power Rangers' most dangerous nemesis, Rita Repulsa, utilizes an ancient artifact to transport herself to an alternate universe that lacks Power Rangers, she is surprised to find herself in a world filled with aliens and kaiju—including Godzilla. Rita orders her fearsome creatures to battle the King of the Monsters. But she never expected the Rangers to follow her to this parallel reality, leading to an epic clash between the Power Ranger's Dinozords and the King of the Monsters.

This mini-series nicely blends the Toho Universe with Power Rangers lore, and seeing the towering Zords go toe-to-toe with Godzilla feels like a perfect fit. After all, the Rangers basically battle giant monsters in their universe on a daily basis.

☢ *Justice League vs. Godzilla vs. Kong* (2023–2024)

Publisher: DC Comics/Legendary Comics
Writer: Brian Buccellato
Penciled artwork: Christian Duce
Inker: Christian Duce
Colorist: Luis Guerrero

▼

The DC Universe and Monsterverse come together in this epic crossover mini-series. When the Justice League and the Legion of Doom accidentally open a barrier portal between dimensions, Godzilla and Kong emerge on Earth in the DC Universe, and chaos reigns.

▼▼ CHARACTERS ▼▼

☢ Starro the Conqueror

Creator: Hajime Isayama
First appearance: *The Brave and the Bold #28* (1960)
Publisher: DC Comics

▼

Starro is a giant alien starfish with a humanoid brain who can also send out smaller starfish that he can control with his mind. The smaller starfish serve as parasites for Starro, as they attach themselves to humans' faces and take control of their brains and bodily functions. Starro can also fly, absorb and project energy, and has incredible telepathic powers. He appeared in the live-action

A model of Godzilla on a Tokyo street at XXI Barcelona Manga Fair in 2015.

film *The Suicide Squad* and the animated *Batman and Superman: Battle of the Super Sons* direct-to-video feature.

☢ Jormungard the Midgard Serpent
First appearance: *Marvel Tales #105* (1952)
Publisher: Marvel Comics

——— ▼ ———

An ultra-giant serpent, Jormungard possesses immense strength and stamina. It is venomous, can breathe lethal fire, and can project powerful illusions. It can also cause earthquakes by flexing its coils around the Earth. Over the last four decades, Jormungard has been seen in some Thor comics published by Marvel Comics. In Norse mythology, the character is known as Jörmungandr, an incredibly large sea serpent or worm that resides

An illustration of Jörmungandr.

in the world sea, encircling the Earth and biting its own tail to form an ouroboros. It is also known as the World Serpent, as it surrounds Midgard (the Earth). If Jörmungandr releases its tail, it is believed that Ragnarök, the world's final battle, will begin.

☢ Ymir
Creator: Jack Kirby and Stan Lee
First appearance: *Journey Into Mystery #97* (1963)
Publisher: Marvel Comics

——— ▼ ———

Loosely based on Norse mythology, Ymir is an immortal frost giant who stands over 1,000 feet tall. He has superhuman strength and can emit immense, deadly cold frosts, and has a large icicle that he can use as a club during battle.

Ymir has appeared in many Marvel Comics, battling Thor, the Avengers, Doctor Strange, and the X-Men. According to Norse mythology, Ymir was the first being and the father of all ice giants. The Norse creation story states that Ymir's body produced numerous beings who went on to bear countless generations.

▾▾ MANGA ▾▾

☢ *Cloverfield: Kinshin* (2008)
Publisher: Kadokawa Shoten
Writers: David Baronoff, Matthew Pitts, Nicole Phillips
Illustrator: Yoshiki Togawa

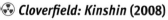

Originally published in four chapters on the Kadokawa Shoten website, *Cloverfield: Kinshin* follows two teenagers, Kishin Aiba and Aiko Sasahara, as they try to uncover the truth behind a mysterious incident that occurred before the Chuai incident (when the monster from the film *Cloverfield* destroyed a deep-sea drilling station in the Atlantic Ocean) and the events of *Cloverfield*, while Tokyo is under attack from a giant, monstrous creature.

☢ *Attack on Titan* (2009–2021)
Publisher: Kodansha
Writer and Illustrator: Hajime Isayama

Attack on Titan is a dark-fantasy, post-apocalyptic story set in a world where humans live in cities protected by three enormous walls from Titans—gigantic man-eating humanoids. The main character, Eren Yeager, promises to destroy the Titans after they kill his mother and destroy his hometown. The story was serialized in Kodansha's monthly magazine, *Bessatsu Shōnen Magazine*, from September 2009 to April 2021, and its chapters were compiled into 34 volumes.

Ymir, the frost giant from Norse mythology, is pictured here, in the background.

Attack on Titan has sold over 140 million copies, making it one of the best-selling manga ever. It has also won several awards, including Kodansha Manga, Attilio Micheluzzi, and Harvey Awards. If *Attack on Titan* had fewer characters and less-deep character development, it's unlikely that the series would have reached the heights it has today. Some fans even argue that Eren Jaeger is one of the most well-developed and memorable characters in all manga.

☢ *Kaiju Girl Caramelise* (2018–)

Publisher: Kadokawa Shoten (Japan), Yen Press (US)
Writer and Illustrator: Spica Aoki

——— ▼ ———

Kuroe Akaishi is an outcast at school, and her classmates call her "Psycho-tan." She suffers from a rare and incurable illness that causes deformations in her body at random times. One day, Arata Minami, a popular guy in her class, starts paying attention to her, which surprises her. She begins to question the strange new feelings she has around him. One night, Kuroe has a realistic dream of transforming into a kaiju and rampaging through Tokyo. The next day, her mother confesses a deep, dark secret: Kuroe *is* a kaiju, which confirms Kuroe's dream. But Kuroe is more concerned that Arata will not accept her for who she truly is.

This story is about the challenges of puberty and first love, viewed through the lens of a kaiju story. It explores the awkwardness we've all experienced, both as teenagers and sometimes even as adults, and the embarrassment that comes with being unable to decipher our hormones and signals. Our emotions might have the power to turn us into uncontrollable monsters—but is there a way to turn that into an advantage?

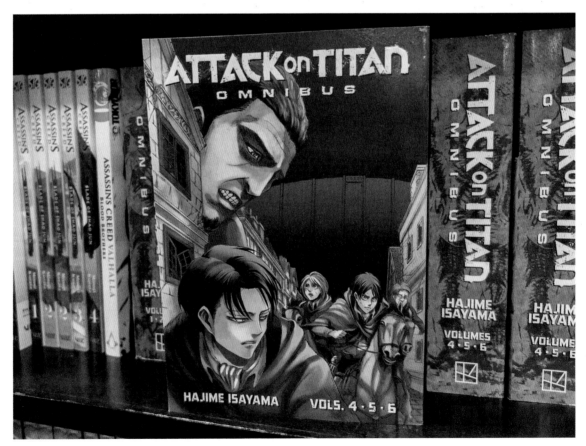

Attack on Titan (2009–2021) manga arranged on a bookstore shelf.

Kaiju No. 8 (2020–)

Publisher: Shueisha (Japan), Viz Media (US)
Writer and Illustrator: Naoya Matsumoto

——— ▼ ———

A man named Kafka Hibino gains the ability to transform into a kaiju after a small kaiju jumps into his mouth and enters his body. He must learn to control his power as he attempts to join an organization that eliminates kaiju. A popular manga, *Kaiju No. 8* also has an English-translated version published by Viz Media and an anime adaptation is set to premiere in 2024.

▼▼ BOOKS ▼▼

Godzilla Returns (1996) by Marc Cerasini

Set in a different continuity than the Toho films, this young adult novel for American audiences introduces Brian Shimura, a Japanese-American college student, who has just arrived in Tokyo to start an internship at a newspaper. His first assignment is to investigate the supposed "return" of a legendary kaiju that Brian feels is a myth. But once he witnesses the destruction caused by Godzilla, Brian's skepticism quickly turns into extraordinary dread.

Meg: A Novel of Deep Terror (1997) by Steve Alten

Seven years ago, Dr. Jonas Taylor, a Navy deep-sea submersible pilot, encountered something that changed his life. Now a marine paleontologist, he firmly believes that a population of prehistoric sharks called *Carcharodon megalodon*, aka MEG, which grow to up to 70 feet in length and feed on whales, still live in the depths of the Mariana Trench, seven miles below the surface of the Pacific Ocean.

When given the chance to return to the depths of the ocean to search for the MEG, Taylor jumps at the opportunity. However, his quest for scientific knowledge and personal vindication soon turns into a desperate battle to survive. There are several books in the MEG series, and two live-action MEG movies have been released (2018's *The Meg* and 2023's *Meg 2: The Trench*).

Clickers (2006) by J. F. Gonzalez and Mark Williams

The residents of Phillipsport, Maine, find themselves in a dire situation when a swarm of creatures called Clickers emerge from the ocean and launch a brutal attack on the town. These Clickers are gigantic, venomous crabs with murderous intentions, and the sound of their claws clicking is a warning of their proximity. However, the Clickers' actions are not without reason: they are being driven onto land by an unknown force of terror. Something ancient and merciless is hunting these creatures down. Reviewer Terry Shiels of the *Midnight Scribe Reviews* says of *Clickers*, "Not for the squeamish, for certain, for the language is terrifyingly explicit in its descriptions. *Clickers* is a tale of sheer horror from start to bloody finish. A right good read . . . for those with no fear of the dark, strong stomachs, and no ocean nearby."

TIM – Defender of the Earth (2008) by Sam Enthoven

TIM (which stands for Tyrannosaurus: Improved Model) is a story about a genetically enhanced lizard that escapes from a top-secret military facility and unintentionally causes destruction all over London. The story has similarities to the old Japanese TV series, *Johnny Sokko and His Flying Robot*, particularly in the connection between one of the main characters (Chris) and his relationship with TIM. Additionally, the book features Big Ben being used as a projectile.

David Gilchrist of *Fantasy Book Review* had mixed feelings about the book, saying, "The book has nice echoes of *War of the Worlds* . . . Unfortunately, these are few and far between. It feels too much like an episode of *Doctor Who*, without the Doctor, with the two children playing the parts of the assistants."

☢ *Project Nemesis* (2012), written by Jeremy Robinson and illustrated by Matt Frank

Heavily influenced by Godzilla and Gamera films, which were favorites of author Jeremy Robinson, in the debut novel of the five-book Nemesis Saga series, Jon Hudson, the lead investigator of Fusion Center-P of the Department of Homeland Security, is faced with a monstrous threat, a kaiju named Nemesis.

Nemesis is an ancient goddess of vengeance who takes the form of a massive kaiju. She has been dormant for thousands of years, but once awakened, she seeks to bring justice to the tormented and destroys anyone who stands in her way. When the consciousness of Maigo, a little girl brutally murdered by her own father, becomes trapped within Nemesis, the kaiju sets out to make the world pay. She begins by targeting large cities, crushing and consuming all the people she can find.

☢ *Kentucky Kaiju* (2016), written by Shawn Pryor and illustrated by Justin Stewart and Tressina Bowling

Kentucky Kaiju is the comprehensive field guide to the kaiju of the Bluegrass state. Borne from love of movies like *Destroy All Monsters*, *Godzilla vs. Mechagodzilla*, *Daimajin*, *All Monsters Attack*, *Gamera: The Giant Monster*, and other classics, the creators of *Kentucky Kaiju* wanted to create never-before-seen kaiju specifically for the state. Each creature has an entry covering their creation, location, and proclivity to violence (or peace), as well as an artist's rendering.

☢ *Ultraman Kaiju Art Works: 1971–1980* (2017)

This art book features conceptual designs and artwork from *Ultraman* and other Ultra Hero series from multiple artists, ranging from 1971 to 1980. It includes sketched designs of the different Ultra Heroes, the menacing kaiju that the Ultra Heroes have faced, and the heroes' vehicles.

☢ *The Kaiju Survival Guide* (2018) by Wes Parker

Fans of kaiju movies and creature features learn helpful tips on what to do when one has an encounter with a kaiju, as told through the lens of the Kaiju Research and Survival Department (KRSD). The guide contains stories about terrifying encounters with monsters without explicitly naming the creatures involved, but kaiju fans may recognize the movies being referenced. Most of the stories in the book are told from the victim's perspective, and the survival tips and information provided can also be useful in the event of actual natural disasters.

☢ *Into the Mist* (2018) by Lee Murray

A group of soldiers are on a mission to escort civilian contractors through a hostile area of New Zealand, filled with militants and other hazards. However, the mission becomes more challenging than expected when a massive creature starts hunting them down individually. Sergeant Taine McKenna leads his crew in the fight against the beast to complete their mission. *Into the Mist* is the first book in a three-book series that blends *Jurassic Park*, *Predator*, *Alien*, and other sci-fi horror into a thrilling story.

☢ *The Kaiju Preservation Society* (2022) by John Scalzi

During the COVID-19 pandemic in New York City, Jamie Gray is going through the motions as a food delivery driver. One day, Jamie delivers food to an old friend named Tom, who is working for an animal rights organization. Tom offers Jamie a job to help his team on their next field visit, and Jamie accepts.

However, Tom doesn't reveal to Jamie that the animals he and his team care for are massive, dinosaur-like creatures called kaiju that exist in an alternate dimension without humans. But the Kaiju Preservation Society is not the only group that has found its way to this alternate world, and

John Scalzi shows off his book, *The Kaiju Preservation Society* (2022).

the careless actions of these others could lead to millions of deaths on Earth if these kaiju are brought into our world.

Critic Adam Morgan wrote in *Scientific American*, "John Scalzi's stand-alone adventure novel is a fun throwback to Michael Crichton's 1990s sci-fi thrillers. . . . Scalzi describes the book as a 'pop song,' and he's right—there are no cerebral messages about animal rights or nuclear proliferation. Written with the brisk pace of a screenplay, it's as quippy as a Marvel movie and as awe-inspiring as *Jurassic Park*."

In an interview with Chris Pickens of Bookpage.com, Scalzi discussed his inspirations: "I think the most obvious inspirations were the classic Japanese kaiju movies, starting with the original *Godzilla*. From there, I worked backward: If you want to have kaiju, how do you build a world where they could not only exist, but in fact, it makes sense that they exist?"

☢ *Anzu the Great Kaiju* (2022) by Benson Shum

In this children's storybook, Anzu is a young kaiju who doesn't want to cause fear and destruction. He would prefer to be happy and to indulge his passion for dance, flowers, and finding the beauty in small things. Anzu wants to be true to himself while also trying to make his family proud of him. A sequel, *Anzu the Great Listener*, was published in 2023.

☢ *Godzilla/Godzilla Raids Again* (2023) by Shigeru Kayama and Jeffrey Angles

The original adapted novellas for the first two Godzilla films, written by Shigeru Kayama, are collected and translated for English-speaking audiences by author Jeffrey Angles. The novellas contain plots and storylines that differ from the films, while making sure that the pro-environment mood is prevalent throughout.

☢ *Klyde the Kraken Wants a Friend* (2023), written by Brooke Hartman and illustrated by Laura Borio

Klyde the Kraken is a friendly creature who loves to give hugs to all the animals in the ocean, but whenever he tries, they all swim away. After Klyde accidentally sinks a pirate ship he was trying to embrace, the shipwrecked buccaneers teach Klyde—and the reader—a valuable lesson in emotional intelligence: not everyone likes to be hugged, and that's okay. (Then again, some adults need to learn about boundaries, too.)

17
KAIJU IN POP CULTURE

Godzilla and other kaiju are more than just characters in their respective films and shows—they are also pop cultural icons. These beasts have been featured in commercials, hotels, amusement parks, museums, toys, board games, and video games. In Japan, Godzilla has been used to sell fast food, toys, clothes, coffee, movies, and electronics over the years, and is still used as a spokesperson to this day. For a long time in America, kaiju merchandise was minimal or non-existent because corporations thought that Americans wouldn't jump on the trend. How wrong they were! Bandai started releasing Godzilla toys in America in 2002, and the character has been a mainstay in American toy aisles ever since.

Kaiju also invaded the world of video games forty years ago. From console and arcade classics to pinball machines, a number of games allow you to either play as a kaiju or hunt these strange beasts. From media tie-ins to tributes to creators' favorite films, much like the many adaptations across media that kaiju have seen over the decades, these games only prove that Godzilla and the gang are a worldwide phenomenon—and they can *sell*.

▼▼ POP CULTURE ▼▼

⊛ Dr. Pepper Godzilla Commercial

Dr. Pepper launched a $10-million advertisement campaign featuring Godzilla in 1985, with two TV commercials for Dr. Pepper and Diet Dr. Pepper. Dr. Pepper was also prominently featured in *Godzilla 1985* (the American version of *The Return of Godzilla*).

OPPOSITE: Visitors can zip-line into Godzilla's mouth on the National Awaji Island Institute of Godzilla Disaster ride at the Nijigen no Mori theme park on Awaji Island, Japan.

Kaiju are everywhere—even on pinball machines!

The first commercial was filmed in black-and-white, to summon up *Godzilla* (1954), and features Godzilla destroying a city. Thirsty from all that destruction, Godzilla drinks a generic cola from a tanker and hates the taste. He then sets a train of lemonade aflame before finding a giant can of Dr. Pepper, the only bit of color in the commercial. Godzilla drinks from the giant can and burps, satisfied.

The second commercial features Godzilla and Newzilla (Godzilla's girlfriend) wreaking havoc on the town as if on a fun date. Trying to find things that will win Newzilla's affection (and failing), Godzilla eventually finds a giant can of Dr. Pepper and gives it to her, which wins her over. This commercial marks the only appearance of Newzilla.

☢ Nike Presents: Godzilla vs. Charles Barkley

Godzilla vs. Charles Barkley is considered one of Nike's most memorable advertising events of

the early 1990s. It was first aired during the 1992 MTV Video Music Awards, preceded by a teaser trailer shown for several weeks leading up to the event. Nike also created tie-in merchandise such as posters, a comic book, and T-shirts.

In the full commercial, a giant-sized Barkley grimaces at Godzilla, challenging him to a gargantuan basketball game in the middle of a devastated city. Slipping on bright pink basketball goggles, Godzilla accepts the challenge and knocks the ball from Barkley's hands with a swipe of his tail. The 11-time NBA All-Star catches the ball and proceeds to elbow Godzilla in the face. As the King of the Monsters falls onto a building and crushes it, Barkley dunks the ball into a giant hoop, winning the match. After the game, Godzilla and Barkley leave together as friends.

The commercial was originally made for Japanese audiences, to air in Japan only. But after seeing the finished commercial, Nike executives were so pleased with the end product that they also decided to use the commercial in the US. For a big corporation such as Nike to air a commercial featuring Godzilla (who, at the time, had last been seen in American movie theaters in 1985) with assistance from Industrial Light and Magic (the special effects powerhouse behind the

A Godzilla action figure.

Star Wars franchise) shows how strong the King of the Monsters' following was in America and the world.

In an interview with Inverse.com, the director of the commercial, Michael Owens, said, "When the commercial aired, it was huge. I don't even watch TV and I was hearing about it all over the place. . . . I knew it was a cool ad, but I had no idea the impact it would have and that it would get all this tie-in merchandise."

☢ Kaiju Big Battel

Kaiju Big Battel is a performance art show created by Rand Borden's New York City-based entertainment troupe. The performances are a parody of professional wrestling and tokusatsu and kaiju films. These "Battels" are presented in the style of professional wrestling events, where the costumed performers play the roles of giant monsters that destroy cities. The show features kaiju characters such as Dusto Bunny, French Toast, Kung-Fu Chicken Noodle, American Beetle, and the villainous Dr. Cube.

☢ Godzilla Interception Operation Awaji and Godzilla Museum

Part amusement park, part museum, these attractions opened at the Nijigen no Mori amusement park on Awaji Island in Hyogo Prefecture. The main attraction is a zipline course 49 feet high and 531 feet long, during which riders zip-line into Godzilla's mouth. The King of the Monsters' head, mouth, neck, and part of the upper body constructed for the zip-line ride measures 82 feet wide and 180 feet long.

The museum showcases all the eras of Godzilla, with large-scale dioramas portraying scenes from Godzilla movies, featuring Godzilla rampaging through some of his favorite cities like Tokyo Station, Otemachi, and Roppongi. Additionally, visitors can explore rotating exhibits often featuring movie props, such as the Godzilla suits used by the actors. The exhibition also

The American Godzilla Museum that Almost Happened

In 1995, an investment group attempted to build a Godzilla Museum in the Little Tokyo area of Los Angeles, with the goal of revitalizing Little Tokyo and boosting the economy in the area. They planned for one part of the museum to cover the history of Godzilla, other Japanese kaiju, and science-fiction projects, while the other part would be a toy museum. There was even the thought of having Godzilla battling a kaiju on top of the museum to catch people's attention. However, the investment group couldn't secure the funding needed to make the museum happen.

includes various friends and foes of the King of the Monsters, including Mothra and Mechagodzilla. Visitors can also enjoy a Godzilla-themed shooting game, in which visitors attempt to stop "Godzilla cells" from spreading inside an inactive Godzilla. The official museum is funded by Toho Studio and Nijigen no Mori amusement park.

☢ The Eiji Tsuburaya Museum

The Eiji Tsuburaya Museum located in the filmmaker's hometown of Sukagawa-shi, Fukushima, is dedicated to Eiji Tsuburaya, also known as the "God of Tokusatsu." The museum depicts the 68 years of Tsuburaya Eiji's life, with interview footage and panels, exhibits, props, and video clips of Tsuburaya behind the scenes during many tokusatsu productions.

☢ Japanese American National Museum – Kaiju vs. Heroes Exhibit, 2018–2019

Godzilla looms over Hotel Gracery Shinjuku in Tokyo.

From September 2018 to July 2019, the Kaiju vs. Heroes exhibition at the Japanese American National Museum displayed a history of Japanese toys, especially vinyl toys. The exhibit featured over one hundred Japanese vinyl toys and explained the historical meaning behind them and the emergence of characters such as Godzilla and Ultraman as pop-culture icons and heroes.

☢ Hotel Gracery Shinjuku

Located in Shinjuku City in Tokyo, this hotel features Godzilla overlooking the city on one side of the hotel, and two special "Godzilla Rooms." The first has a trick wall that reacts to black light, revealing all kinds of Godzilla-related art, a history of Godzilla posters, additional memorabilia, and a massive Godzilla hand emerging through one of the walls. The second is like the first, with the added bonus of seeing Godzilla's head from this room only. In the evening, Godzilla shakes his head and moves briefly, and his eyes flash like lightning. He also emits his atomic breath (which is really just well-lit steam).

☢ Pluto TV's Godzilla and Tokushoutsu Channels

On the Pluto streaming app and website, there is an official Godzilla channel that airs Godzilla films from Toho Studios across multiple eras, twenty-four hours a day, for free. Other Toho kaiju films such are also aired on the channel.

Created by the Shout Factory production company and also found on Pluto, the TokuSHOUTsu channel airs Ultraman, additional Ultra Heroes, many versions of Kamen Rider, kaiju movies, and Super Sentai series, twenty-four hours a day, for free. There's also a talk show that's original to the channel called *Let's Talk Toku*.

▾▾ Toys ▾▾

☢ Vinyl Toys and Sofubi

Vinyl art toys, also known as designer toys or urban vinyl, are typically created by independent artists or small design studios and are often inspired by pop

Godzilla vs. Gamera, in toy form.

culture, underground art, and street art. There have been many vinyl toys and sofubi over the decades in Japan, covering the entire slate of kaiju from all of the Japanese movie studios, the Ultra Heroes, Super Sentai, and more. Sofubi, short for "soft vinyl," is a type of plastic material used to create Japanese vinyl toys. Most of these toys are inspired by classic Japanese monster movies and TV shows from the 1960s and 1970s, which gives them a significant cultural relevance and a link to the past. There are many vinyl toymakers around the world, such as Medicom Toy (based in Japan), Super 7 (based in the US), and the Max Toy Company, to name a few.

Some of the rarer sofubi toys are the Bullmark Ultraman series, produced from the 1960s to the 1970s by Japanese toymaker Bullmark. These Ultra Hero sofubi are very hard to find, with people willing to pay thousands of dollars for them due to their scarcity. The designer/vinyl toy industry has been very strong in Asia, and in the US, a slew of indie artists make limited-run projects.

Shogun Warriors

The Shogun Warriors toy line, created by Mattel, was in stores in America from 1979 to 1981. It was one of the hottest-selling toys in 1979, but the release of *The Empire Strikes Back* in 1980 meant that Star Wars toy sales dominated retail and pushed the Shogun Warriors to obscurity by the end of that year.

The toy line was created from toys produced by Japanese company Popy, based on several anime and tokusatsu shows featuring giant mecha. The mecha had their names changed for American audiences once Mattel made them part of the Shogun Warriors toy line. The most popular Shogun Warriors line was the Jumbo Machinders, 24-inch-tall vinyl figures with moveable arms and wheels on their feet. The Jumbo Machinders also featured spring-loaded launcher weapons such as missiles, shuriken, and battle axes. Some were able to launch their fists.

A selection of toys depicting some iconic manga characters from the 1970s and 1980s.

But what made the Shogun Warriors so popular at their peak was the inclusion of Godzilla and Rodan in the lineup. Godzilla was the same height as the other Jumbo Machinders, could fire off his fist, and had an action button that made his tongue of flames spit forward. Rodan was one of the largest Shogun Warriors ever produced, with a three-foot wingspan that could actually flap, grabbing claws, and a moveable beak. It also made a screeching noise.

☢ Monsterverse Godzilla Toy Line

The latest in the Monsterverse toy line, *Godzilla X Kong: The New Empire* features toys from the movie, created by Playmates, who have made Teenage Mutant Ninja Turtles toys for forty years. Movie versions of Godzilla, Kong, the evil Skar King, additional kaiju, and diorama sets are all part of the first wave of toys for Godzilla X Kong.

Before the Playmates line, the Japanese company Bandai released Godzilla figures in America from 2002 to 2019, with limited articulation that would focus on the titular

character, Mechagodzilla, Jet Jaguar, and a small number of additional kaiju.

▼▼ BOARD GAMES ▼▼

☢ 1960s Godzilla Board Game

The very first Godzilla item ever produced for the United States, the goal of the game was to get your marker to the "Rocket Launch" area so you could fire missiles to stop Godzilla's reign of terror.

☢ 1970s Godzilla Board Game

In this classic, simple, and weird board game from Mattel, your goal is to move your spaceship across the circular board without Godzilla popping up to grab your spaceship with his mouth!

☢ Godzilla: Kaiju World Wars

Released in 2011, Kaiju World Wars uses a battle card system to allow players to combat as Godzilla, Rodan, Gigan, or the menacing King Ghidorah. Destroy buildings and fend off massive military attacks, traps, and other kaiju along the way to be the last kaiju standing.

☢ Godzilla: Tokyo Clash

Released in 2020, this popular board game lets players take on the role of one of four legendary kaiju: Godzilla, Mothra, King Ghidorah, or Megalon. The objective is to battle to become the most terrifying monster in Japan. The game features highly detailed miniatures of the monsters and a modular 3D cityscape that can be destroyed during gameplay.

Each player has a unique card deck corresponding to the kaiju they control. Players can throw trains and tanks at their opponents and attack them directly to cause damage. This burns cards from their opponents' decks, limiting their options on future turns. Additionally, players can earn energy to enhance their kaiju abilities by stomping through the city.

▼▼ ARCADE AND VIDEO GAMES ▼▼

☢ *Rampage* (1986)

In *Rampage*, players take control of a trio of monsters named George (a King Kong analog), Lizzie (a Godzilla analog), and Ralph (a giant werewolf). All three characters were once humans who transformed into these creatures due to experimental mishaps. The purpose of the game is to destroy cities and combat military forces while keeping the monsters' health intact. The game spans 128 days and occurs in various cities across North America, with each cycle repeating five times. The gameplay involves destroying buildings, consuming humans, and avoiding damage.

☢ *Godzilla Arcade* (1993)

Godzilla Arcade is a side-scrolling action game inspired by several of Godzilla's most iconic fights that saw arcade release in Japan. Each stage starts

KAIJU FACT

The *Rampage* arcade game has had over twenty adapted home console versions since its debut in 1986. It has been ported to the Atari 2600, 7800, and Atari Computers, the Atari Lynx, GameCube, Playstation and Playstation 2, Xbox, Commodore 64, MS-DOS, Nintendo Entertainment System, and Sega Master System, among others.

with a warm-up that has the King of the Monsters stomping buildings and smashing the JSDF as humans flee in fear. Once everything is destroyed, Godzilla's opponent will appear, and the two will battle, with combat resembling *Street Fighter II*.

In one-player mode, Godzilla is the only playable character. When no more lives remain, the game is over. Battle mode allows two players to go

Art from *Rampage* (1986).

head-to-head as Godzilla, King Ghidorah, Gigan, Megalon, Mechagodzilla, or Mecha-King Ghidorah. If the time runs out in a battle, the character with the most energy remaining wins.

☢ Primal Rage (1994)

Primal Rage is a classic fighting game, developed and released by Atari Games for arcades in 1994. The game is set in a post-apocalyptic version of Earth called Urth. Players take control of one of seven giant beasts and battle each other to determine the planet's fate. Battles include many standard features of fighting games from that era, such as special moves and gruesome finishing maneuvers. The game was a hit and sold over 1.5 million copies, leading to the production of toys, comics, a novel, and other merchandise.

☢ Godzilla (1983)

Godzilla is a strategy game for solo players, for Commodore 64. Players command the military and must eliminate Godzilla before he destroys Tokyo. The game is set in a large grid on the map of Japan and its nearby waters. The grid is 5x5, containing 25 spaces, with one space containing Tokyo. Godzilla is randomly placed in any of the 25 spaces, except

the one containing Tokyo. The player can choose to attack Godzilla via land, sea, air, or with an atomic bomb, or move troops. After an attack, the game will show the number of attackers killed and how effective the attack was. If Godzilla is on land, he will go on a rampage, resulting in civilian casualties. The atom bomb is the most potent weapon in the game, destroying all life and weapons in the space where the bomb is dropped and the surrounding eight spaces. If the bomb destroys Tokyo or Godzilla reaches the city, the game will end.

☢ The Movie Monster Game (1986)

The Movie Monster Game is a single-player game for Commodore 64 and the Apple II computer. The game features various scenarios, movie monsters to play, and cities to destroy. Locations include famous landmarks such as Tokyo Tower, the Eiffel Tower, the Statue of Liberty, the Golden Gate Bridge, Saint Basil's Cathedral, and Big Ben. The monsters are loosely based on famous movie monsters and mecha like The Blob, Mothra, the Stay Puft Marshmallow Man, and the Transformers. Epyx, the game's developer, obtained the license for Godzilla, which helped boost the game's sales. The gameplay takes place on a movie screen in front of an audience in a movie theater, giving players the feeling of being in an actual monster movie. The game has five different modes: Berserk Mode, in which players accumulate points by destroying as many buildings

The title screen for *Primal Rage* (1994).

KAIJU FACT

The Movie Monster Game was a side sequel to Epyx Software's *Crush, Crumble and Chomp*, which was a 2D grid-based computer game in which players chose a monster to destroy a city.

and vehicles as possible; Escape Mode, in which the monster must flee the city before getting killed by the military; Search Mode, when the monster must rescue its offspring; Destroy Landmark Mode, in which your objective is to destroy a specific landmark within the city; and Lunch Mode, when you satisfy the monster's hunger by eating vehicles and humans.

The title screen from *Godzilla: Monster of Monsters* (1988).

Kaiju Crush (2021)

In this dating sim and visual novel for teens and adults, kaiju have attacked the city, and due to a military accident, you have become just as big as these beasts. As the hero, you can communicate with these kaiju ladies and attempt to reason with them. You choices will determine whether you can save the city—and the world.

GigaBash (2022)

GigaBash is a fighting game in which the player controls a kaiju and fights against other monsters in stages that have destructible environments. These monsters can perform light and heavy attacks and use special moves that are unique to each of them. As the player deals damage to their opponents, they will gain Giga-energy. Once they have enough Giga-energy, the kaiju will become a much stronger S-class kaiju. During a match, a Giga-ball will appear. The kaiju that obtains the Giga-ball can use an ultimate attack that deals massive damage to their opponents.

Godzilla: Voxel Wars (2022)

In this turn-based strategy game, players take control of Godzilla, Mothra, King Ghidorah, and other Toho kaiju on an 8x8 grid to protect the world from the Fungoid mushroom invasion. The game features a unique style, blending *Minecraft* and Chibi aesthetics to create an entertaining strategy game.

▾▾ CONSOLE GAMES ▾▾

Nintendo Entertainment System/ Famicom

Godzilla: Monster of Monsters (1988)

A side-scrolling platform game, *Monster of Monsters* lets players play as Godzilla or Mothra as they battle the dangerous kaiju and the foes of Planet X all over the galaxy. All evil kaiju come from Toho kaiju movies, including Gezora, Moguera, Varan, Hedorah, Baragon, Gigan, Mechagodzilla, and King Ghidorah.

Godzilla 2: War of the Monsters (1991)

An exclusive US release, this sequel to the 1988 NES game is a turn-based strategy game. Players control military forces to prevent Godzilla and other kaiju—such as Mothra, Hedorah, Rodan, Baragon, and King Ghidorah—from destroying Japan.

Magnam, consequianis aliquun dendus ma samendus.

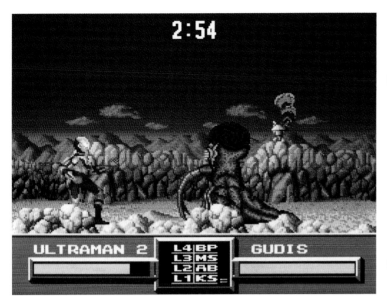

Gameplay from *Ultraman* (1991).

Super Nintendo Entertainment System/ Super Famicom

Ultraman (1991)

In this single-player fighting game, you play as Ultraman and battle his most dangerous kaiju foes. But you also have to balance your power meter and make sure that you have enough energy to use your Specium Beam to defeat your foes. The Japanese version of the game featured the original Ultraman and his nemesis' while the American version featured Ultraman from the TV series *Ultraman: Towards the Future*, which was airing in America at the time.

Super Godzilla (1993)

In this single-player game, the player takes on the role of either Godzilla or Super Godzilla. The player must guide their chosen kaiju into different battles and events by pressing the correct buttons on the gamepad at the appropriate time to advance to battling one of many of Godzilla's kaiju foes. The game is split into two screens: the top one shows Godzilla's actions and the bottom one shows his location on the current level in the game that the King of the Monsters is partaking in. In many ways, the game combines RPG features with moments of standard video game fighting. The game switches into a standard side-view mode when Godzilla finds a monster to battle.

Ultraseven (1993)

Developed exclusively for Japan, this game differs from *Ultraman* in that not only does the game have single-player and multiplayer modes, but it is also both a fighting game and a horizontal shooter. Players can battle through twelve levels based off episodes of the series or play in a Versus Mode against another player.

Gameboy

Godzilla (1990)

In this video game, various kaiju have kidnapped Godzilla's son, Minilla, and hidden him inside the Matrix Labyrinth. Godzilla must fight the monsters, solve puzzles, and navigate a giant maze to rescue his son. The game is a 2D side-scrolling platformer, in which Godzilla can walk around or climb ladders, vines, or crystals. His only attack is a punch that can destroy boulders and kill or push enemies.

Godzilla: The Series (1999)

In this side-scrolling beat-'em-up up for Gamboy Color, based on the animated series, players navigate Godzilla through multiple scenarios, including volcanic islands, underwater trenches, and New York harbors, across twelve levels of gameplay.

Godzilla: The Series – Monster Wars (2000)

Godzilla returns to help H.E.A.T. (Humanitarian Environmental Analysis Team) in this gaming sequel to *Godzilla: The Series* (1999). This side-scrolling game has an open-play environment and features ten levels and sixteen deadly enemies for Godzilla to face.

Godzilla: Domination! (2002)

Domination! has two different playing modes. In Story Mode, Meteor X has appeared over the city known as Tokyo 2 and has started emitting magnetic waves, causing neurological damage to several kaiju, causing them to go berserk. Godzilla remains unaffected and is the only one who can

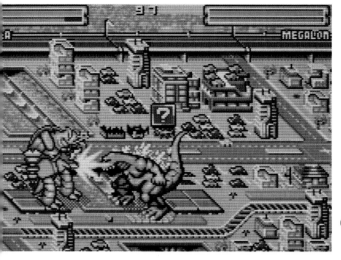

stop the rampage and destroy Meteor X. The second mode is Versus Mode, in which two to four face off via a Game Boy Advance Game Link Cable.

🔘 Kong: King of Atlantis (2005)

A tie-in to the *Kong: The Animated Series* (2000) cartoon and the direct-to-video *Kong: King of Atlantis* animated movie, this is a side-scrolling action platformer in which the player controls Kong, Jason, or Lua. The objective is to fight through each level until the game ends. Each character has a considerable health bar, and Kong can use his fists, while Jason and Lua can kick their way through the game.

🔘 Kong: The 8th Wonder of the World (2005)

A tie-in to the 2005 *King Kong* remake, players take the role of Jack, Ann, or Carl and solve challenging puzzles. As King Kong, you battle planes, tanks, and other enemies.

Nintendo DS
🔘 Godzilla Unleashed: Double Smash (2007)

Double Smash is a 2D sidescroller that features twenty-four monsters, ten of which are playable, while

the rest appear as boss-level enemies. The game requires players to control two monsters simultaneously: one that flies on the top screen and another that walks on the bottom screen. Players will face many challenges besides kaiju, including the military, flying crystals, and buildings that players must destroy using a combo.

Xbox
🔘 Godzilla: Destroy All Monsters Melee (2002)

In *Godzilla: Destroy All Monsters Melee*, you can take part in legendary battles between kaiju in different cities on Earth. You can choose to play as Godzilla or any of his rivals and use hand-to-hand combat and special moves to defeat your opponents. Each monster has unique physical attributes and projectile weapons. The game features realistic building destruction and physics in cities like Tokyo and San Francisco. You can also play with up to four people in multiplayer mode.

🔘 Godzilla: Save the Earth (2004)

In this sequel to *Godzilla: Destroy All Monsters Melee*, you choose one of eighteen monsters, including

Gameplay from *Godzilla: Domination!* (2002).

The start screen for *Godzilla Unleashed: Double Smash* (2007).

Gameplay from *Godzilla: Save the Earth* (2004).

Godzilla, SpaceGodzilla, Mothra, and Jet Jaguar, and rampage through major cities like Tokyo, San Francisco, and New York to protect them from destruction by hostile aliens.

☢ Peter Jackson's King Kong: The Official Game of the Movie (2005)

You can play as either King Kong or Jack Driscoll in this tie-in to the 2005 movie. The game's storyline is based on the movie and was developed in collaboration with its director, Peter Jackson. He expanded the original storyline and introduced

new creatures and locations to make the game even more exciting. The game's cinematic style makes it more immersive.

Playstation

☢ Ultraman: Fighting Evolution (1998–2004)

Ultraman: Fighting Evolution is a series of fighting video games featuring Ultraman, Ultra Heroes, and kaiju from their respective eras. Five games were released between 1998 and 2004, with additional Ultra Heroes and kaiju added to each game.

☢ War of the Monsters (2003)

This game takes place after an extraterrestrial attack on Earth. The aliens' toxic fuels have led to the creation of colossal monsters that engage in fierce battles in urban settings. The game is inspired by kaiju films and creature feature movies.

☢ Monster Hunter (2004)

This series of action and role-playing games has sold close to 100 million copies worldwide. In this game, the player assumes the role of a Hunter,

Gameplay from *War of the Monsters* (2003).

Fans play *Monster Hunter* (2004) at Ani-Com & Games Hong Kong 2019.

tasked with hunting down and defeating giant monsters that inhabit multiple landscapes. The Hunter receives quests from locals, which involve either slaying or trapping monsters. Some quests may also require the Hunter to gather specific items, which puts them at risk of encountering even more monsters. To progress in the game, players must use the loot from slaying monsters, gathering resources, and completing quests to craft better weapons, armor, and other items. These upgrades are necessary to face more powerful monsters and complete more challenging quests. As one of the few games in this list where the human is the protagonist, there are moments when playing the game that you feel that you are immersed in a kaiju film due to the number of quests and monsters that you face, but the hunter, prey, and survival elements of the game are the focus. Since its debut, *Monster Hunter* has spawned multiple sequels over the last twenty years across multiple consoles.

☢ *Godzilla* (2014)

This game has multiple modes of play. In one of the game modes, you get to become a God of Destruction by wreaking destruction across Japan, tasked with destroying cities and environments to eliminate each area's Energy Generator while collecting as much G-Energy as possible. This G-Energy can enhance Godzilla's physical size and offensive and defensive abilities. In the King of the Monsters mode, the game goes through six stages with each stage ending with a big battle against Godzilla's greatest foes. In the Evolution Mode of the game, you play as a chaotic neutral by beating your enemies and only destroying certain structures and buildings.

The game also includes a dynamic Movie-Style Camera Angle System, allowing players to switch between camera angles while destroying various locations and battling classic enemies like Mothra, King Ghidorah, and Mechagodzilla.

Atari 2600
☢ *King Kong* (1982)

Your mission is to rescue a woman held captive by King Kong at the top of the Empire State Building by climbing to the top of the building while avoiding the bombs that King Kong is throwing at you. The faster you save her, the bigger the bonus you receive.

CONCLUSION

From Godzilla's first appearance in 1954, the King of the Monsters (and his friends, foes, and fellow giant folks) has spawned and inspired innumerable influential stories across mediums and genres. The creators behind those stories have brought to life multiple universes, heroes, saviors, and the most dangerous threats to humankind, and the global fandom now has the opportunity to watch their favorite classics on demand or even step into the role of Godzilla in video games across platforms.

Godzilla and other kaiju mean different things to different people around the world. When the first *Godzilla* was released in the 1950s, Japanese filmmakers wanted to make a movie that meant something, that spoke out against the horrors of nuclear war. Sure, the kaiju films and creature features that followed took a turn toward camp for a little while, and they haven't all been winners. But whether a strange beast (or a *really* tall hero) brought you comfort or taught you something new, that just proves the importance of the kaiju genre around the world.

The perception of kaiju films and media has changed significantly in America over the last decade alone. No longer seen as something that's only childish and taboo, the genre is now considered a legitimate place to both craft entertaining stories and delve into the more complex parts of life and humankind. One of the most recent films, *Godzilla Minus One*, even won an Oscar, the highest award in American cinema, for Best Visual Effects in 2024. Kaiju continue to be popular not just because of amazing costumes or brilliant, CGI-laden special effects, but because of the stories they can be used to tell. Kaiju aren't always just cool monsters (though that's reason enough for them to exist). Sometimes, as with the earliest Japanese-made films, they're analogies for the problems and obstacles that we face today.

Even though there have been multiple forms and multitudes of media discussed in this book, there are still so many films, shows, cartoons, and other stories featuring kaiju and other larger-than-life heroes that we have yet to discuss. The goal of this book is to give insight into some of the most important moments in the genre's decades-long history, and I hope you walk away with a new appreciation for these pieces of media and that you continue to explore the ever-expanding world of kaiju. No matter the era, film, cartoon, game, or toy, there is something in the world of kaiju for everyone to enjoy, young and old.

At the end of most Toho Godzilla movies, the titular character, after vanquishing his kaiju foe, makes his way back to the ocean. He plunges into the depths to rest before he's called out again for another adventure. May you find your own moment of peace in which to enjoy a Godzilla movie or an Ultraman episode.

Godzilla in the 1954 film that started it all.

INDEX

Page numbers in **bold** indicate illustrations

SOURCES

Books and Magazines

The Kaiju Film: A Critical Study of Cinema's Biggest Monsters by Jason Barr

Behind the Kaiju Curtain: A Journey Onto Japan's Biggest Film Sets by Norman England

Japanese Special Effects Cinema: Godfathers of Tokusatsu: Vol. 1 by J.L. Carrozza

Ishiro Honda: A Life in Film, from Godzilla to Kurosawa by Steve Ryfle and Ed Godziszewski

Japan's Favorite Mon-Star: The Unauthorized Biography of "The Big G" by Steve Ryfle

Godzilla: The Ultimate Illustrated Guide by Toho Co. Ltd and Graham Skipper

Websites

wikizilla.org

kaijubattle.net

godzilla.fandom.com

ultra.fandom.com

ultraseries.fandom.com

tsuburaya-prod.com

imdb.com

tohokingdom.com

japanbookhunter.com

animebooks.com

boardgamegeek.com

janm.org

ultramanconnection.com

maxtoyco.com

joblo.com

screenrant.com

bleedingcool.com

multiversitycomics.tumblr.com

flickr.com/photos/noger/

criterion.com

afi.com

scifijapan.com

godzilla.com

archive.nerdist.com

alternateending.com

becominggodzilla.com

to-hollywood-and-beyond.fandom.com

superepicfailpedia.fandom.com

juleslcarrozza.medium.com

features.japantimes.co.jp

shinjuku.gracery.com

awn.com

www.stripes.com/living/pacific_travel/quick_trips/2023-06-29/godzilla-zipline-theme-park-japan-10553960.html

reactormag.com/five-giant-monsters-to-make-your-day/

shinjuku.gracery.com/

Videos

The American Godzilla Museum: It Almost Happened - https://www.youtube.com/watch?v=2JRRw3ITvaU

The Evolution Of Godzilla (Animated) - https://www.youtube.com/watch?v=3OGH6PlOiAw

The Evolution of King Kong (Animated) - https://www.youtube.com/watch?v=kmTELp7hfN4

American Godzilla is about Godzilla, Japanese Godzilla is about Life - https://www.youtube.com/watch?v=YJ61QBQfE4o

IMAGE CREDITS

ACKNOWLEDGMENTS

I want to thank my mother and father for their love of science fiction and fantasy and for passing that love along. Without their support, I wouldn't be where I am today. Special thanks to my wife, Dr. Alison Heck, for letting me ramble at her about kaiju history while writing this book. I would also like to thank my late friend, Chris Sweatt, for reintroducing me to comic books and Godzilla movies during our college days and all the fun we had with those stories. A special shout-out to the wonderful people at Quarto; they allowed me to write this comprehensive and thrilling book about the history of kaiju cinema and everything that spawned from it. Thank you to Katie McGuire for being such a fantastic editor and helping me put this massive book in order; you helped make this book shine.

I'd also like to thank Kelly Sonnack and kaiju historians Jason Barr and Steve Ryfle. Their work contributing to the history of kaiju cinema laid a foundation for me and many other creatives who love the genre. And a final thank you to the Shogun Warriors Godzilla toy my uncle let me borrow so I could create my own monster battles in the backyard of my grandma's house.

ABOUT THE AUTHOR

Shawn Pryor's (he/him) work includes the middle-grade graphic novel *Fast Break* (FSG/Macmillan, 2025), the hi/lo reader series *The Gamer* (Capstone Publishing), the *Cash and Carrie* series (Action Lab Entertainment), and several books for Capstone's Jake Maddox Sports and Adventure series, Graphic Library, and the Kids Sports series. In his free time, he enjoys reading, cooking, listening to streaming music playlists, and talking about why Zack from the Mighty Morphin Power Rangers is the greatest Black superhero of all time.

10 9 8 7 6 5 4 3 2 1

ISBN: 978-0-7603-9289-8

Digital edition published in 2024
eISBN: 978-0-7603-9290-4

Library of Congress Control Number: 2024938262

Group Publisher: Rage Kindelsperger
Creative Director: Laura Drew
Managing Editor: Cara Donaldson
Editor: Katie McGuire
Cover Design: Laura Drew
Interior Design: Brad Norr Design
Front and Back Cover Illustrations: Daz Tibbles

Printed in China